THE HOLY RESURRECTION
Arising in Glory

Steven P. Garrett

Text Copyright © 2019 by Steven P. Garrett

All rights reserved. This book or any portion thereof may not be reproduced or used in any manner whatsoever without the express written permission of the author except for the use of brief quotations in a book review.

ISBN Paperback Book 9780578570532
ISBN Electronic Book 9780578570686

Published by Steven P. Garrett
Printed in the United States of America

www.theholyresurrectionarisinglory.com

Abbreviation	Source
D&C	Doctrine and Covenants
DBY	Discourses of Brigham Young
DS	Doctrines of Salvation
HC	History of the Church
JD	Journal of Discourses
JH	Journal of History
JS-History	Joseph Smith History
JSM	Joseph Smith Matthew
JST	Joseph Smith Translation
TPJS	Teachings of the Prophet Joseph Smith

Note: All biblical references are from the Authorized King James Version of the Bible unless noted otherwise. Other scriptural references are from the Standard Works of the Church of Jesus Christ of Latter-day Saints.

Daybreak, by Henry Wadsworth Longfellow

A wind came up out of the sea,
And said, "O mists, make room for me."
It hailed the ships, and cried, "Sail on,
Ye mariners, the night is gone."
And hurried landward far away,
Crying, "Awake! it is the day."
It said unto the forest, "Shout!
Hang all your leafy banners out!"
It touched the wood-bird's folded wing,
And said, "O bird, awake and sing."
And o'er the farms, "O chanticleer,
Your clarion blow; the day is near."
It whispered to the fields of corn,
"Bow down, and hail the coming morn."
It shouted through the belfry-tower,
"Awake, O bell! proclaim the hour."
It crossed the churchyard with a sigh,
And said, "Not yet! in quiet lie

Contents

Chapter 1 - Understanding The Holy Resurrection 1
    Defining Eternal Life 2
    Defining Salvation 3
    Defining the Resurrection 4
    Defining Firstfruits 4
    Defining the Law of Restoration 6
    Defining Perfection 8
    The Resurrection Helps Us Know God 10
    The Resurrections Role in Salvation 12
    The Resurrections Eternal Importance 13
    The Resurrection and Receiving a Fullness of Joy 14
    The Three Estates of Existence, and their Transitional Gateways 15
    Resurrection versus Restoration to life 16
    Resurrection versus Translation 17
    Summary 18

Chapter 2 - Terms of the Resurrection 20
    Juxtapositions for the Resurrection 20
    Synonyms and Verbs for the Resurrection 22
    Summary 22

Chapter 3 - Jesus Christ's Atonement And The Resurrection 23
    Jesus Christ the Only Means of Salvation 24
    Jesus Christ Overcomes Physical Death 25
    Jesus Christ Overcomes First Spiritual Death 26
    Jesus Christ Overcomes Second Spiritual Death 26

Jesus Christ Saves Us Perfectly	28
Jesus Christ's Saving Grace	28
Summary	32

Chapter 4 - Resurrection's Historical Teachings ... 33

The Doctrine of Resurrection Taught in All Ages	33
God's Historical Efforts to Bring Salvation	36
The World's Continued Failure to Recognize the Resurrection	39
Summary	41

Chapter 5 - Doctrines Fundamental to the Resurrection ... 42

Classes in the Resurrection	42
First Resurrection	43
Second or Last Resurrection	45
The First Resurrection as a Title	46
The Morning of the First Resurrection	46
Death a Type of Judgment	47
Resurrection a Type of Judgment	49
Final Judgment and Records of Our Actions	51
All Who Inherit God's Kingdoms Must Repent	53
The Resurrection as a Priesthood Ordinance	55
The End of Our Second Estate, and the Spirit World	56
Eternal Progression	60
Eternal Damnation	62
Summary	63

Chapter 6 - Characteristics of Resurrected Bodies ... 65

Extent of the Resurrection	65
Arising from the Grave	70
We Arise Where Laid Down	72
Childhood Death, Disabilities, and the Resurrection	73
Not All Elements are Resurrected	75
Increased Capabilities	75
Power Over Gravity	78
Power to Pass Through Physical Objects	78

Imbued with Glory, or Light 79
　　Power to Show or Hide Glory 80
　　Ability to Eat and Table Fellowship 80
　　Hunger and Thirst No More 82
　　Power over Suffering and Pain 82
　　Three Grand Keys 84
　　Summary 85
Chapter 7 - The Resurrection and Three Degrees Of Glory 87
　　Timing of Humankind's Resurrection 88
　　Celestial Resurrection Timing and Nature 90
　　Three Degrees within the Celestial Kingdom 95
　　Celestial Marriage 100
　　Celestial Offspring 102
　　A Great Welding Link 104
　　Communication Between Kingdoms 106
　　Terrestrial Resurrection Timing and Nature 107
　　Telestial Resurrection Timing and Nature 113
　　Sons of Perdition Resurrection Timing and Nature 116
　　Summary 119
Chapter 8 - Jesus Christ's Resurrection 122
　　Dating Christ's Birth, Death, and Resurrection 123
　　The Law of Witnesses and the Resurrection 126
　　Christ's Death and Resurrection Day 126
　　Feast of Unleavened Bread 131
　　Feast of Firstfruits 132
　　Summary 133
Chapter 9 - Theories Denying The Resurrection 134
　　Disciples Stole Him Away 134
　　Others Stole Him Away 135
　　The Tomb was not Empty 135
　　Unconscious When Removed from Cross 136
　　Vision Hypothesis 137

Discrepancies in Gospel Accounts 137

The Bible Is Fabricated. 139

Summary. 140

Chapter 10 - Ancient Witnesses of Christ's Resurrection 141

Two Angels at the Tomb 142

Mary Magdalene 143

Mary the Mother of Joses, Joanna, Salome, and the Other Women 144

Simon Peter. 145

Cleopas and Another on the Road to Emmaus. 145

Ten Apostles and Disciples at Jerusalem 146

The Eleven Apostles and Disciples in Jerusalem 147

Seven Apostles at the Sea of Tiberius 148

Eleven Apostles on the Mountain in Galilee. 149

Five Hundred Brethren 150

James the Apostle. 150

Eleven Apostles on the Mount of Olives. 151

Stephen's Stoning. 152

Paul on the Road to Damascus. 152

John on the Isle of Patmos 153

Christ's Appearances at the Temple in the New World 153

The Nephite Twelve. 154

Lost Ten Tribes 155

Other Book of Mormon Prophets 155

Summary. 155

Chapter 11 - Modern Day Witnesses of Christ. 157

Alexander Neibaur's Vision 157

Alfred Douglas Young's Vision 158

Frederick G. William's Vision. 159

Joseph Smith's Vision in the Grove. 159

Joseph Smith and Oliver Cowdery's Vision. 160

Joseph Smith and Sidney Rigdon's Vision. 160

Lorenzo Snow's Vision. 161

    Lyman Wight's Vision 162

    Meeting of the High Priests 1833. 163

    Melvin J. Ballard's Dream 164

    Orson F. Whitney's Dream. 164

    Rebecca Bean's Dream 165

    School of the Prophets Kirtland 167

    Summary. 168

Chapter 12 - Preparing for the Resurrection **169**

    Concepts that Help Us Prepare 172

        Shekhinah, or God's Presence 172

        Preparation and The Five "Ps" 173

        Chaata'ah or Missing the Mark 175

        Hasidut, or Piety and Loving Kindness 177

        Law of the Harvest: You Reap What You Sow 178

        Law of Proliferation 179

    Principles that Develop Christlike Qualities. 181

        Obedience 181

        Keeping God's Commandments 183

        Repentance. 185

        Forgiveness. 186

        Loving All. 187

        Service 189

        Sacrifice 190

        Consecration 191

    Summary. 193

Chapter 13 - Symbols of the Gospel and the Resurrection. **195**

    Animals. 195

    Baptism. 196

    Birth and Death. 197

    Body Parts. 198

    Colors 198

    Heavenly Orbs. 200

Nature	200
Numbers	201
Seasons	203
The Sacrament	204
Vicarious Work	205
Summary	206

Chapter 14 - Parables Applicable to the Resurrection **207**

Cloth and Wineskins	208
Draw Net	210
Invitation to the Wedding Banquet	210
Laborers in the Vineyard	212
Lowest Seat at the Feast	215
Sheep and the Goats	217
Talents	219
Ten Virgins	221
The Sower	224
Unjust Steward/Manager	227
Wheat and Weeds	230
Summary	232

Chapter 15 - Conclusion **234**
About the Author **237**
Endnotes **239**
Bibliography **277**
Index **283**

THE PURPOSE OF THIS BOOK

Have you ever wondered about what awaits you once your life on earth ceases, or have you sat during a funeral and considered God's plan of happiness as your heart ached? In contemplating life after death, the hope of the resurrection is like a calm and gentle breeze that blows through our lives. It arises at birth and meanders through the vicissitudes of life, eventually to seemingly dissipate at death; yet its gentle presence in our lives creates the anticipation of a day when we and our dear departed will arise from the dead.

The birth, life, and death of family members, loved ones, and friends' impact each of us. No one escapes or is untouched by such events. I recall a dear friend's infant son who became sick and over time succumbed to his illness and died. His parents were heartbroken, and we mourned with them. They shared their belief that they would see him again, and his mother spoke of how her arms ached to hold him once more. Despite their mourning, the promise of life's continuance through the resurrection of the dead gave them hope. It provided a salve that helped heal and comfort them in their time of loss and sorrow. Concerning our losses, the Prophet Joseph said, "All your losses will be made up to you in the resurrection, provided you continue faithful. By the vision of the Almighty I have seen it."[2]

But when will the resurrection—that anticipated event—occur? What will it be like? Given its significance, what symbols and testimonies are there of it? What can we learn from Christ's resurrection and from teachings concerning that event? As our reflections about the resurrection turn inward we ask how it will impact our future existence, and how we prepare for it. These along with other questions have answers found in the revelations from God and within the teachings of the prophets.

Jesus Christ's atonement without the resurrection would be of no value to us. The resurrection is the culminating event of His atoning sacrifice and through it we are enabled to return to God's presence. Studying and learning about the resurrection from the scriptures and the prophets is also paramount to our peace and eternal happiness. Joseph Smith spoke of God's desire that His children should know about and understand the resurrection. Joseph said, "It is but reasonable to suppose that God would reveal something in reference to the matter, and it is a subject we ought to study more than any other. We ought to study it day and night, for the world is ignorant in reference to their true condition and relation. If we have any claim on our Heavenly Father for anything, it is for knowledge on this important subject."[3]

The purpose of this book is to encourage a broader study and understanding of the resurrection, the events and principles that encompass it, the testimonies surrounding it, the Savior's teachings and role in it, and how we can prepare ourselves for it. In preparing ourselves, we give ourselves power, because having knowledge of the resurrection gives us choices and helps us discern which course will result in the most favorable outcome. This comprehension illuminates our future potential, focuses our energy, directs our actions, and provides great hope and solace through the endeavors of life. It becomes a catalyst for action and it gives us power to more accurately determine what we can become, since the type of resurrection we experience is tied to our eternal reward and glory.

Among those who may read this book are found four types of learners: the sponge, the funnel, the strainer, and the sieve. "The sponge" soaks up everything. "The funnel" takes things written in one end and lets them out the other. "The strainer" lets out the precious oil and retains the dregs. "The sieve" removes the chaff and retains the fine flour. Upon reflection one realizes it is the sieve and not the sponge that is the best learner. It is my desire that through your study and reflections on this book, like the sieve, you discard the chaff and by the impressions of the Spirit retain the fine flour of the Gospel so that the things written in this book will provide a better understanding of the doctrines surrounding the resurrection, bring peace, communicate our potential, inspire greater commitment, and foster an increased ability to obtain all God makes available to those who love and follow Him.

Finally, this book is not a publication of The Church of Jesus Christ of Latter-day Saints, nor does it necessarily represent the official position of the Church, or that of the book's publisher. I bear sole responsibility for the content of this book.

ACKNOWLEDGEMENTS

In writing a book one is never alone. I would like to thank my wonderful wife who endured thousands of hours of silence over the past years as I wrote, pondered, and produced this book on the resurrection. During the times the silence was broken she was incredibly patient as I would often blurt out, "what do you think about this," and then start reciting a section that I was working on. I am grateful to Hyrum Andrus who kept the flame of interest in the Gospel alive during my years at Brigham Young University. He was complemented by a trove of other religious educators and writers who through the years touched my life and contributed to my understanding of the resurrection. I appreciate Michael Walton's wonderful job of reviewing grammar, style, and composition. Additionally, a warm thanks to Robert Bean for helping catch errors in grammar along with all those who helped contribute to this work. Finally, thanks be to God who is the source of all truth and inspiration.

CHAPTER 1

UNDERSTANDING THE HOLY RESURRECTION

When Jesus comes, the shadows depart.
~ Inscription on a Scottish Castle

WHAT LIES AHEAD after mortality has been for many an awesome mystery, yet God has revealed many truths concerning the resurrection and our eternal reward. In seeking to understand the resurrection, some basic questions arise, which when answered will help us in our exploration of these truths. What is eternal life and salvation? How do we define the resurrection? What does the term firstfruits mean? What is the law of restoration? What does perfection mean? How does the resurrection help us understand God? How does the resurrection fit into the eternal plan of salvation? Why is the resurrection essential to our eternal progression? How does the resurrection relate to receiving a fullness of joy? In what way does the path of progression intertwine with our three estates of existence? And is there a difference between restoration to life, translation, and the resurrection?

Let us briefly examine each of these questions in an effort to lay a stronger foundation for understanding the doctrine of the resurrection.

Defining Eternal Life

Words and phrases often have multiple layers of meaning. For example, there can be a literal, spiritual, general, and specific meaning to a word or phrase. By examining the exegesis, or critical meaning of scriptural passages, and doctrinal concepts, a deeper and richer understanding can result. This is true of the phrase eternal life. All of God's children are eternal in nature. The scriptures tell us that even the elements are eternal.[4] They have no beginning and they have no end. Similarly, our spirits, "have no beginning; they existed before, they shall have no end, they shall exist after, for they are gnolaum, or eternal."[5] In this general sense, all of God's children have eternal life, for they are eternal beings.

Christ has also declared that all those who are on His right hand in the day of judgement inherit eternal life, while the wicked are cast out.[6] This scripture more narrowly defines eternal life as being more than eternal beings. Having eternal life includes occupying one of God's kingdoms of glory.

Yet, in its fullest sense, eternal life is to inherit God's life, or the type of existence He enjoys. It is to dwell in His presence, to inherit all things, and to continue one's posterity throughout eternity.[7] This is what God has foreordained for His children, and for which all true saints are striving. All who receive eternal life in its fullest sense will have no end. They will receive an everlasting, unending, and expanding inheritance with God their Eternal Father. This is what God is referring to when He says, "For behold, this is my work and my glory—to bring to pass the immortality and eternal life of man."[8] It began before this earth was formed and for the faithful saints will go on through eternity. God views this as His greatest gift for we are told that, "if you keep my commandments and endure to the end you shall have eternal life, which gift is the greatest of all the gifts of God."[9]

The Savior's parable of the pearl of great price applies to the gift of eternal life. He taught, "the kingdom of heaven is like unto a merchant man, seeking goodly pearls: Who, when he had found one pearl of great price, went and sold all that he had, and bought it."[10] All who inherit the fullness of eternal life, having given all to obtain it, will find themselves experiencing a fullness of joy and eternal progress throughout the eternities, having obtained this precious pearl.

The gift of eternal life is synonymous with the gift of salvation, which also is said to be the greatest of all the gifts of God. Next let's examine the definition of salvation, a companion concept of eternal life.

Defining Salvation

The scriptures teach us that salvation is also the greatest gift of God.[11] It is made available to all of humankind as a gift from a loving Heavenly Father. Jesus Christ is the author of humankinds' salvation, which is brought about through His Atonement. As Paul teaches in his letter to the Thessalonians, "For God hath not appointed us to wrath, but to obtain salvation by our Lord Jesus Christ."[12] In its broadest sense, salvation is to be saved within God's realm, which encompasses three kingdoms of glory, whether it be the celestial, terrestrial, or telestial kingdom.[13] We read that even those who inherit the telestial kingdom, the least of the three, will be heirs of salvation and will be redeemed.[14]

This general salvation is not the type of salvation that the saints of God should desire or seek. Settling for such salvation would be like gaining entrance to a coveted event with the anticipation of being seated on the front row, but upon arrival finding oneself only qualified to be seated on the row farthest back and behind a pillar. In its fullest sense, similar to eternal life, salvation is to be saved through the Atonement of Jesus Christ and live in the presence of God and Christ—to dwell with them eternally, becoming a joint heir with Christ, and receive all power. It is to have not only immortality, but eternal lives.[15] Full salvation comes through faith in the Lord Jesus Christ, repentance, good works, obedience to the Gospel, and obtaining all the ordinances and obeying all the principles required for a person to receive their exaltation. This type of salvation is what all true saints seek and what most scriptures concerning salvation allude to.[16]

Since the resurrection is an essential part of our salvation it is important to define the nature of the resurrection.

Defining the Resurrection

We know that through birth into mortality, humankind's spirit bodies are combined with physical bodies, helping humankind progress and become more like their Heavenly Father, who possesses an exalted body of flesh and bones.[17] But that uniting of spirit and body at birth is temporary due to the separation of the spirit and body at death. Following death, the resurrection reunites humankind's spirits and bodies for eternity.[18] Thus, we can define the resurrection as the reunion of a spirit body and physical body in its perfected and eternal state.[19]

Jesus Christ was the first to be resurrected and is called the firstfruits of the resurrection. Let's analyze the meaning of the phrase "firstfruits" as it pertains to Jesus Christ and to humankind.

Defining Firstfruits

As mentioned previously, words and phrases often have layers of meaning. The term "firstfruits" also can be viewed in different ways.

Literally, the term firstfruits referred to a Jewish festival. Shortly after God gave Israel the Ten Commandments, He gave another commandment to them saying, "Three times thou shalt keep a feast unto me in the year. Thou shalt keep the feast of unleavened bread…And the feast of harvest, the firstfruits of thy labours, which thou hast sown in the field: and the feast of ingathering, which is in the end of the year."[20] These celebratory events were to help the Israelites give thanks and remember their God and His blessings, while acknowledging that He was the creator and owner of all things. The feast of firstfruits involved making an offering late in the spring from the barley harvest, the first grain to ripen. The priest would wave a sheaf of green barley from side to side, to the four points of the compass, seeking acceptance from God, which was followed by the offering of a year-old male lamb without blemish. The lamb represented the coming Messiah. The ritual helped develop grateful hearts by acknowledging the gift of fruitfulness, life, and that God was the Lord of the harvest. Today through tithing, fast offerings, and other donations, we give of our harvest, recognize our blessings, show our gratitude, and acknowledge that all things belong to God.

The term firstfruits has another meaning and includes a component of time when referring to Jesus Christ. He was the firstfruits of God in the pre-earth existence, being the Firstborn. Specifically, Christ is described as the firstfruits, of them that slept.[21] We read that Christ, "layeth down his life according to the flesh, and taketh it again by the power of the Spirit, that he may bring to pass the resurrection of the dead, being the first that should rise. Wherefore, he is the firstfruits unto God.[22] He is the first to come forth as an eternal, perfected, and exalted being. Thus, He was the first born in mortality to obtain exaltation. He becomes, in a very personal sense, our Mentor, teaching us how to join Him eternally in God's presence, and like Him become the firstfruits of God's harvest.

With humankind, the term firstfruits is not time-related, but rather event-related. It refers to what is being produced and denotes that other fruits will be harvested later. It is part of a total harvest. Spiritually speaking, those who have passed through mortality and have obtained exaltation are called the firstfruits. As James writes that God, "Of his own will begat [sic] us with the word of truth, that we should be a kind of firstfruits of his creatures."[23] In this light as a general group, exalted humankind is the first of God's harvest amongst His children, no matter when the timing of their resurrection and exaltation is, when compared to those who come forth in a later harvest and do not obtain all that God has to offer His children. Jacob, a Book of Mormon prophet, said, "Wherefore, beloved brethren, be reconciled unto him through the atonement of Christ, his Only Begotten

Son, and ye may obtain a resurrection, according to the power of the resurrection which is in Christ, and be presented as the first-fruits of Christ unto God."[24] Like the first harvest of berries, which are the most succulent and flavorful, we should all strive to become the firstfruits of Jesus Christ's salvation and grace and inherit exaltation or God's life.

Having analyzed the meaning of firstfruits, let's now review how the law of restoration has a critical impact on the future and nature of humankind's resurrection.

Defining the Law of Restoration

Have you ever seen someone receive a reward they did not deserve, or perhaps more challenging, not receive one they did deserve? In our egalitarian society, although life is not fair, fairness is viewed as an important component of life. Most want to be treated fairly, or justly, and likewise try to treat others the same. While others may not always be fair to us, we know our God is perfectly fair, just, and merciful.[25] The law of restoration is a law whose foundation is based on these principles of fairness, justice, and mercy. It is a guiding and overarching principle that impacts the resurrection. In doing so, the law of restoration encompasses three broad areas. It restores us back to the presence of God to then be judged according to our works, it restores to us our physical bodies to then arise according to our works, and it restores our knowledge of our pre-earth existence works while maintaining a knowledge of our mortal existence and works. This threefold impact connotes divine backing and influence.[26] Let us examine each of these three areas.

First, the law of restoration restores us to the presence of God for judgment. Humankind having been cut off from God's presence by the fall of Adam is restored to that which was lost. Because of the Atonement of Jesus Christ, we are able to stand again in His presence. As Helaman taught, "But behold, the resurrection of Christ redeemeth mankind, yea, even all mankind, and bringeth them back into the presence of the Lord."[27] However, although the resurrection restores us back to God's presence that situation is only temporary. Our ability to remain with God is based upon how we have conducted our lives while in mortality. The law of restoration thus restores to humankind only what they are entitled to. Alma the Younger captured this idea by teaching, "And it is requisite with the justice of God that men should be judged according to their works; and if their works were good in this life, and the desires of their hearts were good, that they should also, at the last day, be restored unto that which is good. And if their works are evil they shall be restored unto them for evil. Therefore, all things shall be restored to their proper order."[28]

Second, the resurrection restores our physical bodies to us following death. Death, which comes upon all humankind through the fall of Adam, is overturned and all of humankind receive their bodies once again. We read that, "it is requisite and just, according to the power and resurrection of Christ, that the soul of man should be restored to its body, and that every part of the body should be restored to itself."[29] However, the law of restoration also requires that the type of body we receive in the resurrection be based upon our faith in Christ, acceptance of the Gospel, and our good works–restoring to humankind only that which they merit. The Doctrine and Covenants teaches this when it says, "For he who is not able to abide the law of a celestial kingdom cannot abide a celestial glory. And he who cannot abide the law of a terrestrial kingdom cannot abide a terrestrial glory. And he who cannot abide the law of a telestial kingdom cannot abide a telestial glory; therefore he is not meet for a kingdom of glory. Therefore he must abide a kingdom which is not a kingdom of glory."[30]

Finally, with the law of restoration, the characteristics and knowledge that we develop in mortality through our earthly experiences will arise with us. For, "Whatever principle of intelligence we attain unto in this life, it will rise with us in the resurrection."[31] The law of restoration also means that our memories of our premortal existence will be restored to us. As Nephi teaches, after the resurrection, we will, "become incorruptible, and immortal…having a perfect knowledge like unto us in the flesh, save it be that our knowledge shall be perfect."[32] It rightly restores that which we have obtained through our efforts and diligence. It does not restore that which we have not previously gained or sought to obtain. Thus the law of, "restoration more fully condemneth the sinner,"[33] and justifies the faithful while undergirding the justice and mercy of God.

Let's now consider the concept of perfection and its role in the resurrection.

Defining Perfection

In reviewing perfection perhaps, it is best to begin at the starting point. We are not perfect now, we were not perfect in the pre-earth existence, and will only become perfected after the resurrection when we become eternal, exalted, and glorified beings. As members of the Church we often obsess about perfection here in mortality, while inherently realizing it is not going to happen. Yes, we may be able to be perfect in some areas like paying tithing but the overall reality is that perfection in this life is not going to happen. Our faults are often exaggerated in our own eyes, especially while comparing ourselves to others who we perceive as perfect. In truth neither perspective is accurate. We are not as hopeless as we may think and no one gets through this life unscathed by sin and transgression. That is not to say we should not seek to live lives free from sin and error. The Savior and the prophets frequently admonished us to keep His commandments, sin no more, and do works of righteousness.[34] But it is to say we should realize that perfection is not obtainable during our lifetime and we should enjoy the journey of life, versus agonizing over our shortcomings as we do our best to overcome them and repent as we fall short.

What then did Jesus Christ mean when He Said, "Be ye therefore perfect, even as your Father which is in heaven is perfect.[35] Did He mean that God's focus and expectation was that we could be perfect during this mortal life despite the realities of our existence? That we through our efforts could be perfect in our daily walk? If so why was there the need for the Savior's expansive atonement? Why do the scriptures indicate that we all fall short of perfection, as John said, "If we say that we have not sinned…his word is not in us."[36] If we can find salvation in mortality through becoming perfect why does Paul state, "For by grace are ye saved through faith; and that not of yourselves: it is the gift of God."[37]

Let's take a closer look at the Savior's message about perfection. The Greek word for perfection in the bible is *teleios* pronounced (tel'-i-os) and signifies having reached an end or completion. It means to be finished, complete, or finally perfected. The Hebrew for perfection is *tamin* pronounced (taw-meen') and means sound, whole, complete, and entire. Neither of these are the same as todays definition of perfection, which is faultless, never making mistakes, or never needing correction. It is of interest that Christ, during His mortal ministry excluded Himself and only referred to God as the perfect example we should emulate. However, later following His resurrection when speaking to the Nephites He said, "Therefore I would that ye should be perfect even as I, or your Father who is in heaven is perfect."[38] Here He included Himself. What had occurred that changed His directive? When He appeared to the Nephites He was a resurrected, glorified, exalted, and eternal being. Prior to His resurrection He was still in a mortal unperfected state. This would suggest that Christ's admonition to become perfect like God was focused on humankind's final potential state of being. He was pointing our attention to the obtaining of our exaltation. To one day live as God lives as resurrected, glorified, immortal, and exalted beings enjoying the eternal presence and glory of God. To become perfected, eternal, exalted children of our loving Father in Heaven.

Sometimes we sin through mistakes of omission, sometimes commission. Other times the inherent weakness of mortality or the lack of knowledge leads us to err, etc. One time I remember being asked to address a group of Stake Presidents regarding a missionary program. My wife and I had to take a flight from where we were serving up to where the meeting was being held. As we were about to board our flight my wife asked, "Steve where is your suit coat?" My mouth dropped open and I said, "on the bed at home." When we arrived at the meeting I was dressed in slacks and a sweater. Everyone else including two members of the Area Seventies were dressed in suits. Clearly, I was dressed too casually for the meeting. Though certainly not a sin it was an error. As I addressed the group I said, "life has a way of humbling you. I forgot my suit coat at home. As I reflected on this I began to consider if my glass was half empty or half full. I concluded it was half full. I remembered my pants." We all had a good laugh. Enjoy the journey, no one can claim to be perfect.

The Resurrection Helps Us Know God

As we strive for eternal perfection understanding the resurrection's place in the plan of salvation is essential to gaining a correct comprehension of who and what God is. As God's children, this knowledge in turn reveals what we can become and gives us hope and consolation.

The more you take time to get to know another person, the more your ability to understand, relate, and communicate with them increases. Knowing that God is a resurrected, exalted man and our Father allows us to more intimately know Him, and increases our faith in Him, and improves our ability to communicate with Him. He is not some unknown God who is, "an infinite sphere, whose centre is everywhere and whose circumference is nowhere."[39] But He occupies space as a distinct being who, "has a body of flesh and bones as tangible as man's,"[40] exalted, glorified, divine, and dwelling in everlasting burnings.[41] As the Prophet Joseph Smith declared, "we know that there is a God in heaven, who is infinite and eternal, from everlasting to everlasting the same unchangeable God, the framer of heaven and earth, and all things which are in them; And that he created man, male and female, after his own image and in his own likeness, created he them."[42] Joseph Smith went on to teach that God is a resurrected, exalted, and glorified man, and that we have the potential to become as He is. Joseph said, "God himself was once as we are now, and is an exalted man, and sits enthroned in yonder heavens…God himself, the Father of us all, dwelt on an earth, the same as Jesus Christ Himself did…and you have got to learn how to be Gods yourselves, and to be kings and priests to God, the same as all Gods have done before you."[43] Since God dwelt on an earth "the same as Jesus Christ Himself did" and, "was once as we are now," He like Christ, is acquainted with our suffering, grief, and He knows how to succor us. Knowing this increases our love for, desire to communicate with, and ability to understand God.

Understanding God better can also give us a godlier perspective, one that provides consolation for the loss of loved ones. The Prophet Joseph Smith taught, "How consoling to the mourners when they are called to part with a husband, wife, father, mother, child, or dear relative, to know that, although the earthly tabernacle is laid down and dissolved, they shall rise again to dwell in everlasting burnings in immortal glory, not to sorrow, suffer, or die anymore; but they shall be heirs of God and joint heirs with Jesus Christ."[44] The sorrow and empathy that arises in our hearts due to the suffering and death of those around us can be swallowed up in the hope and healing of the promised glorious resurrection, and the knowledge that God is our Father, and understands us. As the Psalmist says, "weeping may endure for a night, but joy cometh in the morning."[45]

In thinking about how the resurrection brings us hope, my thoughts turn to Dan. Dan had served a faithful mission for the Church. When he returned home from his mission, a friend took him for a ride on a motorcycle, and unfortunately Dan was thrown off. As a result of that accident, he suffered spinal injuries that left him unable to walk and with little use of one arm and limited use of the other. As his home teachers, we felt great empathy for Dan and decided to hold a three-day fast to see if God would heal him. Following the fast, we met with Dan and blessed him according to the promptings of God's Spirit—but not with healing. As we left, my companion and I talked about our feelings and how the blessing had turned out. We felt a bit discouraged but trusted in God's will.

Later Dan shared a dream he had where, following death, he found himself sitting up as his grave was opened. It was in a beautiful grove surrounded by trees. He watched the ground fall away as he arose, fully restored to health. He greeted loved ones who were interned near him and who arose with him.

Following his story, Dan spoke to us of his longing to be healed, but found solace in the fact that, as he learned in his dream, one day he would joyously come forth in the resurrection and be restored to health. Dan has continued to serve faithfully in the Church; he now attends the temple many days a week. There he participates in multiple temple sessions providing saving ordinances to those who have died. He is an inspiration to all who know him. His attitude and actions serve as an example that in the face of difficult, continual, and daunting challenges, hope in Christ and the resurrection can inspire us to find ways to contribute to building God's kingdom and find meaning in life as we endure our challenges.

Understanding the resurrection not only helps us to understand God but it is an essential part of the plan of salvation.

The Resurrections Role in Salvation

It is human nature to seek happiness no matter if one lived today or two thousand years ago. There are many diverse sources of happiness. A number are fleeting like the thrill of bungee jumping or racing a car at high speed. Others are eternal in nature, such as the peace of knowing that one's life is in harmony with God or the joy a couple feels when they are sealed together eternally in marriage in the Lord's temple. God's plan of salvation, which is also aptly called the plan of happiness, brings true joy that is lasting in nature, and that doesn't fade with the lights and the music. Through it we can find eternal happiness, or a fullness of joy.[46] The resurrection as part of that plan of salvation is an essential part of humankind's progression and is a fundamental part of

Christ's Atonement.[47] Its absence would make death permanent, which means the separation of our body and spirit would also be permanent.[48] Without our bodies, we cannot continue to progress toward becoming like our Heavenly Father. Because the resurrection is an essential part of Christ's Atonement, its absence would mean that God's plan of salvation would be frustrated. Without the Atonement of Christ, we would be shut out from God's presence eternally. Our sins could not be forgiven, and sorrow would be humankind's eternal fate rather than happiness.

In discussing the resurrection, we can also benefit from exploring the importance of it in our lives.

The Resurrections Eternal Importance

A song contains a stanza that essentially says that though our bodies have been a friend, we won't need them when we reach the end. However, contrary to that message, we will need our physical bodies following mortality because they are essential to our eternal salvation and will allow us to become like our Heavenly Father, who possesses an exalted, divine body of flesh and bones. Since our spirts and bodies are separated when death occurs, the resurrection is essential to rejoin them so that we can become more like God and enter eternity to experience "a fulness of joy."[49]

Long-term, the absence of our physical bodies means we would become like Satan and his followers, who lost the opportunity to come to mortality because they rebelled against God in the pre-earth existence.[50] The scriptures tell us that without the resurrection, "our spirits must have become like unto him, and we become devils, angels to a devil, to be shut out from the presence of our God, and to remain with the father of lies, in misery, like unto himself."[51] Indeed, the dead looked upon the absence of their bodies as bondage,[52] for when their spirits and bodies are separated, they cannot receive a fullness of joy.[53] Following death, without the resurrection, as spirits we would be destined to an eternal existence with Satan and his followers, never to enjoy the pleasures and enhancements to our senses or the knowledge and capabilities of the resurrection, and never to be added upon throughout all eternity. Why? Because without the resurrection there would be no atonement, and due to Adam's transgression, in our fallen state we would be cut off from God's presence eternally for, "no unclean thing can inherit the kingdom of heaven."[54] We would be spirits separate and distinct throughout eternity. To be damned without any claim on Christ's atonement, without any hope of salvation, never to dwell in God's realm.[55] It would be an awful and unimaginable state. Clearly the resurrection, whereby we regain our then perfected physical bodies, and continue along the path of the plan of salvation, is a merciful event that allows us to enjoy the blessings of eternity.

Another purpose of the resurrection is to bring humankind lasting joy. Let's turn and explore what it means to receive a fullness of joy.

The Resurrection and Receiving a Fullness of Joy

The fullness of joy encompasses the absence of mortality's pain, suffering, and temptations,[56] coupled with the benefits brought by the enhancement of our senses, knowledge, sociality, and learning capabilities that are part of our eternal state of being. Thus, the eternally combined body and spirit in an exalted state brings about an increase and fullness of joy, which is not available when the body and spirit are separated. As mentioned previously, the dead looked upon the absence of their bodies as bondage, and when their spirits and bodies are separated they cannot obtain a fullness of joy. In trying to understand this concept, it may be helpful to consider how the absence of our bodies would affect us. Have you ever been unable to do something that brings you pleasure? Like smelling the rich fragrance of a summer rose, or experiencing the swelling feeling of joy in your heart at a glorious sunset as the amber glow of the sun warms your skin, or the gentle touch of moisture from a soft tepid rain on your uplifted face? This is like the bondage spirits experience in the absence of their bodies. Conversely, when our bodies and spirits are united and exalted, our capabilities are increased. This includes additional abilities that allow us to enjoy the interaction with matter around us, the enhancement of our emotional sensitivity, the ability to continue to create, the ability to organize matter, increased abilities to think and reason on multiple levels, enlarged access to and understanding of eternal laws and realities, and enhanced personal associations and relationships. All of these things and more contribute to humankind experiencing a fullness of joy. In our exalted eternal state, Parley P. Pratt explained that, "Eternal man in possession of eternal worlds, in all their variety and fullness, will eat, drink, think, converse, associate, assemble, disperse, go, come, possess, improve, love, and enjoy. He will increase in riches, knowledge, power, might, majesty and dominion, in worlds without end."[57] The Lord adds, "The wonders of eternity shall they know."[58] All of these things and more, coupled with a fullness of the spirit, contribute to exalted humankind experiencing a fullness of joy.[59]

Let's now examine the three estates of existence pre-earth life, mortality, and our post-resurrection eternal life, and the transitional gateways associated with each of these phases of existence.

The Three Estates of Existence, and their Transitional Gateways

The number three is biblically symbolic and signals divine backing, guidance, and influence.[60] The First Estate of existence was when, as spirit children of our Heavenly Parents, we dwelt with them in the pre-earth existence.[61] There, all the children of God possessed spirit bodies. These spirit bodies were tangible and made up of refined matter. As the Prophet Joseph Smith taught, "There is no such thing as immaterial matter. All spirit is matter, but it is more fine or pure, and can only be discerned by purer eyes; We cannot see it; but when our bodies are purified we shall see that it is all matter."[62] While there, we were tried, tested, and we exercised our agency choosing to follow God's plan of salvation. Satan and his followers did not. They were cast out and denied the opportunity to come to the second estate of mortality.[63] Those who were faithful in their first estate became heirs of the three transitionary gateways of mortality: birth, death, and the resurrection. All of humankind will experience them. Through them, humankind progresses along the plan of salvation to exaltation.

As spirit children, we must have looked in awe at our Heavenly Parents with their spirits clothed in glorified, exalted, eternal, bodies of flesh and bones. We would have hoped for the day we could come to mortality and become more like them. And in part, that day came as we left our premortal life. Through the gateway of birth, humankind leaves their pre-earth life, or their first estate, as spirits. We enter mortality, beginning our second estate.

Here, we gain our earthly bodies, are again added upon, tried, and tested to see if we will follow God. This mortal period also gives us the opportunity to continue to prepare ourselves for immortality.[64] This mortal existence is described as corrupt because of humankind's fallen nature.[65] At the gateway of death, humankind leaves the mortal portion of their second estate and enters the spirit world to await the resurrection.[66] Here our Second Estate continues. Yet even out of mortalities corruption and death, God in His infinite goodness and mercy creates the genesis of our third and final estate of existence.

Through the gateway of the resurrection, humankind leaves their second estate and enters their third estate as immortal, perfected beings, never to have their bodies and spirits separated again.[67] In the scriptures, this transition into the third estate is referred to as the "mortal putting on immortality."[68] This recombined spirit and physical body is called "the soul of man."[69] In the scriptures the resurrection is also termed "the redemption of the soul,"[70] since death brings a separation of "the soul of man," or the separation of the spirit and physical body. Thus, the third transitional gateway of the resurrection redeems our souls—it brings our spirits and bodies together eternally in a perfected state. This is the third estate of humankind's existence.

Having reviewed the three states of existence and their transitional gateways, let's look at how the restoration to life is different from the resurrection in relationship to the second gateway of death.

Resurrection versus Restoration to life

Some people have equated the phenomenon of restoration to life with the resurrection. An example of restoration to life occurs in the Bible's record of the miracle where Lazarus died and was brought back to life by Jesus Christ.[71] Another occurred when Jesus Christ raised the nobleman's son to life after his death.[72] And in the Old Testament, we learn of Elijah raising a widow's son from death to life.[73] Although each of these represents a miracle and demonstrates the power of God over death, they are not the same as being resurrected. In each case, Lazarus, the nobleman's son, and the widow's son, the person who was raised from the dead was raised up with their mortal body. They were still subject to all the vicissitudes of life and to death at a later date. They had not been raised from mortality to immortality in their final, perfected, and glorified state, never to die again. They were not resurrected.

Some characters in the scriptures, however, experienced an even more miraculous transformation called translation. What makes translation different from resurrection?

Resurrection versus Translation

Translation describes a change in an individual's condition such that they do not feel pain or suffer death. Satan also has no power over a translated being. But it is not the same as being resurrected. One example of translation is the three Nephites who were disciples of Christ. They requested to remain on the earth until Christ's Second Coming so they could bring souls unto Him. Mormon wrote of them, "I have inquired of the Lord, and he hath made it manifest unto me that there must needs be a change wrought upon their bodies, or else it needs be that they must taste of death…Now this change was not equal to that which shall take place at the last day; but there was a change wrought upon them, insomuch that Satan could have no power over them, that he could not tempt them; and they were sanctified in the flesh, that they were holy, and that the powers of the earth could not hold them. And in this state they were to remain until the judgment day of Christ; and at that day they were to receive a greater change, and to be received into the kingdom of the Father to go no more out, but to dwell with God eternally in the heavens."[74] As Joseph Smith stated, "men having this faith, coming up unto this order of God, were translated and taken up into heaven."[75] Enoch and his city, Melchizedek and his people, Elijah, John the Beloved, as well as others all experienced this process of translation.[76]

Joseph Smith additionally taught, "Many have supposed that the doctrine of translation was a doctrine whereby men were taken immediately into the presence of God, and into an eternal fullness, but this is a mistaken idea. Their place of habitation is that of the terrestrial order, and a place prepared for such characters He held in reserve to be ministering angels unto many planets, and who as yet have not entered into so great a fullness as those who are resurrected from the dead. ... This distinction is made between the doctrine of the actual resurrection and translation: translation obtains deliverance from the tortures and sufferings of the body, but their existence will be prolonged as to the labors and toils of the ministry before they can enter into so great a rest and glory."[77] These individuals, though translated, still need to go through the process of death and resurrection. For, as we learned from Mormon, this change was not equal to that which shall take place at the last day.

Summary

The resurrection provides a means to return to the presence of God and gain salvation. This prevents us from ultimately becoming subject to and like Satan. Gaining an understanding and knowledge of the resurrection is integral to worshipping God in faith and truth. With this insight, God becomes a loving, corporeal, and concerned father whom we can relate to. It reveals our divine potential to overcome life's challenges and become like God. The resurrection provides comfort and consolation for life's trials as we experience the tragedies of mortality. The three transitional gateways of mortality—birth, death, and the resurrection—are tied to our three estates of existence—pre-earth life, mortality, and eternity and provides a passage between them. They lay out a path of progress toward becoming like our Heavenly Father. And the number three testifies of their divine origin. The application of the law of restoration in our lives, along with our works, and the Atonement of Christ, determines what type of existence we enjoy in the eternities. Perfection is to one day live as God lives as resurrected, glorified, immortal, and exalted beings enjoying the eternal presence and glory of our Father in Heaven.

The resurrection is neither a translation or a resuscitation, but a reuniting of our body and spirit in an eternal, perfected, glorified state. As resurrected eternal beings in the kingdom of our God, we will be added upon again. We will experience a fullness of joy as our abilities, senses, and opportunities are increased. The solemnities and wonder of eternity await us.

CHAPTER 2

TERMS OF THE RESURRECTION

That which we call a rose by any other name would smell as sweet

~ Romeo and Juliet by William Shakespeare

Juxtapositions for the Resurrection

THROUGHOUT THE SCRIPTURES, the Lord often uses a comparison of two distinct words to highlight the differences between the righteous and the unrighteous. In making these comparisons, the Lord uses the number two, which is a symbol for separation or division. These two divergent words form a juxtaposition that leaves a strong impression of how the Lord views these two separate classes and how He contrasts their differences. Comparisons using juxtapositions are common in the scriptures and are filled with meaning. The juxtaposition of the wheat and the tares demonstrates this. Wheat—the righteous—is a crop upon which humankind has relied for sustenance for millennia. It provides nourishment and is the basis for life in many areas. Tares—the wicked—are injurious weeds that invade wheat fields and look like wheat when they are young. Tares are identified as darnel seed and actually uproot the wheat if they are left to grow. One way of interpreting Christ's parable of the "Wheat and the Tares" is that a competitor, or an enemy, sowed the tares among the wheat. This suggests that Christ as the faithful farmer sowed the wheat, and that Satan the competitor sowed the tares in an attempt to uproot the wheat, or the righteous. This parable seems to hearken back to the pre-earth life where Satan sought to supplant Jesus Christ as our Savior. It also has application to the resurrection—Christ is planting the true seed that will bring eternal life, while Satan plants a counterfeit seed that leads to eternal destruction.

The following is a chart of some of the common juxtapositions the Lord uses in describing these two main classes, the righteous and the wicked, in the resurrection and provides places where these comparisons can be found.

Happiness & Misery	Alma 40:17, 41:4; Mormon 8:38
Just & Unjust	Acts 24:15; Alma 12:8; D&C 76:17
Life & Damnation	John 5:29; Helaman 12:26; Mosiah 16:11; 3 Nephi 26:5
Right Hand & Left Hand	D&C 29:27; Matthew 25:33
Sheep & Goats	Matthew 25:32–33
Spiritual & Carnal	Romans 8:6; 2 Nephi 9:39

Illustration 2.1 Schedule of Juxtapositions

In these comparisons, "Happiness" describes the joyful state of the righteous. "Just" means they are justified through Jesus Christ. "Life" is eternal life, or God's life which they inherit. The "Right Hand," is a figure of speech that represents God's ultimate power and authority, where the exalted Jesus Christ now sits, and where those whom God loves and owns are to be found. "Sheep" refer to God's people, a prized possession, centered around Christ as the Lamb of God. "Spiritual" refers to their inherent thoughts and character as being pure and clean, without spot or blemish.

Conversely, "Misery" is the reward of the wicked. They are "Unjust," having failed to qualify for Christ's Atonement. They are damned, having suffered themselves to be overcome by the world. They are on God's "Left Hand," in the day of judgment, and which He is ashamed to own having denied His power and authority. And like "Goats," they may be head strong, but are not centered in Christ the "Lamb." "Carnal" is the nature of their character.

In describing the resurrection, God also uses pairs when He speaks of "Mortality" putting on "Immortality"[78] and "Corruption" putting on "Incorruption."[79] The resurrected are "Quickened" or "Rise" (past tense "Raised") becoming a "Spiritual Body" or "Spiritual," highlighting the change in humankind's physical condition.[80]

Synonyms and Verbs for the Resurrection

God also uses synonyms to describe the difference between two classes of humankind. An example would be those that are righteous receive the "First Resurrection,"[81] while those that are wicked receive the "Next, or Last Resurrection."[82]

God also uses verbs to identify the resurrection. On their resurrection day, the graves are "Opened,"[83] the people are "Lifted Up,"[84] they have "Risen,"[85] and they are deemed "Glorious."[86] All of which uplift our sights and inspire our thoughts concerning that event.

Summary

All of these comparisons, and more, represent a loving God trying to help His divine children comprehend the consequences of their choices, and the value and importance of His message of eternal salvation. They bring the message of salvation to each of us in a personal and individual way, challenging us to contemplate the impact on our lives and encouraging us to choose His path.

CHAPTER 3

JESUS CHRIST'S ATONEMENT AND THE RESURRECTION

He changed sunset into sunrise

~ Clement of Alexandria

THE SCRIPTURES MAKE clear that Jesus Christ is the author of our salvation and only through the Atonement of Jesus Christ can salvation come. In His divine role, as in all things, He is our exemplar, showing us the way for, "he is the life and the light of the world."[87] He is the divine prototype, and like a beacon, He streams a glorious beam of truth that illuminates the path back to God. And as death came through one, Adam, the father of us all born into mortality, redemption comes through one, Jesus Christ, who can spiritually redeem all who will receive Him. For as King Benjamin taught his people, "ye shall be called the children of Christ, his sons, and his daughters; for behold, this day he hath spiritually begotten you; for ye say that your hearts are changed through faith on his name; therefore, ye are born of him and have become his sons and his daughters."[88] As the author of our salvation, He overcame both the physical and spiritual barriers keeping us from returning to God's presence. He overcame the physical barrier, death, through the resurrection. The spiritual barriers He overcame through His Atonement and suffering for sin. He saves us perfectly physically, spiritually, and socially through His amazing grace.

Let's first examine the doctrine that Jesus Christ is the only means of salvation.

Jesus Christ the Only Means of Salvation

God in the pre-earth life, in His infinite goodness brought forth His firstborn son, Jesus Christ.[89] Jesus Christ was foreordained to the role of Redeemer in the pre-earth life.[90] The truth God gave Him there, which He taught us, was so powerful that He became known as "The Word."[91] All knew of His preeminent role. Those who were to be born into mortality accepted, followed, and trusted Him and God's plan of salvation. We rejoiced as we received knowledge and understanding of God's plan of salvation, which included our Savior's role as our Redeemer.

As part of the Atonement, He was foreordained to bring about the resurrection of humankind, "which was to be brought to pass through the power, and sufferings, and death of Christ, and his resurrection and ascension into heaven."[92] As a result of Jesus Christ's Atonement and resurrection, He holds the keys of the resurrection, death, and hell. These powers resided with the Father, and Jesus Christ through His Atonement and resurrection received them from God. When Jesus appeared to His disciples, He said, "All power is given unto me in heaven and in earth."[93] To John on the Isle of Patmos, Christ declared, "I am he that liveth, and was dead; and, behold, I am alive for evermore, Amen; and have the keys of hell and of death."[94]

Satan masquerades as the prince of this world, seemingly holding sway in hell, but he is not even a shadow of our great Lord and King, nor the ruler of these. Isaiah, in reference to Satan, stated, "They that see thee shall narrowly look upon thee, and consider thee, saying, Is this the man that made the earth to tremble, that did shake kingdoms;

That made the world as a wilderness, and destroyed the cities thereof; that opened not the house of his prisoners?"[95] Unlike Christ, the devil does not support or redeem his followers, as many have sadly learned.[96]

As mentioned, Christ provides the only way to obtain salvation for humankind. As a result, "There shall be no other name given nor any other way nor means whereby salvation can come unto the children of men, only in and through the name of Christ, the Lord Omnipotent."[97] No other person or source has or will exist with the power to bring our salvation to fruition. The plan of salvation is intended to redeem humankind from physical and spiritual death and return them to the presence of God in a resurrected, glorified, and eternal state. Let us now explore Christ's role in overcoming physical death brought by the fall of Adam as part of that plan of salvation.

Jesus Christ Overcomes Physical Death

Adam and Eve, along with all humankind, became subject to physical death as a result of the fall, becoming corruptible and mortal. Jesus Christ's Atonement brings salvation by overcoming the physical fall of Adam and Eve or death. As the prophet Jacob proclaimed, "O how great the plan of our God! For on the other hand, the paradise of God must deliver up the spirits of the righteous, and the grave deliver up the body of the righteous; and the spirit and the body is restored to itself again, and all men become incorruptible, and immortal, and they are living souls."[98] During His mortal ministry, all of His disciples struggled with the realization that Christ would and did physically rise from the dead.[99] In all of earth's roughly four thousand years of recorded history, no one had come back from the grave as a resurrected and perfected being, who promised the same reward for all humankind. No one had the power or the keys to overcome death and to change death into life, until Christ blazed a trail through death's sorrows, leading to a future of indescribable joy and rejoicing. As Isaiah proclaimed, "The people that walked in darkness have seen a great light: they that dwell in the land of the shadow of death, upon them hath the light shined."[100] The gift of overcoming physical death through Christ's resurrection, is given to all who enter mortality, regardless of their beliefs, the life they live, or their spiritual standing. It is the gift of a loving God made through the sacrifice of His Son, Jesus Christ.

As part of the plan of salvation, Jesus Christ also overcame the first spiritual death that was caused by the fall of Adam and Eve.

Jesus Christ Overcomes First Spiritual Death

God knew that the fall of Adam and Eve would bring about a spiritual death where humankind would be cut off from His presence. The Bible states that Adam was expulsed from the presence of God as he and Eve were driven out of the Garden of Eden.[101] And in being driven from the Garden of Eden, "the fall came by reason of transgression; and because man became fallen they were cut off from the presence of the Lord."[102] This estrangement meant that Adam and all his descendants were cut off from God's presence due to their transgression—we call this the first spiritual death.

Through the Atonement of Jesus Christ, this first spiritual death is overcome, "for all mankind, by the fall of Adam being cut off from the presence of the Lord, are considered as dead, both as to things temporal and to things spiritual. But behold, the resurrection of Christ redeemeth mankind, yea, even all mankind, and bringeth them back into the presence of the Lord."[103] Like Christ's gift of overcoming physical death, this gift of overcoming the first spiritual death is made for all who enter mortality. However, it does not guarantee they will remain in God's presence since humankind is responsible for the consequences of their own sins, and no unclean thing can dwell in the presence of God.

Thus, a means of overcoming humankind's sins had to be provided.

Jesus Christ Overcomes Second Spiritual Death

God saw that sin would enter the world and that humankind would be cut off from His presence as a result of their own sins, as opposed to Adam's—we call this the second spiritual death. Thus, for some of humankind, this re-instatement brought about by Jesus Christ overcoming the first spiritual death will be temporary due to an individual's failure to have faith in Christ, repent, accept the Gospel, and do good works. They will be judged, cast off from God's presence, and will receive according to their evil works. This is called the law of restoration. As Mormon said, "And then cometh the judgment of the Holy One upon them; and then cometh the time that he that is filthy shall be filthy still; and he that is righteous shall be righteous still; he that is happy shall be happy still; and he that is unhappy shall be unhappy still."[104]

However, this second spiritual death can be overcome through Christ's Atonement since He has paid the price of all humankind's sins.[105] It is a gift from Christ, which we qualify for through repentance. Those who repent and avail themselves of Christ's Atonement are washed clean through His atoning blood, and inherit a reward based on their worthiness. As Helaman taught concerning Christ's Atonement, "Yea, and it bringeth to pass the condition of repentance, that whosoever repenteth the same is not hewn down and cast into the fire."[106] Those who reject His Atonement must suffer for their own sins. "For behold, I, God, have suffered these things for all, that they might not suffer if they would repent; But if they would not repent they must suffer even as I."[107] And these having suffered, "after they have paid the penalty of their transgressions, and are washed clean, shall receive a reward according to their works, for they are heirs of salvation."[108]

Those who fail to repent either through the Atonement of Christ or by their own suffering will receive what their lack of action, or rebellion has earned—spiritual death. Concerning the unrepentant, Helaman said, "but whosoever repenteth not is hewn down and cast into the fire; and there cometh upon them again a spiritual death, yea, a second death, for they are cut off again as to things pertaining to righteousness."[109] Christ adds, "For what doth it profit a man if a gift is bestowed upon him, and he receive not the gift? Behold, he rejoices not in that which is given unto him, neither rejoices in him who is the giver of the gift."[110] Why are these individuals cut off? Because they will not repent and the Atonement of Christ cannot cleanse them for they choose to remain filthy still, and appalling is their final state.[111]

For those who accept Jesus Christ as their Redeemer and keep His commandments not only does He spiritually save us, but His Atonement saves us perfectly.

Jesus Christ Saves Us Perfectly

Through His Atonement and through the resurrection, Jesus Christ redeems us perfectly—physically, spiritually, and socially. He demonstrated His ability to completely redeem and heal us through many of the divine miracles He performed among the Jews during His mortal ministry. When Jesus Christ healed the man with an infirmity at Bethesda, He restored his physical abilities, "Jesus saith unto him, Rise, take up thy bed, and walk."[112] He also healed him spiritually, for later at the temple, Jesus told him, "Behold, thou art made whole: sin no more, lest a worse thing come unto thee."[113] But Jesus also healed him socially. As a Jew, he could now perform his obligations at the temple, whereas before he, "was there [Bethesda]…thirty and eight years," being infirmed.[114] Now healed, he could be gainfully employed providing for himself, and if he had a family, he could provide for them, fulfilling his societal obligations. This was also true of the widow's son,[115] the ten lepers,[116] and the woman with an issue of blood.[117] It is true for all those He touched with His divine power. It is also true for all the righteous in the resurrection: He restores our previous mortal body to an immortal state, spiritually heals us by cleansing us of all our sins, and socially brings us back into God's presence. He heals all who come unto Him with full purpose of heart, physically, socially, and spiritually—by removing all barriers for returning to our Father in Heaven's presence. Praise His holy name!

Those who choose to follow Jesus Christ will find hope in His amazing grace.

Jesus Christ's Saving Grace

Through Christ's Atonement and resurrection, His grace blesses each of our lives in numerous untold ways. Grace is defined as free and unmerited favor of God, undeserved divine assistance, and sanctification enjoyed through divine assistance. Each of these definitions reflects the grace of Christ that He bestows upon humankind.[118] An interesting exchange is recorded in the New Testament between a rich young man and Christ that bears upon the discussion of Christ's grace. The rich young man asks Christ what he needs to do to inherit eternal life. As the conversation progresses, Christ counsels him, "one thing thou lackest: go thy way, sell whatsoever thou hast, and give to the poor, and thou shalt have treasure in heaven: and come, take up the cross, and follow me." The young man's reaction is telling, "And he was sad at that saying, and went away grieved: for he had great possessions."[119] The rich young man's response challenges us all to ask ourselves where our priorities lie. Do we trust in our wealth or in God's direction for our lives? Then comes a key question that many ask themselves. His disciples inquired, "who then can be saved?" In response, Jesus declares this divine truth, "With men it is impossible, but not with God: for with God all things are possible."[120]

So, it is with exaltation. We cannot work our way there or achieve our desires without the grace of Christ. Have you ever heard it said that by our works we can get most of the way to exaltation, and the Savior's grace will make up the difference? This is a false and fallacious belief. Christ does not just help us over the final hurdle, He is there every step along the way. He is the life and light of the world, blessing us throughout our lives through His mercy and love with forgiveness, hope, insight, strength, peace, and guidance. We do not earn it, but it is a gift from a loving Savior who paid for it with the price of His blood, suffering in Gethsemane and on the Cross, and ultimately giving His life. This is what the Prophet Enoch was referring to when he said, "thou hast made me, and given unto me a right to thy throne, and not of myself, but through thine own grace."[121]

King Benjamin helped us understand that works by themselves will not save us. He proclaimed, "I say unto you that if ye should serve him who has created you from the beginning, and is preserving you from day to day, by lending you breath, that ye may live and move and do according to your own will, and even supporting you from one moment to another—I say, if ye should serve him with all your whole souls yet ye would be unprofitable servants."[122] Humankind does not, cannot, and will not earn their way to heaven—with men it is impossible. Rather, our works are a manifestation of our love and faith in Christ and are required for us to prove ourselves worthy of Christ's grace. We cannot be saved without good works, "For as the body without the spirit is dead, so faith without works is dead also."[123] Just as faith and works are tied together, grace and works are tied together. For through our works we open the door to the grace of Christ and show our willingness to follow Him. We conform our lives and mold our character to meet the requirements for His grace to apply in our lives in regards to the reward we will inherit. As Moroni, a Book of Mormon prophet taught, "come unto Christ, and be perfected in him, and deny yourselves of all ungodliness; and if ye shall deny yourselves of all ungodliness, and love God with all your might, mind and strength, then is his grace sufficient for you, that by his grace ye may be perfect in Christ."[124]

In this capacity, our works also justifies and sanctifies us through the grace of Christ.[125] We are commanded to grow from grace to grace just as Jesus Christ did.[126] Grace in this context can be related to the pure love of Christ.[127] It creates within us the genesis of our justification, in that we merit our reward, and sanctification as we become more like Jesus Christ and He purifies us. As the Doctrine and Covenants teaches, we must grow in grace for, "we know that justification through the grace of our Lord and Savior Jesus Christ is just and true; And we know also, that sanctification through the grace of our Lord and Savior Jesus Christ is just and true, to all those who love and serve God with all their mights, minds, and strength."[128] For with God all things are possible.

The following popular poem reminds me of the grace of Christ, His vigilant care and love for us, and how that blesses each of our lives.

FOOTPRINTS IN THE SAND, BY MARY STEVENSON

One night I dreamed a dream.
As I was walking along the beach with my Lord.
Across the dark sky flashed scenes from my life.
For each scene, I noticed two sets of footprints in the sand,
One belonging to me and one to my Lord.

After the last scene of my life flashed before me,
I looked back at the footprints in the sand.
I noticed that at many times along the path of my life,
especially at the very lowest and saddest times,
there was only one set of footprints.

This really troubled me, so I asked the Lord about it.
'Lord, you said once I decided to follow you,
You'd walk with me all the way.
But I noticed that during the saddest
and most troublesome times of my life,
there was only one set of footprints.
I don't understand why, when I needed You the most,
You would leave me."

He whispered, "My precious child, I love you and will never leave you
Never, ever, during your trials and testings.
When you saw only one set of footprints,
It was then that I carried you."

Summary

Jesus Christ is the only source of salvation and the divine prototype for how to return to and live with God eternally. His Atonement redeems us from physical death and the first spiritual death. He also delivers us from the second spiritual death brought about by our own sins, based upon repentance. Through His Atonement, we are holistically saved physically, spiritually, and socially. His grace blesses all our lives and assists us throughout our journey along the path of salvation towards exaltation. Christ's grace will eventually exalt us if we let it. In that process of salvation, the resurrection transforms us from our earthly to our eternal existence. Through faith in Jesus Christ and His atonement we can like the Anti–Nephi–Lehi's in the Book of Mormon and never, "look upon death with any degree of terror, for [our] hope and views of Christ and the resurrection; therefore, death [is] swallowed up to by the victory of Christ over it."[129]

CHAPTER 4

RESURRECTION'S HISTORICAL TEACHINGS

How oft would I have gathered you...and ye would not

~ 3 Nephi 10:5

DUE TO THE resurrection's essential role in salvation, it is important to realize that the resurrection has been taught down through the ages. It was not first introduced by Jesus Christ during His mortal ministry. Despite God's efforts to disseminate information concerning the plan of salvation and the resurrection, much of the world fails to comprehend or accept Jesus Christ's Atonement and His literal resurrection.

The Doctrine of Resurrection Taught in All Ages

The doctrine of the resurrection was not first introduced by Christ during His mortal ministry nor was it conceived after His death by His followers as some have supposed. Rather, this doctrine was first revealed by God in the pre-earth life. As Alma explained concerning our pre-mortal foreknowledge of the plan of salvation and the resurrection, "if it had not been for the plan of redemption, which was laid from the foundation of the world, there could have been no resurrection of the dead; but there was a plan of redemption laid, which shall bring to pass the resurrection of the dead, of which has been spoken."[130]

The resurrection has also been preached throughout the history of humankind. For example, the Lord through Ezekiel, who lived hundreds of years before Christ, declared, "Therefore prophesy and say unto them, Thus saith the Lord God; Behold, O my people, I will open your graves, and cause you to come up out of your graves, and bring you into the land of Israel. And ye shall know that I am the Lord, when I have opened your graves, O my people, and brought you up out of your graves."[131]

The reality of the resurrection was also taught to the people in the Book of Mormon before the coming of Christ. Lehi explained, "Wherefore, how great the importance to make these things known unto the inhabitants of the earth, that they may know that there is no flesh that can dwell in the presence of God, save it be through the merits, and mercy, and grace of the Holy Messiah, who layeth down his life according to the flesh, and taketh it again by the power of the Spirit, that he may bring to pass the resurrection of the dead, being the first that should rise."[132] We find the word "resurrection" used fifty-two times before the coming of Christ in the Book of Mormon, not counting other synonyms for the resurrection, such as "risen," or "incorruption."

In the New Testament, it is apparent that the Jews had at least some knowledge of the resurrection, for different sects of Jews had differing beliefs on the afterlife, as illustrated during Christ's mortal ministry. The Sadducees, for example, did not believe in resurrection.[133] They would ask, where in the law could it be proved? Whereas, the Pharisees did believe in afterlife and a physical resurrection,[134] though they had many misconceptions, such as a person would not be healed, but would rise with the same bodily defects, or all the pious would arise in Palestine, after they had rolled through cavities under the earth till they arrived there.[135] There are other sources that demonstrate the belief in the resurrection at the time of Christ. One of these is the Amidah.

The Amidah, meaning standing, pronounced (ah–mee–DAH), is a prayer currently offered three times daily by observant Jews, as they stand. Also called the Shemoneh Esrie, it is a series of eighteen blessings formalized in 70 CE, but that have their origin in pre-70 CE Jewish worship. Different forms and parts of these blessings are found in various ancient sources.[136] Jesus would have been very familiar with a variation of this prayer. Blessing two contains the concept that God raises the dead. There, we read:

> You are powerful, humbling the proud;
> Strong, and judging the violent;
> Alive, forever, raising the dead;
> Making wind blow, and dew fall;
> Sustaining the living, reviving the dead;
> Like the fluttering of an eye,
> make our salvation sprout.
> Blessed are you Lord, reviving the dead[137]

Although the form and exact wordage may have varied down through the ages it illustrates that the resurrection was believed, taught, and anticipated at the time of Jesus Christ's ministry. In the face of these differing views and opinions, Christ clearly proclaimed the resurrection during His ministry. To Martha He said, "I am the resurrection, and the life: he that believeth in me, though he were dead, yet shall he live."[138]

We also find this doctrine was being preached in the spirit world, for while the righteous spirits awaited the Savior's appearance following His crucifixion we learn, "that they were filled with joy and gladness, and were rejoicing together because the day of their deliverance was at hand. They were assembled awaiting the advent of the Son of

God into the spirit world, to declare their redemption from the bands of death. Their sleeping dust was to be restored unto its perfect frame, bone to his bone, and the sinews and the flesh upon them, the spirit and the body to be united never again to be divided, that they might receive a fulness of joy."[139] There is clear scriptural evidence that the knowledge of the resurrection was among God's children from the pre-earth life down to our day and will continue in the future. The fact that this knowledge of the resurrection has continued to exist shows God's desire for His children to understand and partake of this promised blessing.

I recall being in the mission field in England and with my companion teaching investigators. We had collapsible felt illustration boards that worked like an umbrella. When opened, we would put words and small pictures that stuck on the felt board. When we got to the plan of salvation, and placed images of the pre-earth existence, mortality, and the three degrees of glory, it often spurred their interest and discussions about our eternal destiny ensued. When we spoke of the resurrection we often heard them say, "I have always believed in that."

As members of the church, we also have the blessing of additional insight into the resurrection, which should motivate us to study and learn about it as a means to increase our faith in Jesus Christ, and to look for God's efforts to bring about our salvation.

God's Historical Efforts to Bring Salvation

Our vision is often focused on the times in which we live and our efforts to obtain salvation. We often fail to see what has already been done to assure God's plan for His children is not frustrated. Historically, the past shows that God has already done much to fulfill humankind's eternal destiny, which efforts also display His commitment and determination. Throughout the scriptures, the number seven represents perfection. From that perspective, let us examine seven things that God has done to bring salvation to His offspring.

First, in the pre-earth life, God brought us forth as His children and taught us the Gospel, which was the beginning of our progress in becoming like Him. Abraham gave us insight into this when he said, "Now the Lord had shown unto me, Abraham, the intelligences that were organized before the world was; and among all these there were many of the noble and great ones; And God saw these souls that they were good, and he stood in the midst of them, and he said: These I will make my rulers."[140] Thus from the pre-earth life, God was active in preparing His children for salvation.

Second, through Jesus Christ, God created this earth, and our birth provides us a physical body like our Father's as we are added upon, although we may be corruptible and unglorified at the present. John told us, "All things were made by him; and without him was not any thing made that was made. In him was life; and the life was the light of men."[141] Through the creation, God formed humankind's dwelling place as part of the plan of salvation.

Third, the unprecedented gift of His Son, Jesus Christ, and His Atonement and resurrection provides the means to redeem us and bring us back to God's presence with a resurrected, perfected, and glorified body. As Christ declared, "Behold, I am he who was prepared from the foundation of the world to redeem my people. Behold, I am Jesus Christ. I am the Father and the Son. In me shall all mankind have life, and that eternally, even they who shall believe on my name."[142] Our Heavenly Father provided the means for all to gain salvation through the gift of His only begotten son.

Fourth, God has provided the scriptures and prophets to show us the way to become like Him and return to His presence. For, "All scripture is given by inspiration of God, and is profitable for doctrine, for reproof, for correction, for instruction in righteousness."[143] God has also disseminated His word through His servants. In Ephesians we learn that, "he gave some, apostles; and some, prophets; and some, evangelists; and some, pastors and teachers; For the perfecting of the saints."[144] God has not kept the essential knowledge of the plan of salvation to Himself but has in all ages unselfishly revealed it to His children.

Fifth, God has revealed Gospel ordinances like baptism and the gift of the Holy Ghost to prepare for the resurrection and qualify us to return to live with Him. For we are told that, "in the ordinances thereof, the power of godliness is manifest."[145]

Sixth, through obedience to the laws and ordinances of the Gospel, we are cleansed, sanctified, and prepared to return to Him. In the Doctrine and Covenants, we read, "verily I say unto you, that which is governed by law is also preserved by law and perfected and sanctified by the same."[146] Not only has God shown us the path to perfection, but He has also provided the knowledge that allows us to cleanse and sanctify ourselves.

Seventh, God has sent the Holy Ghost to testify and guide us to all truth, "And by the power of the Holy Ghost ye may know the truth of all things."[147] Through the Holy Ghost, God has provided a direct conduit to His knowledge and gifts and has sent the Holy Ghost as a witness to testify of Him and His Son.

These seven things, though not a complete listing of God's efforts to bring us salvation, show God's undeviating and perfect effort to provide a way for humankind to progress, and to understand and obtain salvation. There are many other things that witness to God's undeviating commitment to redeem His children through all ages of time. Truly, He is a God of mercy and love, and does nothing save it is for the salvation of humankind.

In regards to God's effort to bring salvation to humankind, a member of a temple presidency shared a situation he experienced. One day he was called to the temple reception desk and found a person there who spoke no English. After listening to him, the member of the presidency decided the man was probably Japanese and said, "One minute," holding up one finger. He returned to his office, called the mission president of the area the temple was in, and told him that he had a non-member at the temple who spoke Japanese. The mission president said he had two Elders who spoke Japanese and could be at the temple within twenty minutes. My friend said he would call him back if he required anything, and, picking up a temple brochure in Japanese, returned to the front reception desk. He gave the man the brochure, who upon examining it said, "Mandarin." My friend realized the man was actually Chinese, and again excused himself and called the mission president again. The mission president said, "I have two missionaries who speak Mandarin. They have just finished lunch and are within five minutes of the temple. I will have them come right over." The member of the temple presidency took a brochure that this time was written in Mandarin, which the visitor gratefully received. The missionaries arrived and met with the man, who agreed to receive the missionary discussions. He was baptized a member of the Church two weeks later. The work of salvation continues all around us and we are often unaware of the many tender mercies God extends toward His children in helping them find salvation. If we open our eyes and hearts, we will see God's hand working in our lives to bring about our salvation, and also doing the same in the lives of many around us.

Yet the world as a whole continues to ignore the eternal truths of the Gospel, including the resurrection.

The World's Continued Failure to Recognize the Resurrection

The world's failure today to understand and recognize the resurrection continues to mimic the past—like when the Jews rejected their Savior. Today, only 31.2 percent of the world's population is Christian, which as a religious class has a focus on Christ and His resurrection. The following pie chart illustrates this fact:

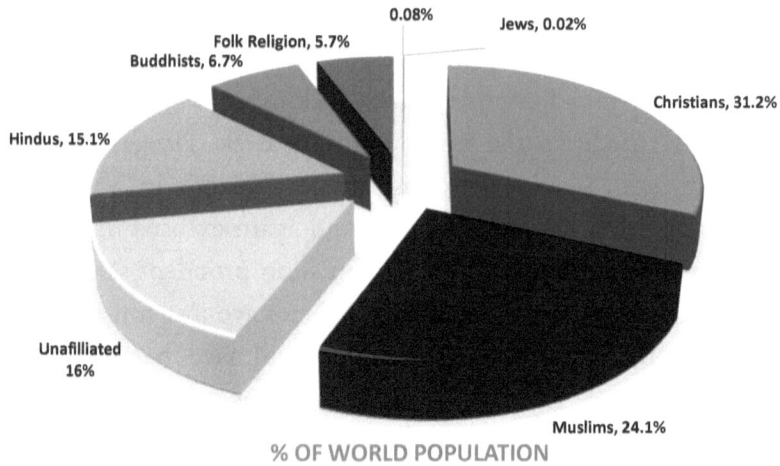

Illustration 4.1 World Religions

Another recent Harris poll shows that 65 percent of Americans believe Christ was resurrected.[148] However, most Americans don't believe that they will personally be resurrected.[149] A BBC poll shows 25 percent of Christians in Great Britain do not believe in the resurrection.[150] Some believe there is no physical resurrection, but the spirit continues on. Some don't believe in life's continuance but believe that at death everything ends. Others subscribe to the idea of reincarnation or other non-resurrection doctrines. The world as a whole continues to misunderstand or reject the truth of the resurrection. As the book of Proverbs points out, "The fear of the Lord is the beginning of knowledge: but fools despise wisdom and instruction."[151]

A close associate, who was a member of our Church, shared with me how one day he was having lunch at a restaurant where many business people met and ate. Suddenly, as he sat there having his lunch, like a switch turning the lights off, everything went dark for about five minutes. He could not see, hear, or perceive anything. Then just as suddenly, like flipping the light switch on, things returned to normal. His assessment following this event was that when life ends, that is it;

nothing continues. I thought how sad it was that a single event in his life would lead to a lack of faith in Jesus Christ and the eternal nature of man. He has since died and passed on to the world of spirits. I have often thought of how surprised he must have been when he found the "light switch" still on—that our existence continues beyond the grave. With all the evidence that testifies to the reality of the continuation of life, we should first doubt our doubts before doubting the truth.

Summary

The doctrine of the resurrection, which is required for exaltation, has been taught in all ages. God historically has made a voluminous effort to teach salvation and the resurrection of humankind. Satan in opposition to God's efforts has been very successful in creating confusion and misunderstandings throughout humankind's existence concerning the plan of salvation and the resurrection. He has been active in spreading lies about the reality of it, including teaching falsehoods concerning it, and generating false concepts foreign to it in order to dissuade humankind from believing in God. The Book of Mormon teaches, "Wherefore, men are free according to the flesh; and all things are given them which are expedient unto man. And they are free to choose liberty and eternal life, through the great Mediator of all men, or to choose captivity and death, according to the captivity and power of the devil; for he seeketh that all men might be miserable like unto himself."[152] True followers of Jesus Christ must always examine their beliefs and lives to be sure they are following true principles that will prepare them for a glorious resurrection and will lead them back to God's presence.

CHAPTER 5

DOCTRINES FUNDAMENTAL TO THE RESURRECTION

*For the Lord giveth wisdom: out of his mouth
cometh knowledge and understanding*

~ Proverbs 2:6

IN ORDER TO continue to expand our understanding of the resurrection, let's build upon what we have already discussed and examine what general classes of humankind will rise in the resurrection. We will explore what the terms first, second, and morning of the resurrection mean, in what ways the death and the resurrection are partial judgment, and what records play a role in the resurrection and final judgment day. We will also discuss the importance of repentance, how the resurrection is a priesthood ordinance, and when our second estate ends. Finally, we will examine what is meant by eternal progression and eternal damnation.

Classes in the Resurrection

Within the resurrection there are classes of people. For our purposes here, a class is a set or group of people having certain attributes in common. Before discussing this, we must first remember that God's realm includes three different kingdoms: the celestial, terrestrial, and telestial realms. All are kingdoms of glory.[153] Each kingdom differs in glory, and the gradation, attributes, and traits of those who inhabit them is just as different as the variance in the luminosity of the sun, moon, and stars. Satan has a kingdom of no glory. While there are three different kingdoms within God's realm of glory, and one of no glory that Satan rules, there are two main classes of people that will be resurrected and inherit the four kingdoms. As we explored previously, the number two symbolically infers a separation, three divine guidance, while the number four means completeness. In these two classes of beings there are those who achieve the First Resurrection, and those who obtain the Second or Last Resurrection.

Let's examine the First Resurrection and the class of people it encompasses and the kingdoms they inherit.

First Resurrection

Illustration 5.1 The First Resurrection

The first class constitutes the resurrection of humankind who will inherit the celestial and terrestrial kingdoms, the number of kingdoms being two again signals a separation. This is called the First Resurrection. All who arise in the First Resurrection are part of the resurrection of the "Just," because they are justified by their faith in Jesus Christ.[154] One way to confirm who takes part in the First Resurrection is to begin with who will take part in the Second, or Last Resurrection. In the Doctrine and Covenants in speaking of those who inherit the telestial kingdom, it states, "These are they who shall not be redeemed from the devil until the last resurrection, until the Lord, even Christ the Lamb, shall have finished his work."[155] Since those who are raised in the telestial resurrection belong to the Second, or Last Resurrection it leaves those who belong to the celestial and terrestrial kingdom as participants in the First Resurrection. For the resurrected celestial saints this is reaffirmed by the Lord when He said in reference to those who He will bring with Him in the clouds at His return, "These are they who shall have part in the first resurrection."[156] For those of the terrestrial kingdom the Lord in speaking of the resurrection said that, "then shall the heathen nations be redeemed, and they that knew no law shall have part in the first resurrection; and it shall be tolerable for them."[157] Scripturally we know that the heathen nations and those who knew no law come forth in the terrestrial resurrection,[158] hence we know that the terrestrial resurrection is included in the first resurrection.

The defining features for those who take part in the First Resurrection, inheriting the celestial kingdom, is that they have demonstrated faith in and have a testimony of Jesus Christ, accepted the Gospel of Jesus Christ and all its ordinances, demonstrated good works, and endured to the end.[159] The features that define those who inherit the terrestrial kingdom is that they have faith in and a testimony of Jesus Christ but have rejected the Gospel of Jesus Christ. They are the good people of the earth who have been blinded by traditions or the craftiness of humankind or knew no law. They also include those who have accepted the Gospel and its ordinances but unlike those who inherit the celestial kingdom have not proved valiant in their faith.[160]

Next let's review the second class who take part in the Second or Last Resurrection and the kingdoms they inherit.

Second or Last Resurrection

Illustration 5.2 The Second or Last Resurrection

The second class consists of humankind who are part of the Second, or Last Resurrection. They inherit the telestial kingdom, or Satan's kingdom of no glory. Again, the number two symbolically signaling a separation. It is second because they have proved themselves less worthy than those of the First Resurrection and is called the Last Resurrection because these eventually will be the last to be resurrected. They also include those who are last within the realm of God. It is the resurrection of the "Unjust," or "Damnation," because they are not justified by their faith in Jesus Christ.[161] We read that, "another trump shall sound, which is the fourth trump, saying: There are found among those who are to remain until that great and last day, even the end, who shall remain filthy still."[162] This indicates that included in the Second Resurrection are two groups. The first group who inherit the telestial kingdom have rejected the Gospel of Jesus Christ, and do not have a testimony of Christ, but acknowledge Him as their King and Sovereign. They have repented of their sins through their sufferings and will be found on Christ's right hand in the day of judgment.[163] The second group rejects the Gospel, does not accept Jesus Christ as their Savior or King, and will not submit to His rule or dominion. They refuse to repent and remain condemned by their sins or as the scriptures describe they remain filthy still. These inherit

Satan's kingdom of no glory. They are not part of God's realm and are found on Christ's left hand in the day of judgment.[164]

This understanding leads us next to consider the meaning of the term First Resurrection as a title.

The First Resurrection as a Title

A member in Sunday School once asked why it is called the "First Resurrection," since Jesus Christ and the saints already arose in the meridian of time. Our society is so driven by the passage of time that it is easy to understand the confusion over the term "First Resurrection." "First" denotes an initial event. However, its meaning also can relate to a class, or title for which time may not be the identifying factor. For the people who died prior to Christ's coming in the flesh, it was the "First Resurrection;" none had risen before.

But today the term "First Resurrection" more aptly applies as a title, with time being a less important element. It began with Christ's resurrection and continues through earth's temporal existence. Hence, it applies to all those who come forth in the first class to be resurrected—those of a celestial and terrestrial nature—regardless of the time period.

What then does it mean to arise in the morning of the First Resurrection?

The Morning of the First Resurrection

Another individual asked what it means when you are told in your patriarchal blessing that you will come forth in the morning of the First Resurrection, if you are faithful. Clearly, it means to come forth in a celestial resurrection. "Morning" can refer to the glorious dawning of a new day for humankind as they arise in a perfected, immortal, glorified, and exalted state. Inherent in this promise is the idea that one will have prepared and proved themselves to be worthy of that event. Thus, it can be said that all who arise in a celestial resurrection come forth in the morning (new day) of the First Resurrection. It could also refer to those who will be resurrected at the time of Jesus Christ's Second Coming, or arise shortly thereafter, as in the dawn of the millennium. Some express concern because their patriarchal blessing does not mention this. The presence or absence of specific language does not foretell what resurrection one will experience. Rather, it is faith in Christ, obedience to the Gospel and its ordinances, good works, and enduring to the end that will ultimately determine the type of one's resurrection.

Let's now turn to the role of death as a type of judgment in the resurrection.

Death a Type of Judgment

We often like to rehearse the quote that says, "Judge not that ye be not judged," when people are critical of us or of others. Yet in life we are constantly judging or being judged. We might consider whether someone we deal with is trustworthy, or if we feel safe in another's presence. Someone might judge whether the credit card we are presenting is ours. Likewise, there are many spiritual types of judgments that occur in life. For example, birth into mortality is an indication of a judgment, for those in the pre-earth life who were unworthy of their second estate forfeited the right to be born here. Most Christian churches have moral standards that their members are expected to follow to be in good standing in their faith. For members of the Church of Jesus Christ of Latter-day Saints, a temple recommend is a judgment of one's spiritual status in God's kingdom. To obtain one, a person must be able to respond positively when asked if they have a testimony of Jesus Christ and the restored Gospel in these latter days. They are also asked if they are keeping His commandments, if they are paying an honest tithe, and if they are faithful to their spouse, etc. For male members, holding the priesthood of God is a judgment of one's standing before God. A calling as the president in the Relief Society could be an indication of a sister's positive spiritual standing before God. These are just a few examples of the many types of spiritual judgments that occur.

Following death, we also experience a partial spiritual judgment.

At death, we enter the world of spirits. There we reside in one of two realms—paradise or prison. Where we reside is based on our faith in Christ, our acceptance of the Gospel of Jesus Christ, the desires of our hearts, and the quality of the life we lived. Those who faithfully accepted the Gospel of Jesus Christ and were baptized for the remission of sins will be judged worthy to reside in paradise with the saints. This includes little children who die before they could accept the Gospel or be baptized. All others enter spirit prison. Alma taught this when he said, "Now, concerning the state of the soul between death and the resurrection...then shall it come to pass, that the spirits of those who are righteous are received into a state of happiness, which is called paradise, a state of rest, a state of peace, where they shall rest from all their troubles and from all care, and sorrow. And then shall it come to pass, that the spirits of the wicked...shall be cast out into outer darkness; there shall be weeping, and wailing, and gnashing of teeth, and this because of their own iniquity, being led captive by the will of the devil."[165] Outer Darkness, in this context, refers to spirit prison, where those sent there are condemned by their own conscience and where looking forward to fiery indignation of God is like a lake of fire and brimstone. Like the teachings of Alma, the Savior's parable of Lazarus the beggar, and the Parable of the Ten Virgins all plainly point to the great divide between the righteous who are at peace and the wicked who are in torment in the spirit world. President Joseph Fielding Smith added the following insight, "It is the righteous who go to paradise. It is the righteous who cease from those things that trouble. Not so with the wicked. They remain in torment. They have their anguish of soul intensified, if you please when they get on the other side, because they are constantly recalling to mind their evil deeds. They are aware of their neglected opportunities, privileges in which they might have served the Lord and received a reward of restfulness instead of a reward of punishment...All spirits of men after death return to the spirit world. There, as I understand it, the righteous—meaning those who have been baptized and who have been faithful—are gathered in one part and all the others in another part of the spirit world."[166] Here, President Joseph Fielding Smith clearly points out that baptism and keeping the commandments are two critical requirements for entering paradise instead of spirit prison.

For humankind, another partial judgment is the resurrection.

Resurrection a Type of Judgment

Like death, one's resurrection is a partial judgment of an individual's standing before God. The scriptures are clear that there is only one resurrection for an individual. Regardless of when they are resurrected, once the spirit and the body are united in an immortal and eternal state, there will be no more death, hence no other resurrection. Alma taught this when he said, "Now, behold, I have spoken unto you concerning the death of the mortal body, and also concerning the resurrection of the mortal body. I say unto you that this mortal body is raised to an immortal body, that is from death, even from the first death unto life, that they can die no more; their spirits uniting with their bodies, never to be divided; thus the whole becoming spiritual and immortal, that they can no more see corruption."[167]

The scriptures declare that there are different types of bodies in the resurrection.[168] Since there is only one resurrection, the nature of our resurrected bodies becomes important. Each type of resurrected body has the ability to endure a specific degree of glory and those below it. So, our resurrection limits what type of glory, or kingdom, we will inherit due to the nature of our resurrected bodies. Just as someone born into mortality might have greater or lesser physical abilities, so a resurrected body will have different physical abilities to endure different environments depending on the nature of one's final being.

In addition, the state of our own consciences will affect where we will feel accepted and the glory we inherit. Mormon taught this when speaking of dwelling in the presence of God. He said, "Do ye suppose that ye shall dwell with him under a consciousness of your guilt? Do ye suppose that ye could be happy to dwell with that holy Being, when your souls are racked with a consciousness of guilt that ye have ever abused his laws? Behold, I say unto you that ye would be more miserable to dwell with a holy and just God, under a consciousness of your filthiness before him, than ye would to dwell with the damned souls in hell. For behold, when ye shall be brought to see your nakedness before God, and also the glory of God, and the holiness of Jesus Christ, it will kindle a flame of unquenchable fire upon you."[169] If our minds and hearts are not purified, we will not desire to dwell in the presence of our Holy God.

Our actions also are a contributing factor in what type of resurrection we will come forth in, and whether we will dwell with God. They determine the amount of light and truth we are imbued with and govern the purity of our minds. Those governed by laws are sanctified by them, and hence the fewer the laws we are willing to obey, the less light and truth we will possess and the less our purification and sanctification will be. Conversely, the more of God's laws we are willing to obey, the greater the light and truth we will be invested with and the purer and more sanctified we will become. Thus, the type of heavenly laws we obey establishes the type of resurrection we will experience and the type of body we will receive. We will arise as celestial beings if we have been imbued with the light and truth of a celestial spirit or arise as terrestrial beings if we have been imbued with less light and truth than a celestial spirit, but concurrent with a terrestrial spirit. Likewise, with telestial beings.[170] In reflecting on the differences between the types of bodies in the resurrection, Orson Pratt said, "there will be several classes of resurrection bodies; some celestial, some terrestrial, some telestial, and some sons of perdition. Each of these classes will differ from the others by prominent and marked distinctions; yet in each, considered by itself, there will be found many resemblances as well as distinctions. There will be some physical peculiarity by which each individual in every class can be identified."[171]

Some may think they can receive a resurrection to a lesser kingdom, and over time move up to a higher kingdom. There is no scriptural support for this concept. For example, we are told that those who receive the telestial kingdom, "shall be servants of the Most High; but where God and Christ dwell they cannot come, worlds without end."[172] This clearly shows that those of a telestial resurrection will never be able to live in God's presence in the celestial kingdom. It would also apply to those of a terrestrial resurrection due to the nature of their resurrected bodies, which cannot endure a celestial glory.[173] Elder Bruce R. McConkie emphasized this by stressing that although there may be progression within a kingdom individuals do not progress from one kingdom to another in eternity neither does one ever progress from a lower kingdom to where a higher kingdom once was.[174] Because the resurrection is a partial judgment, it has eternal consequences that reflect one's eternal reward and which kingdom they will inherit.

Since our reward is based on the number of God's laws we are willing to obey, all of God's children receive the ultimate desires of their hearts. "For every man receiveth wages of him whom he listeth to obey, and this according to the words of the spirit of prophecy."[175] In God's perfect mercy and love, no one is resurrected until they have reached their fullest spiritual potential and have been cleansed by the Atonement, or have paid for their sins in preparation for their resurrection, or have chosen not to repent.

This brings us to the final judgment and records of our actions which will reflect our eternal reward.

Final Judgment and Records of Our Actions

As we go through life, there are many judgments. As mentioned, our death and resurrection are partial judgments. The Lord's Second Coming is described as a day of judgment.[176] Yet there is a day of final judgment. Of this day, Mormon wrote, "ye must all stand before the judgment-seat of Christ, yea, every soul who belongs to the whole human family of Adam; and ye must stand to be judged of your works, whether they be good or evil."[177] This day, we read in the Doctrine and Covenants, "shall come at the end of the earth."[178] John the Revelator described this final day of judgment when he said, "And I saw a great white throne, and him that sat on it, from whose face the earth and the heaven fled away; and there was found no place for them."[179] At that time, the records of heaven and earth are opened and the judgment takes place. John goes on to say, "And I saw the dead, small and great, stand before God; and the books were opened: and another book was opened, which is the book of life: and the dead were judged out of those things which were written in the books, according to their works."[180]

The book of life is the record in heaven of all humankind's deeds from which humankind will be judged. In Revelation we read, "He that overcometh, the same shall be clothed in white raiment; and I will not blot out his name out of the book of life, but I will confess his name before my Father, and before his angels."[181] Indicating that in addition to those who overcome and are included in the book of life, there will be those who will not be included in the book of life. In the Book of Mormon, Alma says this is done so, "that the word of God may be fulfilled, which saith: The names of the wicked shall not be mingled with the names of my people."[182] As we will discuss later, an inheritance on God's right hand means to be saved in any of His kingdoms, and encompasses those found in the book of life. The Sons of Perdition do not inherit a kingdom of God and are found on His left hand, and these are they who Christ will be ashamed to own before the Father. They suffer the second death.[183] John indicates that those who suffer the second death are not found in the book of life, he says, "And death and hell were cast into the lake of fire. This is the second death. And whosoever was not found written in the book of life was cast into the lake of fire."[184] Thus the Sons of Perdition are not written in the book of life for their names will be blotted out, assuring that the names of the wicked are not mingled with the names of God's children who inherit a kingdom of glory in His realm.

John also says that prior to the book of life, other books were opened. Of these books, Joseph Smith said, "You will discover in this quotation that the books were opened; and another book was opened, which was the book of life; but the dead were judged out of those things which were written in the books, according to their works; consequently, the books spoken of must be the books which contained the record of their works and refer to the records which are kept on the earth."[185] These I would suppose include individual, church, and public records. Then there are our own memories. A personal record that we each carry of our thoughts, emotions, deeds, and interactions. This too will be weighed in the day of the final judgment. Finally, we are told of another book, the book of the sanctified in which the prayers of the heirs of the celestial kingdom are recorded. Of this book the Lord said, "the alms of your prayers have come up into the ears of the Lord of Sabaoth, and are recorded in the book of the names of the sanctified, even them of the celestial world."[186] It will also play a role in our final judgment along with the book of life, earthly records, and our own memories, etc. When judgment day comes none will be able to refute or claim that God's judgments are not just.

Although we all will be judged, we also have the opportunity to repent before that day comes.

All Who Inherit God's Kingdoms Must Repent

As a child, I imagined that the telestial kingdom would be inhabited by a class of liars and thieves going around taking advantage of one another. In my mind's eye it reflected what many experience here in mortality. As the years have passed, I have come to realize that God saves no one in their sins. As Amulek stated, "And I say unto you again that he cannot save them in their sins; for I cannot deny his word, and he hath said that no unclean thing can inherit the kingdom of heaven; therefore, how can ye be saved, except ye inherit the kingdom of heaven? Therefore, ye cannot be saved in your sins."[187] Thus, it behooves us to repent now because we will eventually have to do so in order to dwell in any of God's kingdoms.[188]

Postponing the process of repentance is an all too common trait.

One day, a seminary teacher shared his frustration with some of the youth he had known, who were postponing repentance. He said some youth would engage in sexual sin and justify it by saying God would forgive them, and so they could wait to repent until just before it came time to serve a mission, or to be married in the temple. I recall my surprise and sorrow at hearing about their self-centered attitude. We talked about how, by their actions, they had forfeited the opportunity to be an example of good at that time of their life, which opportunity could never be reclaimed. We contemplated how they had lost the fellowship of God—for those who are in a carnal state are without God in the world.[189] We reflected on how they lost God's spiritual blessings that could help them with the challenges and decisions they would face. We discussed the poor example they were setting for their partner in sexual sin. How their repetition of sexual sin was setting a pattern of behavior that would be hard to change, and that could lead to them fathering children outside the marriage covenant, which children in turn would suffer because of their poor decisions. They might even lose the desire to repent and find themselves falling away from the Church. In addition, God would not be pleased with their "gaming" the process of repentance and minimizing the seriousness of their sin for, "the Lord looketh on the heart," and will not be mocked.[190]

Through our daily actions and choices, we are either refining our character or degrading it. We are either moving towards a glorious eternal reward or distancing ourselves from it. We are either decreasing the time and effort required to become Christlike, or we are increasing our burden and the effort required to do so. None of us know when our time on earth will end and we will be ushered into the world of spirits where we either will be consigned to dwell with the righteous or the wicked based on our worthiness to await the resurrection.

In addition, the law of restoration tells us that the characteristics we have when we die will be restored to us.[191] That is a somber warning that this life is the time to prepare to meet God. Once we die and enter the spirit world, we will have to continue to repent and perfect ourselves, but without the benefit of our mortal body. Elder Melvin J. Ballard highlighted how this makes the process more difficult when he said, "every man and woman who is putting off until the next life the task of correcting and overcoming the weakness of the flesh are sentencing themselves to years of bondage, for no man, or woman will come forth in the resurrection until he has completed his work, until he has overcome, until he has done as much as he can do."[192] Mortality is the best time to repent; eternity will be the best time to learn."

This is not to say that we can achieve our desires and destiny through our works alone, "for we know that it is by grace that we are saved, after all we can do."[193] However, this doctrine gives great emphasis and urgency to Joshua's challenge for each of us to, "choose you this day whom ye will serve," and appreciation for the wisdom of his decision, "but as for me and my house, we will serve the Lord."[194]

This brings us to the next point: the resurrection is a priesthood ordinance, which confirms that God's house is a house of order.

The Resurrection as a Priesthood Ordinance

The act of being resurrected is tied to a priesthood ordinance. Priesthood, being the power of God, is connected with the Resurrection, just like it is with all the other ordinances within God's kingdom. The Doctrine and Covenants elucidates that the Saint's resurrection is a priesthood ordinance. In speaking concerning the dead and Christ's ministry among them, as He laid in the tomb, it reads, "These the Lord taught, and gave them power to come forth, after his resurrection from the dead, to enter into his Father's kingdom, there to be crowned with immortality and eternal life."[195] How does the Lord give power unto men? Just as we have seen His servants do: through the laying on of hands and the bestowal of the power and keys of the priesthood. The power to use the priesthood to bring about the resurrection requires a person to receive the power and authority to perform this ordinance from one who has the keys, or right, to give this power to others. Concerning the keys of the resurrection, Brigham Young taught, "We have not, neither can we receive here, the ordinance and the keys of the resurrection. They will be given to those who have passed off this stage of action and have received their bodies again, as many have already done and many more will. They will be ordained, by those who hold the keys of the resurrection, to go forth and resurrect the Saints."[196] On this subject, he also said concerning Joseph Smith, "He is the man who will be resurrected and receive the keys of the resurrection, and he will seal this authority upon others, and they will hunt up their friends and resurrect them when they shall have been officiated for, and bring them up."[197]

Those who inherit a terrestrial resurrection come forth by God's divine decree rather than by an individual priesthood ordinance. These do not accept the Gospel and it's saving ordinances, or are unworthy of them.[198] Like the terrestrial resurrection, the Second Resurrection arises by God's immutable decree, rather than through an individual priesthood ordinance.[199] They have rejected the Gospel and its ordinances and do not have a testimony of Jesus Christ. They do not recognize and will not accept the priesthood ordinances of salvation. In a vision given to Wilford Woodruff of the Second Resurrection he recounts, "Vast fields of graves were before me, and the spirit of God rested upon the earth like a shower of gentle rain, and when that fell upon the graves they were opened and an immense host of human beings came forth."[200] Again illustrating that they will be called forth as a group, rather than by an individual ordinance. I suppose we would be amazed if we could roll back the starry heavens and view the amount of effort that is going on to bring about the salvation of God's children. Great is our God.

Given God's ongoing effort to bring about humankind's salvation and the timing of the resurrection, the question can be asked, when does our probationary second estate end?

The End of Our Second Estate, and the Spirit World

Many assume that our second estate—which begins at our birth into mortality—ends at death. Based on that assumption, many often feel that if someone loses one's faith and dies, has not yet cleansed their life of sin before they die, or has rejected the Gospel message here in mortality, have had their chance at being saved and only damnation awaits them. Sometimes they quote passages from the Book of Mormon that on the surface seem to support this concept, but upon deeper reflection do not.[201] This perception shortens God's mercy and narrowly defines God's ability and opportunity to save His children. It also disregards the vagaries of mortality and the challenges inherent with one having an opportunity to hear or accept the Gospel. God, in His love and mercy, desires to extend multiple opportunities to each of His children to gain exaltation.

In the mission field as a young missionary, I witnessed many reject our invitation to hear about the Gospel of Jesus Christ. In frustration, some missionaries would say, "they had their chance to hear the Gospel," as though the missionary's invitation constituted the only chance to hear and accept the Gospel of Jesus Christ. This comment was shortsighted then and remains so now. Certainly, gaining a testimony of the Gospel in this life is very important, as is remaining faithful to the end. Those in this life who merit the blessings that come through a Christ-centered Gospel focus receive the saving and purifying ordinances of the Gospel. They gain more insight and truth concerning the Gospel, and they die with the promise of exaltation. They are far better prepared to enter the spirit world and continue the work of salvation on the behalf of others, while they await a glorious resurrection and their third estate. But to limit our second estate to mortality, or to argue that humankind has only one opportunity to hear and receive the Gospel, is too narrowly defining it. God's invitation to His children to come unto Him is continuous.[202]

The spirit world is also a place where humankind can be tried and faith can be exercised as a part of humankind's second estate, allowing them to accept the Gospel, repent of their sins, and potentially receive exaltation. The scriptures teach that while Jesus Christ was in the spirit world, "from among the righteous, he organized his forces and appointed messengers, clothed with power and authority, and commissioned them to go forth and carry the light of the gospel to them that were in darkness, even to all the spirits of men; and thus was the gospel preached to the dead. These were taught faith in God, repentance from sin, vicarious baptism for the remission of sins, the gift of the Holy Ghost by the laying on of hands, And all other principles of the gospel that were necessary for them to know in order to qualify themselves that they might be judged according to men in the flesh, but live according to God in the spirit."[203] This clearly states that the Gospel is taught in the spirit world and the spirits who heed the message can qualify for the ordinances and blessings that accompany it. It is here that the majority of mankind will hear the Gospel and determine if they will heed the invitation to have faith in Christ, repent of their sins, and accept the Lord's Church.

Since the wicked will have the opportunity to accept or reject the Gospel in the spirit world, we can assume that the knowledge of the pre-earth life is not returned until after the resurrection. Otherwise, if the knowledge of the premortal life was returned in the spirit world, those in spirit prison would not have to be taught the Gospel or exercise faith for they would have a knowledge of God and His plan of salvation. However, the veil separating them from God will continue to be present in the spirit world. This allows them to exercise faith in God and Christ while in the spirit world and accept the Gospel. To have their second estate end at death while there is still an opportunity to act in faith in the spirit world, accept the gospel, and obtain exaltation would be neither merciful or just.

It is when humankind is resurrected that they will have a perfect knowledge of their pre-earth existence.[204] In addition to the foreknowledge from the pre-earth life that will be restored in the resurrection, what we have learned in mortality and the spirit world will rise with us.[205] With the prior knowledge of the pre-earth life united with the experiences gained in mortality and the spirit world, our journey will no longer be a test. We will be able to recall and understand our pre-earth relationship to God and others, what we accomplished, and the knowledge we obtained throughout our existence. We will act based on this greater knowledge rather than the circumstances that make mortality a test. The veil between us and God will be removed. Thus, it seems clear that our second estate ends when we are resurrected, not at death. Neal A. Maxwell said, "We tend to overlook the reality that the spirit world and paradise are part, really, of the second estate. The work of the Lord, so far as the second estate is concerned, is completed before the judgement and Resurrection."[206] This doctrine expands the reach of God, and Christ's mercy, and their ability to save humankind. It gives greater hope to all who struggle with wayward children or other lost loved ones and provides support and efficacy for the missionary work that goes on in the spirit world, and the impact it has on the inhabitants there.

Often, here in mortality, one is not ready when first approached about the Gospel, but over time something changes and they become receptive to the message. Many of us have seen this happen. I recall a wonderful man who was not a member of the Church, although his wife was. She was a faithful, engaged, and committed member of the Church. His children were raised in the Gospel. Some of his children served missions and some were married in the temple. Over the years, the Elders had taught him the Gospel on several occasions, but he had rejected their invitations. Decades passed. Later in his life he began attending Church and paying his tithing but remained unbaptized. During this time, his wife was called as Relief Society president and received the ordinances of the temple. Something changed within him and the missionaries once again came into his home to teach him the Gospel. This time he accepted their message and was baptized. Later he was sealed to his wife in the temple and they and many of their family rejoiced at the blessing of being sealed together as a family for eternity. We cannot know when someone will heed the Lord's call to come and be healed. Sometimes that process takes decades. As the Lord said, "for unto such shall ye continue to minister; for ye know not but what they will return and repent, and come unto me with full purpose of heart, and I shall heal them."[207]

We should always be accepting of others and respectful of their beliefs, yet ready to invite them with love to hear the glorious message of the Gospel. Who knows when their hearts will be softened, or when they will be open to hear the Gospel message? It may not even be in this life but may come after they die and enter the spirit world.

This brings us to the principle of eternal progression: what does eternal progression mean and how does it apply to the resurrection and eternity?

Eternal Progression

The opportunity to progress is neither new to our existence, nor unique to mortality. As children of our loving Father in Heaven, we inherited the capacity to progress in our pre-earth existence. There we were added upon and gained a spirit body with all its additional capabilities, and we progressed. Here in mortality we are again added upon and gain a physical body with all of its capabilities. Each of us has personally experienced progression and are very familiar with it. Progression is a process of change. For example, here in mortality, the growth we experience in our transition from birth to adulthood results in change. It encompasses the growth in our sensual, physical, emotional, social, intellectual, and spiritual capabilities. These changes affect each of us differently, and along with our environment, and our spiritual beings, contributes to the variety of personalities we see in humankind. This change can be positive or negative depending on our focus, attitudes, and desires. But change, or progression, is inevitable.

The acquiring of knowledge is another catalyst for change. Understanding the world around us, politics, science, the heavens, and other studies, is important for our progression. Joseph Smith emphasized this when he declared, "if a person gains more knowledge and intelligence in this life through his diligence and obedience than another, he will have so much the advantage in the world to come."[208] Knowledge can contain truths of eternal value that contribute to our progression towards exaltation. But knowledge alone is not sufficient; we have to be able to apply that knowledge in a way that leads to exaltation. Joseph F. Smith addressed this when he said, "There is a difference between knowledge and pure intelligence. Satan possesses knowledge, more than we have, but he has not intelligence, or he would render obedience to the principles of truth and right. I know men who have knowledge, who understand the principles of the Gospel, perhaps as well as you do, who are brilliant but who lack the essential qualifications of pure intelligence. They will not accept and render obedience thereto. Pure intelligence comprises not only knowledge, but also the power to properly apply that knowledge."[209] Properly applying the knowledge we gain in our process of eternal progression is essential for our success in obtaining exaltation. God has placed us here to provide the opportunity to experience positive change, gain knowledge, and within that mortal context, to become more like Him.

In our third estate as exalted beings, we will be added upon once more as our mortal bodies become perfected, glorified, and eternal. Our senses, emotions, attributes, and opportunities will be enhanced once more, and we will continue to progress eternally. Those who follow the straight and narrow path of salvation laid out by Jesus Christ enjoy the blessings and opportunities eternal progression provides just like our Heavenly Father experiences.[210] Joseph Smith addressed God's and the Lord's progression when he said, "What did Jesus do? Why; I do the things I saw my Father do when worlds come rolling into existence. My Father worked out his kingdom with fear and trembling, and I must do the same; and when I get my kingdom, I shall present it to my Father, so that he may obtain kingdom upon kingdom, and it will exalt him in glory. He will then take a higher exaltation, and I will take his place, and thereby become exalted myself. So that Jesus treads in the tracks of his Father, and inherits what God did before; and God is thus glorified and exalted in the salvation and exaltation of all his children."[211] Likewise we tread in the path towards exaltation that those before us took. As they take a higher station so we take their place in the ongoing path of eternal progression. As part of this we also increase in glory.[212] The Lord declared, "and they who keep their second estate shall have glory added upon their heads for ever and ever."[213] In a similar sense Jesus Christ increases in glory through our glorification. In the Doctrine & Covenants, we read of the Lord visiting His servants, "that his lord might be glorified in him, and he in his lord, that they all might be glorified,"[214] showing that the Lord in turn is glorified from those He glorifies. It is not a case of a limited pie being sliced ever thinner, but rather as more obtain exaltation the limitless pie grows bigger. This eternal growth in glory and station is part of the eternal opportunities for progression. Encompassed in this is the eternal increase in posterity which those who obtain the highest degree of the celestial kingdom will experience, which we will discuss in greater detail later.[215] To experience eternal progression is to grow in power, glory, posterity and dominion forever.

If eternal progression is a reward for the faithful saints, then what awaits the unfaithful?

Eternal Damnation

The Lord defines eternal damnation as God's punishment. "Again, it is written eternal damnation…For, behold, I am endless, and the punishment which is given from my hand is endless punishment, for Endless is my name. Wherefore—Eternal punishment is God's punishment."[216] What is this endless punishment? It is the eternal limiting of progression and opportunity. Satan and those who follow him are defined as receiving eternal punishment where their worm dieth not and their fire is not quenched.[217] They did not keep their first estate and were denied mortality, and their eternal progress ended. In regards to these punishments, the Lord said, "and they who keep not their first estate shall not have glory in the same kingdom with those who keep their first estate."[218] Those who fail to keep their second estate, or mortality, will also have their eternal progress limited. For where God and Christ dwell, they cannot come, and by being outside of God's immediate presence, their progression is eternally finite.

God has identified many situations that lead to damnation, which is ultimately a failure to obtain all He has made available to His children and continue to progress. For example, those who need to be commanded in all things and act with slothfulness of heart are damned.[219] Their lack of commitment to Christ results in damnation and they forfeit their eternal progression. Those who fail to repent and accept the Gospel ordinances of baptism and receipt of the Holy Ghost will be damned and cannot dwell with God and Christ.[220] Thus their eternal progression is limited. Those who do not accept the New and Everlasting Covenant of Marriage will be damned, and they will remain single throughout eternity. Again, their eternal progression is limited.[221] The Lord emphasized that obedience to Him and His laws is key to eternal progression. For, "Broad is the gate, and wide the way that leadeth to the deaths; and many there are that go in thereat, because they receive me not, neither do they abide in my law."[222] In this declaration, Christ is not referring to physical death, but a spiritual one where eternal progression is limited. Thus, eternal damnation is the limiting of our opportunities and the inability to obtain all that God has and makes available to His children.

Summary

As stated before, knowledge is power. A knowledge of the doctrines of the resurrection gives us insight into the principles that surround it, and that knowledge can become a catalyst that motivates us to continue and enhance our process toward achieving perfection. It replaces the unknown with principles of truth that change our fears and doubts into hope and faith. Understanding the First and Second Resurrections as titles that encompass more than a single temporal event gives us greater insight into the meaning of the scriptures.

We will be judged by the record of our lives, which is kept in heaven and our acts will impact our eternal reward. All must repent who wish to inherit a kingdom of glory. Death is a partial judgment where the spirits of humankind who are righteous and have obeyed the Gospel go to paradise, and the wicked go to spirit prison. The resurrection is a type of judgment that determines what type of glory one can endure. The resurrection finds its genesis in a priesthood ordinance and ends our Second Estate. Those who come forth in a celestial resurrection to God's highest reward will have the blessing of eternal progress. God continues to progress through His posterity. As His posterity, to have our progression limited is to be damned. These doctrines associated with the resurrection can and will help us in our efforts to obtain eternal life by providing insight and knowledge about our potential future estate in eternity, and the cost of failing to obtain it.

CHAPTER 6

CHARACTERISTICS OF RESURRECTED BODIES

*Arise, shine; for thy light is come, and the
glory of the Lord is risen upon thee*

~ Isaiah 60:1

HOW EXTENSIVE IS the resurrection and what will we be like when we are resurrected? A complete understanding of this will only come when we have risen ourselves in the resurrection. However, we can learn about the extent, nature of, and some of the characteristics of resurrected beings through recorded appearances, and from statements found in the scriptures.

This leads us to our next consideration: what is the reach of the resurrection upon Christ's creations?

Extent of the Resurrection

What if there were some event in earth's history that had the power to impact its inhabitants—past and future—regardless of any other events that may, or had, occurred? What would that event be? How would it be made known to those of the past? How would it be viewed by all ages? Who would accept it? What power would be able to accomplish it?

In considering the resurrection as part of the Atonement of Jesus Christ, we find just such an event. Through prophets, God has made this event known in all ages. For example, Abinadi, a Book of Mormon prophet who lived before the birth of Jesus Christ, taught, "And there cometh a resurrection, even a first resurrection; yea, even a resurrection of those that have been, and who are, and who shall be, even until the resurrection of Christ—for so shall he be called."[223]

The resurrection also reaches proactively forward from the time of Christ's resurrection until the end of the earth. All of humankind, since the time of Christ through the end of the earth who have not yet arisen, will be resurrected.[224] As the Lord revealed through Joseph Smith, "But, behold, verily I say unto you, before the earth shall pass away, Michael, mine archangel, shall sound his trump, and then shall all the dead awake, for their graves shall be opened, and they shall come forth—yea, even all."[225] Thus the resurrection touches all of humankind regardless of when they were born, their view of the resurrection, or acceptance of it. For as Samuel the Lamanite taught, "the resurrection of Christ redeemeth mankind, yea, even all mankind, and bringeth them back into the presence of the Lord."[226] This occurs as a result of Jesus Christ's Atonement. Jesus Christ, having completed the Atonement, passed through death, arose, and was given the keys of death and hell. Just as humankind will eventually die, God gave power to Christ to bring humankind forth from that death. No other event that has or will occur has the ability to stop it. Its occurrence is as immutable as the sun shining in the heavens, even more so for, "though the heavens and the earth pass away, my word shall not pass away, but shall all be fulfilled."[227] But what about other life here upon the earth? Will the animals, plants, or the earth be resurrected?

In answer to this question, while attending a religion class at Brigham Young University, a student asked a professor what would be resurrected. The professor's reply was very apropos. He said, "Everything that has a spirit." In the Doctrine and Covenants we read, "For all old things shall pass away, and all things shall become new, even the heaven and the earth, and all the fulness thereof, both men and beasts, the fowls of the air, and the fishes of the sea; And not one hair, neither mote, shall be lost, for it is the workmanship of mine hand."[228] Through a conversation recorded in the Doctrine and Covenants, Joseph Smith reinforced that beasts and other life will be resurrected and are part of God's eternal kingdom. In explaining The Book of Revelation, Joseph Smith responded to questions and emphasized this. He said:

"Q. What are we to understand by the four beasts, spoken of in the same verse?

A. They are figurative expressions, used by the Revelator, John, in describing heaven, the paradise of God, the happiness of man, and of beasts, and of creeping things, and of the fowls of the air; that which is spiritual being in the likeness of that which is temporal; and that which is temporal in the likeness of that which is spiritual; the spirit of man in the likeness of his person, as also the spirit of the beast, and every other creature which God has created.

Q. Are the four beasts limited to individual beasts, or do they represent classes, or orders?

A. They are limited to four individual beasts, which were shown to John, to represent the glory of the classes of beings in their destined order, or sphere of creation, in the enjoyment of their eternal felicity."[229]

To which kingdom will these animals and creatures be resurrected to? Like humankind, the beasts and creatures will arise in the resurrection based on their nature and their obedience to the laws God has given for their existence. The law of restoration will apply to them as well as humankind. President Joseph Fielding Smith said: "As to where the beasts, birds, and fish, and all other creatures will go after the Resurrection we can only express an opinion. John saw many of them in heaven in the presence of God. It is very probable that they, like mankind, will be distributed in the various kingdoms, celestial, terrestrial, and telestial. We may well believe that in each of these kingdoms such creatures will be assigned."[230]

These scriptures indicate that not only those creatures and creations that inhabit the earth will be resurrected, but the earth itself will be resurrected. In the Pearl of Great Price, Enoch writes of a unique vision where he heard the spirit of the earth mourning the wickedness that had gone forth from it. We read, "And it came to pass that Enoch looked upon the earth; and he heard a voice from the bowels thereof, saying: Wo, wo is me, the mother of men; I am pained, I am weary, because of the wickedness of my children. When shall I rest, and be cleansed from the filthiness which is gone forth out of me? When will my Creator sanctify me, that I may rest, and righteousness for a season abide upon my face?"[231] At Jesus Christ's Second Coming, the earth will be cleansed of evil, sanctified, and find a season of righteousness during the Millennium.[232] But later, John the Beloved saw the day when the earth would ultimately die and be resurrected. He wrote, "And I saw a new heaven and a new earth: for the first heaven and the first earth were passed away; and there was no more sea."[233] This event is to prepare the earth as the future habitation of God's children who merit this reward. For as the Lord revealed through Joseph Smith, "it is decreed that the poor and the meek of the earth shall inherit it. Therefore, it must needs be sanctified from all unrighteousness, that it may be prepared for the celestial glory…That bodies who are of the celestial kingdom may possess it forever and ever; for, for this intent was it made and created."[234] It will be perfected and be brought back into the presence of God.[235] The Lord adds, "For after it hath filled the measure of its creation, it shall be crowned with glory, even with the presence of God the Father."²³⁶ Brigham Young taught that this meant the earth would return to occupy a place near God. He said, "The earth will abide its creation, and will be counted worthy of receiving the blessings designed for it, and will ultimately roll back into the presence of God who formed it."²³⁷ As John declared, there will be a new heaven displayed in the skies of a perfected, celestial earth when it is returned to God's presence and crowned with the glory of God.

The Atonement and resurrection apply not only to this earth and its inhabitants, but to all of Christ's creations, which encompasses worlds without end. While all creation is subject to entropy's process of decline, Christ's Atonement will reverse this process and return all of Christ's creations to a state of perfection. He literally is the life and light of the world.²³⁸ Speaking of Christ, the scriptures say, "Who glorifies the Father, and saves all the works of his hands, except those sons of perdition who deny the Son after the Father has revealed him."²³⁹ In the poetic version of Doctrine and Covenants 76, called the "The Vision," we find this same concept. We read:

> "And I heard a great voice bearing record from heav'n,
> He's the Saviour and only begotten of God;
> *By him, of him, and through him, the worlds were all made,*
> *Even all that career in the heavens so broad.*
> *Whose inhabitants, too, from the first to the last,*
> *Are sav'd by the very same Saviour of ours;*
> And, of course, are begotten God's daughters and sons
> By the very same truths and the very same powers."
> [Italics added for emphasis]²⁴⁰

In the face of the Atonement and the resurrection's epic and comprehensive nature, all of humankind's combined achievements pale in insignificance. As Ammon said, "Therefore, let us glory, yea, we will glory in the Lord…we will praise our God forever…Yea, who can say too much of his great power, and of his mercy, and of his long-suffering towards the children of men?"[241]

What will the resurrection day be like in our lives and how shall we arise from our graves?

Arising from the Grave

In what form will the dead arise from the grave? Joseph Smith taught, "As concerning the resurrection, I will merely say that all men will come from the grave as they lie down, whether old, or young; there will not be added unto their stature one cubit, neither taken from it; all will be raised by the power of God."[242] Some have suggested we come forth as we are laid down and somehow over time evolve into perfection. How foolish a supposition. Could a perfectly just and merciful God be so preferential? We will arise from the grave as laid down for there is no growth in the grave, but upon arising will be immediately made perfect. One of the clearest statements on this comes from Joseph Fielding Smith; he said, "Bodies will come up, of course, as they were laid down, but will be restored to their proper, perfect frame immediately. Old people will not look old when they come forth from the grave. Scars will be removed. No one will be bent, or wrinkled. How foolish it would be for a man to come forth in the resurrection who had lost a leg and have to wait for it to grow again. Each body will come forth with its perfect frame. If there has been some deformity, or physical impairment in this life, it will be removed."[243] This echoes what Alma taught about this doctrine when he wrote, "The soul shall be restored to the body, and the body to the soul; yea, and every limb and joint shall be restored to its body; yea, even a hair of the head shall not be lost; but all things shall be restored to their proper and perfect frame."[244] We will come forth as tangible, perfected, eternal beings, as the Lord demonstrated when He challenged His disciples, "Behold my hands and my feet, that it is I myself: handle me, and see; for a spirit hath not flesh and bones, as ye see me have."[245] We will come forth, be changed, and become perfect, devoid of scars or imperfections.[246]

What a glorious and wonderful promise. All our mental and physical pains, deformities, and impairments will be done away with. We will be in the prime of life, freed from the effects of old age and mortality's limitations. Our appearance will be the same as in mortality, only perfected, and others will recognize us. The scriptures teach concerning our bodies and spirits appearance, "that which is spiritual being in the likeness of that which is temporal; and that which is temporal in the likeness of that which is spiritual; the spirit of man in the likeness of his person."[247]

In considering that impact of the resurrection on a person's life, a dear sister comes to mind. She was a vivacious, active, and outgoing person. She would always have a smile and a warm greeting, and she would lead our music in sacrament meeting with vigor. She would not hesitate to chastise us if we were not singing loud enough. One day she noticed a weakness in her foot and ankle that caused her to not to be able to raise her foot. We noticed her illness as she stumbled in church wearing a brace around her ankle to help her walk. Over time, she graduated to a cane and then crutches as the disease progressed. We were heartbroken watching her struggle to maintain her balance and dignity. Then she was confined to a wheel chair. But come Sunday, we would find her chatting away with anyone near her, especially new members. Her excitement and positive attitude prevailed over her disease.

Then, to us quite suddenly, she was unable to leave her home. Her family rallied around her, washed, fed, and dressed her, and moved her frequently to avoid sores. Often friends would visit and we would gather at her home to enjoy a family home evening with others. She continued to radiate joy and her laughter often cackled throughout the house. Near the end I was at her home, and for a moment time stopped. I was in a holy place and saw her radiant and resplendent, made perfect and glorious through the things she had suffered. As I left that evening, I stopped to kiss her forehead and she said, "I am ready to go." She passed away a few days later. She and her family had a firm hope of the resurrection and talked of when they would one day stand, walk, and run together again. Like my friend, we must all be patient in our afflictions as God refines and makes us glorious, and as we await our time to arise in perfection.

That brings us to the next point to consider if it matters where we are laid down in death.

We Arise Where Laid Down

In ancient times, the saints made a great effort to be buried with their kindred. We know the Iron Age tombs, for example, would hold numerous members of a family. One might argue this was for convenience because of the effort to construct or obtain a tomb. However, the reason went far beyond convenience: they wished to be buried with those they loved and knew. They understood the doctrine of the resurrection and that one day they would arise, and they wanted to rejoice with family members when that day came. We read that Jacob spoke with his sons, "And he charged them, and said unto them, I am to be gathered unto my people: bury me with my fathers in the cave that is in the field of Ephron the Hittite."[248] He told them that, "There they buried Abraham and Sarah his wife; there they buried Isaac and Rebekah his wife; and there I buried Leah."[249] Joshua was another Old Testament prophet who likewise was buried with his fathers, as were others.[250]

Joseph Smith helped us appreciate this concept more when he shared that, "I have said, Father, I desire to die here among the Saints. But if this is not Thy will, and I go hence and die, wilt Thou find some kind friend to bring my body back, and gather my friends who have fallen in foreign lands, and bring them up hither, that we may all lie together. I will tell you what I want. If tomorrow I shall be called to lie in yonder tomb, in the morning of the resurrection let me strike hands with my father, and cry, 'My father,' and he will say, 'My son, my son,' as soon as the rock rends and before we come out of our graves."[251] Can you conceive of the joy and love that will be shared by faithful kindred as they arise and greet each other on the day of their resurrection? To embrace our family members once again in our perfected and eternal bodies, knowing we had overcome the world and obtained the desire of our hearts, on that special day would indeed be a great blessing.

But what of those whose remains are scattered for various reasons? My sister, who died prematurely due to cancer, was a member of the Neptune Society. She did not want a funeral or a lot of attention paid to her upon her passage. When she died, the Neptune Society immediately came to her home, placed her body in a vinyl bag, and swept her away. By the time we were notified of her death, her body was long gone. The Neptune Society cremated her remains and spread her ashes upon the ocean. Where is her final resting place? I certainly could not tell. However, it seems certain that the same God who made the world and all things in it could call her elements back together on the day of her resurrection. President Joseph Fielding Smith said, "It is true that the mortal body in due time returns to the earth as the Lord predicted that it should. Much of the cremated body is carried off into the air and only a small portion of ash remains. However it is impossible to destroy a body. It makes no difference whether a body is consumed by fire, buried in the depths of the sea, or placed in the tomb, the time will come when every essential particle will be called back again to its own place, and the individual whose body was laid away, or scattered to the winds, will be reassembled with every essential part restored."[252]

This restoration of our bodies has special application in regards to the promises made to little children who die young.

Childhood Death, Disabilities, and the Resurrection

Many families have been touched by devastating loss of a child or have children with developmental issues. How does Christ's Atonement and resurrection impact these individuals?

The sorrow and bereavement engendered by the loss of a child is truly heart wrenching for all those affected. Yet through the law of restoration, a loving and merciful God has provided a source of comfort and hope to all those affected by this. In a vision given to Joseph Smith, he was shown, "that all children who die before they arrive at the years of accountability are saved in the celestial kingdom of heaven."[253] They will receive exaltation in the kingdom of God and be given all that God has provided for the faithful. As Moroni declared, "But little children are alive in Christ, even from the foundation of the world."[254]

In addition, little children will arise from the grave as they were laid down: as children. And in the resurrection, their faithful mothers will have the blessing and privilege of raising them to adulthood. Joseph F. Smith stated, "Joseph Smith taught the doctrine that the infant child that was laid away in death would come up in the resurrection as a child; and, pointing to the mother of a lifeless child, he said to her: 'You will have the joy, the pleasure, and satisfaction of nurturing this child, after its resurrection, until it reaches the full stature of its spirit.' There is restitution, there is growth, there is development, after the resurrection from death. I love this truth. It speaks volumes of happiness, of joy and gratitude to my soul."[255] What a tremendous blessing of comfort and mercy from our God. The arms that ached to hold their child will once again be filled. There as part of the family unit, they will be nurtured by exalted loving parents, grow to adulthood, and enjoy eternal progression with all the faithful.

This is also true of the mentally deficient. Of them, the Lord said, "And, again, I say unto you, that whoso having knowledge, have I not commanded to repent? And he that hath no understanding, it remaineth in me to do according as it is written."[256] Those with developmental or other mental impairments who lack comprehension are saved through the atonement of Christ. They never reach the years of accountability, "For behold that all little children are alive in Christ, and also all they that are without the law. For the power of redemption cometh on all them that have no law."[257] They will arise in the resurrection whole and complete with no impairments. They, like little children who die young, will be exalted and saved in the highest kingdom of our God. There they will be part of the family unit and enjoy all the blessings God has for the faithful.

Next, let us discuss the principle that not all elements of our mortal bodies will be resurrected?

Not All Elements are Resurrected

It seems apparent that not all the elements of our bodies will be resurrected. For example, we know blood will not be a part of resurrected beings. When Jesus Christ appeared to His Apostles, He said He had a body of "Flesh and bones," not one of flesh, bones, and blood.[183] As Joseph Smith taught, "God Almighty Himself dwells in eternal fire; flesh and blood cannot go there, for all corruption is devoured by the fire.[258] Our God is a consuming fire. When our flesh is quickened by the spirit, there will be no blood in this tabernacle."[259] Beyond that, we are not told what elements of this earth will or will not arise in the resurrection, but it will be only those fundamental elements required to provide us with a refined, perfected, eternal, and glorified body. Reflecting on this, Brigham Young commented, "the peculiar fundamental particles that organized our bodies here…though they be deposited in the depths of the sea, and though one particle is in the north, another in the south, and another in the east, and another in the west, will be brought together again in the twinkling of an eye…This body must be changed, else it cannot be prepared to dwell in the glory of the Father."[260] We will remain corporeal beings, but be more pure and refined as we walk in the newness of eternal life.

In addition, as part of this renewal we will have an increase in our senses, abilities, and capabilities.

Increased Capabilities

As we examine the scriptures, it becomes apparent that resurrected beings have increased capabilities. We know this because individuals have experienced them here in mortality when they have been filled with God's spirit. If they can be bestowed upon mortal humankind they are certainly available to resurrected, perfected, and eternal beings.

When Moses was caught up to an exceedingly high mountain he was filled with the spirit and was shown the earth and all its inhabitants. We read that, "Moses cast his eyes and beheld the earth, yea, even all of it; and there was not a particle of it which he did not behold, discerning it by the spirit of God. And he beheld also the inhabitants thereof, and there was not a soul which he beheld not; and he discerned them by the Spirit of God; and their numbers were great, even numberless as the sand upon the sea shore."[261] At this time, his intellectual ability was expanded to behold every particle of the earth and every inhabitant of it. Have you ever sat and read a book in its entirety at one time? Then tried to remember every concept, idea, principle, sentence, or word contained between its covers? As resurrected beings filled with the fullness of God's spirit, our ability to retain information, to comprehend, and to discern will be greatly expanded just as Moses experienced.[262] Not only was Moses's intellect increased, but his vision was expanded as well. He was able to see down into the opaque earth and discern every particle. Orson Pratt referred to this when he said, "We may expect that the immortal being will have his vision so enlarged that he can, not only look with all ease upon every particle of this earth, but on the particles of millions of worlds like this."[263]

Not only will our intellectual ability and vision increase, but our emotional capacity will also improve. Enoch, who was labeled "the weeping prophet," had a unique experience. He had witnessed the Lord weeping over the wickedness of the children of men and asked, "how is it thou canst weep?"[264] The Lord then explains to him how this was possible: "And it came to pass that the Lord spake unto Enoch, and told Enoch all the doings of the children of men; wherefore Enoch knew, and looked upon their wickedness, and their misery, and wept and stretched forth his arms, and his heart swelled wide as eternity; and his bowels yearned; and all eternity shook."[265] Enoch's ability to feel, empathize, and love was enhanced to such a degree that Enoch's heart expanded and his bowels yearned in sorrow over the children of men, and all eternity shook in consequence with him. His emotions were greatly expanded.

As resurrected beings, humankind will experience a similar emotional enhancement, for both happiness and sorrow. Elder Orson Pratt, in speaking to the increased emotions we would experience as resurrected beings, said, "Do you suppose that we shall get up out of the grave, male and female, and that we shall not have the same kind of affections, and endearments, and enjoyments that we have here? The same pure feelings of love that exist in the bosoms of the male and female in this world, will exist with seven-fold intensity in the next world."[266] We should probably not take the term "seven-fold" too literally, but we should realize that our relationships, affections, endearments, and enjoyments will be amplified and more refined than what we now experience. Doubts, misunderstandings, ailments, pains, disabilities, jealousy, fear, envy, along with all the other host of mortalities challenges will be done away with. We shall see as we are seen and know as we are known.[267]

Resurrected beings will also have the ability to move great distances in a relatively short time. After teaching the Nephites in the New World, the Savior said, "prepare your minds for the morrow, and I come unto you again. But now I go unto the Father, and also to show myself unto the lost tribes of Israel."[268] The risen Lord was going from the New World to see His Father in Heaven, then to visit the lost ten tribes of Israel and teach them, and then to return back to the New World, all in less than a twenty-four-hour period! His ability to move swiftly over great distances illustrates that resurrected beings have an increased power of movement that far surpasses anything known to man. Orson Pratt said, "They will have the same power of locomotion, the same power to pass through space (almost in the twinkling of an eye) that our Father has—that his Son Jesus Christ has—that all celestial beings who are exalted in his presence have."[269] These and other abilities will be added, increased, and enhanced when the body and spirit are joined eternally in their exalted state. While mortality is a time for preparation, exaltation is a time for learning.

In addition to these increased capabilities, we also know that resurrected beings are not bound by gravity.

Power Over Gravity

The natural laws of gravitation that we all are subject to do not inhibit resurrected beings. Resurrected beings are able to levitate and move about without having solid objects to stand on. Jesus Christ demonstrated this when, after speaking to His Apostles, He ascended into heaven for, "while they beheld, he was taken up; and a cloud received him out of their sight."[270] Similarly in the New World, when Jesus Christ appeared to the Nephites, "they cast their eyes up again towards heaven; and behold, they saw a Man descending out of heaven; and he was clothed in a white robe; and he came down and stood in the midst of them."[271] Moroni, Peter, James, and John, along with others, all demonstrated this mastery over gravity when they appeared to Joseph Smith.

A story comes to mind when considering the effects of gravity. One day during the Christmas season, my wife and I decided to take a walk after it had snowed. Our driveway has a downward slope from our house to the street. As we stepped onto the driveway, I slipped and fell down. My wife who was right behind me also fell down. There was a sheet of ice underneath the snow that we did not see. I broke my wrist, and she broke her ankle. Somehow between our tears and laughter we were able to get up and hobble back to our home. Later when we went to the store to Christmas shop, with both of us wearing casts, the crowds parted around us like the Red Sea did for the children of Israel, and their expressions reflected a painful empathy for us. Though we laugh about it now, I envision the benefits when gravity does not have the same effect upon us that it now exerts.

Next let's examine examples where resurrected bodies had the power to penetrate physical walls.

Power to Pass Through Physical Objects

Following His resurrection, we find Jesus Christ appearing to His disciples within a secured and locked room. We read that, "Then the same day at evening, being the first day of the week, when the doors were shut where the disciples were assembled for fear of the Jews, came Jesus and stood in the midst, and saith unto them, Peace be unto you."[272] His disciples had shut the doors and made the room secure due to a fear of persecution from the Jewish leaders. Those material objects of stone and wood that secured the disciples within a room offered no barrier to the resurrected Christ. He passed right through them to appear to His disciples inside. Moroni also showed this same trait when he appeared to Joseph Smith while Joseph was praying in his bedroom. Joseph Smith wrote that, "While I was thus in the act of calling upon God, I discovered a light appearing in my room, which continued to increase until the room was lighter than at noonday, when immediately a personage appeared at my bedside, standing in the air, for his feet did not touch the floor."[273] Clearly, locked doors and the limitations of mortality in respect to physical objects no longer apply to resurrected beings.

Additionally, like Moroni's appearance to Joseph Smith, the scriptures show that resurrected persons are imbued with glory, or light.

Imbued with Glory, or Light

When resurrected beings appear to humankind, they are often enveloped in glory. The angel Moroni, a resurrected person, appeared to Joseph Smith in 1823 in his glory. Joseph recorded that when Moroni appeared, "Not only was his robe exceedingly white, but his whole person was glorious beyond description, and his countenance truly like lightning. The room was exceedingly light, but not so very bright as immediately around his person."[274] Earlier, when God the Father and Jesus Christ appeared to Joseph Smith, they also were surrounded by glory, "whose brightness and glory defy all description."[275] This glory, light, and truth seems to center in a resurrected person and shines outward so that they appear enveloped in light. In the Doctrine and Covenants, the Lord teaches us that as we develop Christlike qualities, we grow in glory: "That which is of God is light; and he that receiveth light, and continueth in God, receiveth more light; and that light groweth brighter and brighter until the perfect day."[276]

When we are resurrected in the celestial kingdom and our spirits and bodies are eternally joined, it will be "the perfect day" and we will be filled with the glory of Christ. "And he who receiveth all things with thankfulness shall be made glorious."[277] Just as the three kingdoms of God are likened to different luminescent objects—the sun, moon, and stars—the glory their inhabitants are imbued with also varies in intensity. Those inhabitants of the celestial kingdom eclipse in luminosity those of lower kingdoms. Just as the moon is eclipsed by the sun, appearing as a mere shadow of itself, or the stars which during daylight can no longer be seen due to the sun's radiant nature.

Resurrected beings not only have the power to display but also withhold their glory.

Power to Show or Hide Glory

We see a good example of the ability to hide glory when the resurrected Lord appeared to the two disciples on the road to Emmaus: "And it came to pass, that, while they communed together and reasoned, Jesus himself drew near, and went with them. But their eyes were holden that they should not know him."[278] Here we see that the Lord appeared like a man, without showing His glory. He also hid His identity from them as they walked and talked. This is in contrast to when Jesus Christ's appeared in the Kirtland Temple to Joseph Smith and Oliver Cowdrey in His radiant glory and, "His eyes were as a flame of fire; the hair of his head was white like the pure snow; his countenance shone above the brightness of the sun."[279]

In addition to appearing mortal, we read about other mortal traits that resurrected beings appear to have, such as the ability to eat food.

Ability to Eat and Table Fellowship

The enjoyment of food and the sociality that accompanies it has been a tenant of, and present within, humankind down through the ages. In ancient and modern eastern cultures, "Table Fellowship" has been a way of life, honored, and followed, and will be present at future events involving the resurrected Lord and His saints. Anciently, it was supported by a dependence on those around you. When one traveled in the desert, an unwelcoming host could be a matter of life and death for the visitor, where temperatures exceed one-hundred degrees Fahrenheit and water is often scarce. As part of this ancient custom, people often hosted strangers at their dinner tables. These guests were under the care and protection of their host. We read how Abraham hosted three holy men in Table Fellowship and received the promise that Sarah his barren wife would have a son.[280] Another interesting event surrounding Table Fellowship appears in the Old Testament. Moses, along with the seventy Elders, met with God and ate in His presence. We read, "Then went up Moses, and Aaron, Nadab, and Abihu, and seventy of the elders of Israel: And they saw the God of Israel: and there was under his feet as it were a paved work of a sapphire stone, and as it were the body of heaven in his clearness. And upon the nobles of the children of Israel he laid not his hand: also they saw God, and did eat and drink."[281] Moses and the elders sat down at a heavenly table and ate and drank in the presence of God under His divine protection. The fact that they had a meal surrounding this event in God's presence was not a coincidence, but a celebration meal of the covenant they had made with Him.

Jesus Christ demonstrated this ability to eat after His resurrection when He appeared to His disciples, "He said unto them, Have ye here any meat? And they gave him a piece of a broiled fish, and of an honeycomb. And he took it, and did eat before them."[282] In another future scenario, we are told that the great prophets and faithful will sit down with Christ and partake of the fruit of the vine in a great sacrament meeting. "Behold, this is wisdom in me; wherefore, marvel not, for the hour cometh that I will drink of the fruit of the vine with you on the earth…And also with all those whom my Father hath given me out of the world."[283] Think of the power and majesty of that gathering. To sit in the presence of all those who have faithfully discharged their divine commission, whether great or small, and through partaking of the sacrament renew our covenants with Jesus Christ and be reconciled to Him in a divine setting. Somehow, over time, many have lost sight of the sociality and holiness of eating a meal together, but in eternity Table Fellowship will be renewed as we eat and drink together in faith.

But will hunger and thirst be a part of life in the resurrection?

Hunger and Thirst No More

Here in mortality, God declared to Adam and Eve, "By the sweat of thy face shalt thou eat bread, until thou shalt return unto the ground."[284] The obtaining and production of food and the search for water to satiate one's hunger and thirst is a driving force in society. For many, hunger and thirst are too frequent visitors. Yet it will not always be this way. In the Book of Revelation, John, in descriptive terms, defines the happy state of the faithful in eternity. He says, "They shall hunger no more, neither thirst any more; neither shall the sun light on them, nor any heat. For the Lamb which is in the midst of the throne shall feed them, and shall lead them unto living fountains of waters: and God shall wipe away all tears from their eyes."[285] In the eternities, if needed, the ability to satisfy one's hunger and thirst will be within each of our powers. Christ demonstrated the power to transform and duplicate matter when He changed water into wine,[286] and transformed a few fish and loaves of bread into sufficient to feed over five thousand.[287] One day that power will be ours. With the social blight of hunger and thirst absent, eternal life certainly takes on a more warming tone.

If hunger and thirst will have no place after the resurrection, what about pain and suffering?

Power over Suffering and Pain

We all have suffered pain of one kind or another—none of us is a stranger to it. Some is social, perhaps brought by the inconsideration of others, or as a result of the loss of those we have loved, or because of estrangement from someone we care for. Some is spiritual suffering caused by the effects of sin, or by poor choices made by ourselves or those around us. And some is physical as a result of disease, injury, or some other consequence of mortal life. Regardless of its source, or who and what originates it, the consequences are real and painful. In regards to sorrow, Robert Browning Hamilton's poem "I walked a mile with Pleasure" comes to mind. It reads:

I WALKED A MILE WITH PLEASURE, BY ROBERT BROWNING HAMILTON

> I walked a mile with Pleasure;
> She chatted all the way;
> But left me none the wiser
> For all she had to say.
>
> I walked a mile with Sorrow;
> And ne'er a word said she;
> But, oh! The things I learned from her,
> When Sorrow walked with me.

Through our sorrows and pain come learning, wisdom, and experience. However, the Lord has indicated this will not be the vehicle of character growth for the resurrected saints in the eternities. As the Book of Revelation teaches, "And I heard a great voice out of heaven saying, Behold, the tabernacle of God is with men, and he will dwell with them, and they shall be his people, and God himself shall be with them, and be their God. And God shall wipe away all tears from their eyes; and there shall be no more death, neither sorrow, nor crying, neither shall there be any more pain: for the former things are passed away. And he that sat upon the throne said, Behold, I make all things new."[288] It indeed will be a new and glorious experience for the faithful as the peace and joy of eternity pervades their being.

With these increased abilities, worthy resurrected beings are uniquely prepared to act as agents for God in the work of salvation.

Three Grand Keys

God has sent and does send resurrected beings and the spirits of the dead, on missions to visit humankind, as His divine purposes dictate.[289] As Moroni wrote concerning the angels they, "minister according to the word of his command, showing themselves unto them of strong faith and a firm mind in every form of godliness."[290]

Satan and his minions, who are ever trying to deceive and thwart God's work, also appear to humankind in opposition to God.[291] How can one tell the difference between righteous and unrighteous spirits, mortals, and resurrected beings, who have different characteristics, some of which we have discussed? With mortals who act as messengers, their true nature is more easily discerned based on their message and the spirit they project. If one can determine that they are resurrected, then their messages are from God. With a spirit, it can be more challenging since both good and evil spirits can appear to humankind.

Joseph Smith provided three keys to help saints determine what type of non-mortal being they are interacting with, and if they are from God. He said, "There are two kinds of beings in heaven, namely: Angels, who are resurrected personages, having bodies of flesh and bones—For instance, Jesus said: Handle me and see, for a spirit hath not flesh and bones, as ye see me have. Secondly: the spirits of just men made perfect, they who are not resurrected, but inherit the same glory. When a messenger comes saying he has a message from God, offer him your hand and request him to shake hands with you. If he be an angel he will do so, and you will feel his hand. If he be the spirit of a just man made perfect he will come in his glory; for that is the only way he can appear—Ask him to shake hands with you, but he will not move, because it is contrary to the order of heaven for a just man to deceive; but he will still deliver his message. If it be the devil as an angel of light, when you ask him to shake hands he will offer you his hand, and you will not feel anything; you may therefore detect him. These are three grand keys whereby you may know whether any administration is from God."[292]

The test as outlined is simple: by asking the being to shake your hand, you will find whether they are from God, or from the adversary. Spirits sent from God will appear in their glory and will not agree to shake your hand, because to do so would be an attempt to deceive you, which is contrary to the law of God. If they extend you their hand and you feel it, you know they are a resurrected being and they have been sent from God. If it be an evil spirit, which also can appear as an angel of light in an attempt to placate you, they will extend their hand but you will feel nothing. You then know they are a messenger from Satan and can dismiss them in the name of Jesus Christ.

One can also tell based on the purpose of a being's visit. Messengers from God deliver His instructions.[293] "The office of their ministry is to call men unto repentance, and to fulfil and to do the work of the covenants of the Father, which he hath made unto the children of men, to prepare the way among the children of men, by declaring the word of Christ unto the chosen vessels of the Lord, that they may bear testimony of him."[294] Thus they proclaim the Gospel.[295] They restore priesthood keys.[296] They usher in Gospel events and help humankind prepare for future events.[297] They protect and comfort.[298] They reveal Satan.[299] They do not come for vain purposes such as séances, personal whims, intellectual questions, or signs. Finally, they will not reveal anything that is contrary to the Gospel of Jesus Christ.

Summary

The resurrection extends to all of Christ's creations on the earth and in the starry heavens above. We will arise from the grave in perfection where we were laid down. Not all the elements found in our bodies will be resurrected, only those needed to perfect us. Little children will come forth in the resurrection as laid down and will mature during the millennium. As resurrected beings our senses, abilities, and capabilities will be added to and expanded upon. Those natural laws of gravity that we all are subject to will no longer bind us as resurrected beings. Locked doors and other limitations of mortality in respect to physical objects no longer apply. The enjoyment of food and the sociality that accompanies existence will continue after the resurrection. In the eternities, the ability to satisfy one's hunger and thirst will be within each of our powers, and we will hunger and thirst no more. Suffering and pain will be done away with and will not be the vehicle of character growth in the eternities. Resurrected persons are imbued with glory, or light, through the grace of Christ, and have power to hide or display their glory. Since both God and Satan send spirits with messages for humankind, Joseph Smith provided three keys to help saints determine what type of being these spirits are, and if they are from God. The characteristics of resurrected beings give us a comfort and hope that the travails of mortality will one day end.

CHAPTER 7

THE RESURRECTION AND THREE DEGREES OF GLORY

Eternity Sketched in a Vision from God

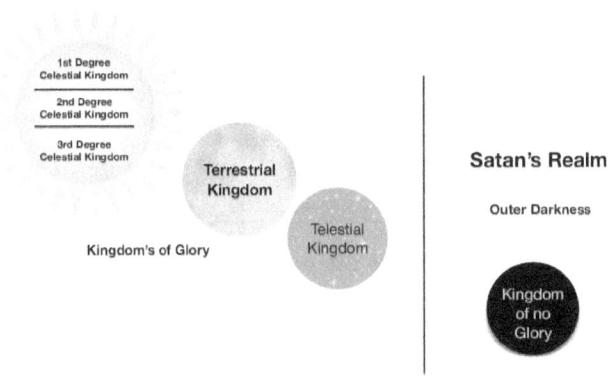

Illustration 7.1 God's Realm and Satan's Realm

THE NUMBER THREE symbolizes the Godhead and signals the divine backing of the Godhead, guidance, and influence. This symbolism of three repeats itself in many different forms: the three members of the Godhead, three kingdoms of glory, three degrees within the celestial kingdom, three estates of existence, three gateways of mortality, and more. Clearly, God is in charge of the plan of salvation and directs, guides, and influences all things concerning it.

The timing and nature of the resurrection is intrinsically tied to the three kingdoms, or the three degrees of glory, within God's realm. By examining the timing and nature of the resurrection for each of the three kingdoms of glory, the celestial, the terrestrial, and the telestial, and Satan's kingdom of no glory, we can gain a better appreciation for the differences between them and how that difference is manifest in the resurrection for those who inherit them.

First, let's discuss humankind's overall resurrection and look at a Chart showing an overview of the resurrection's timing, which we will discuss in detail shortly.

Timing of Humankind's Resurrection

Have you ever pondered the timing of humankind's resurrection? Perhaps this is a pastime of those who are experienced in life's journey. As life continues and loved ones pass into the world of spirits, it becomes a more frequent consideration for many. When will parents and siblings arise from the grave? What will occur if we live to see the Savior's Second Coming? If we do, will we also die and be buried? As Paul said, "For now we see through a glass, darkly."[300] Time reveals all things, yet God has foretold many things including the timing of humankind's past and future resurrection.

Regardless of our considerations, persuasions, or views, the resurrection will occur for all humankind born into mortality. None can escape it and none are exempt. However, not all humankind has been, or will be resurrected at the same time. The following is a chart outlining the different times that humankind's resurrection has and will take place.

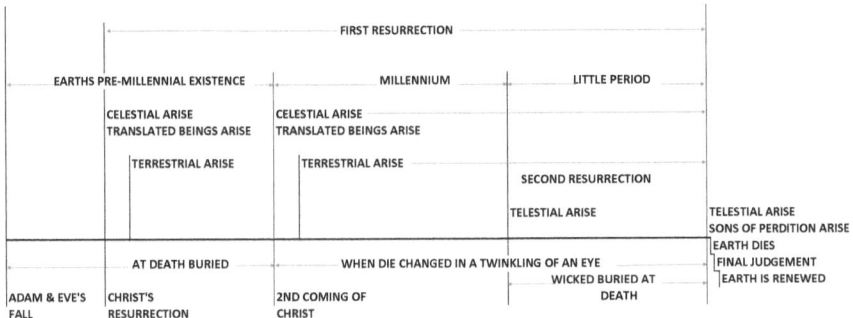

Illustration 7.2 Humankind's Resurrection Timing

As the chart indicates a resurrection took place at the time Jesus Christ was resurrected. It encompassed celestial and translated beings. It was shortly followed by the resurrection of terrestrial humankind who resided in spirit prison at that time of which we will speak more about shortly. After earth's pre-millennial existence another future resurrection awaits humankind at His Second Coming. Like the first it includes celestial and translated beings. Following this, the resurrection of celestial beings continues till the end of the earth as they die and are changed in the twinkling of an eye. The next group is the resurrection of terrestrial beings that occurred just after Christ's resurrection and will happen again just after Christ's Second Coming. Following this the resurrection of terrestrial beings continues till end of the earth as they are individually changed in the twinkling of an eye. Another resurrection will occur at the end of the Millennium and focuses on telestial humankind. This is the first of two groups to come forth in the Second Resurrection. Finally, at the end of the little period the last resurrection occurs and encompasses the rest of telestial humankind, including the Sons of Perdition. It is the second group to come forth in the Second Resurrection.

If you count those who arise during the millennium for both the celestial and terrestrial kingdoms as one unique process, you get seven times or periods when humankind will come forth in the resurrection, indicating perfection. Conversely if you count them as separate events you get eight times or a new beginning for humankind. Finally, there are four main bodies of humankind resurrected, celestial, terrestrial, telestial, and sons of perdition. The number four signifying completeness.

Let us now look in more detail at the timing and nature of the resurrection starting with those who inherit a celestial glory.

Celestial Resurrection Timing and Nature

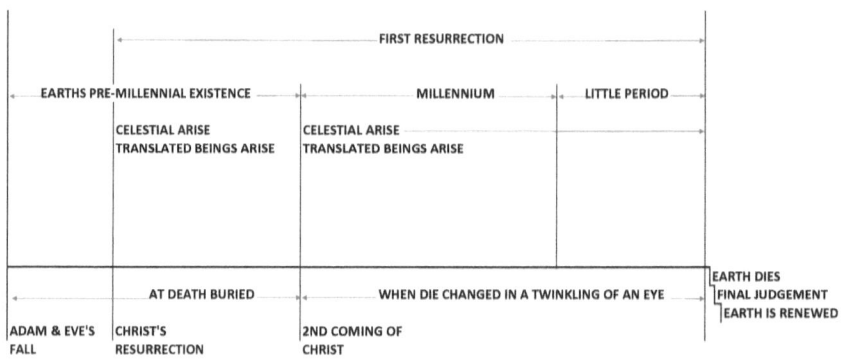

Illustration 7.3 Celestial Resurrection Timing

Historically, the righteous who died prior to Jesus Christ's advent had their resurrection occur just after He arose from the dead. As Paul declares, "For as in Adam all die, even so in Christ shall all be made alive. But every man in his own order: Christ the firstfruits; afterward they that are Christ's at his coming."[301] Concerning those who were Christ's at His coming, in the New Testament it reads, "The graves were opened; and many bodies of the saints which slept arose, And came out of the graves after his resurrection."[302] Joseph Smith said, "Now, we read that many bodies of the Saints arose at Christ's resurrection, probably all the Saints."[303]

We additionally read in the Book of Mormon of an interesting exchange between the resurrected Lord and Nephi that also speaks of this resurrection. The Lord said, "I commanded my servant Samuel, the Lamanite, that he should testify unto this people, that at the day that the Father should glorify his name in me that there were many saints who should arise from the dead, and should appear unto many, and should minister unto them. And he said unto them: Was it not so? And his disciples answered him and said: Yea, Lord, Samuel did prophesy according to thy words, and they were all fulfilled."[304] This fact was not written down in their records and Jesus commanded them to write it. It is apparent that the Lord wanted to assure that this critical event was recorded as a witness that all the righteous, throughout the world, who had died prior to His resurrection arose at that time. The prophet Abinadi confirmed this when he prophesied, "And there cometh a resurrection, even a first resurrection; yea, even a resurrection of those that have been, and who are, and who shall be, even until the resurrection of Christ—for so shall he be called. And now, the resurrection of all the prophets, and all those that have believed in their words, or all those that have kept the commandments of God, shall come forth in the first resurrection; therefore, they are the first resurrection."[305] One could read the last part of this scripture as applying to all the saints who will ever be resurrected, when considering the First Resurrection as a title, however the opening sentence of the verse clearly ties it to those who died prior to the time of Jesus Christ's resurrection. For those who were translated before Christ's birth on earth, their resurrection happened with the saints at the time of Christ's resurrection. We know that they arose at that time because we read that when Christ returns again, He will bring with Him the faithful saints who have previously been resurrected. Included in this group is Elijah and, "Enoch also, and they…who were with Christ in his resurrection."[306] Both Elijah and Enoch were translated beings, which illustrates that translated beings were part of the resurrection at the time of Christ.

For those righteous saints who die after Christ's first coming, but before Christ's return in glory, the celestial resurrection happens at the time of Christ's Second Coming. For those people translated after His coming in the flesh, it will also happen at this time, or as Mormon indicates at the "Judgment day of Christ."[307] Concerning this resurrection the scriptures declare, "And then they shall look for me, and, behold, I will come; and they shall see me in the clouds of heaven, clothed with power and great glory; with all the holy angels; and he that watches not for me shall be cut off. But before the arm of the Lord shall fall, an angel shall sound his trump, and the saints that have slept shall come forth to meet me in the cloud."[308] And again we read that at the Lord's return, "the trump of God shall sound both long and loud, and shall say to the sleeping nations: Ye saints arise and live; ye sinners stay and sleep until I shall call again."[309] Of this day, Orson Pratt wrote, "When the great Redeemer shall roll back the curtains of heaven, and unveil his glorious face, an angel shall sound his trump, both long and loud, which will cause the whole earth to quake: then will the graves of the saints be opened, and their sleeping bodies will come forth, clothed in all the beauty and freshness of immortality; arrayed in beautiful garments and white robes, and encircled with pillars of light, their glory will be as the dazzling sun. These shall all be caught up from the earth, and be wafted from the four winds towards the great central gathering place in the clouds of heaven, where the Redeemer will be seen, armed with Omnipotent power."[310]

What a glorious day that will be. To have one's hope and faith vindicated. To arise with our loved ones, perfect and complete in celestial glory. To meet our glorious King in the clouds of heaven, rejoicing in the triumph and coming of our Savior, as He appears in great glory and power. In a revelation to Joseph Smith, regarding this glorious return, the Lord said, "And it shall be said: Who is this that cometh down from God in heaven with dyed garments; yea, from the regions which are not known, clothed in his glorious apparel, traveling in the greatness of his strength? And he shall say: I am he who spake in righteousness, mighty to save. And the Lord shall be red in his apparel, and his garments like him that treadeth in the wine-vat. And so great shall be the glory of his presence that the sun shall hide his face in shame, and the moon shall withhold its light, and the stars shall be hurled from their places."[311] What a different event than what occurred at Jesus Christ's first coming, when He was born in a manger in humble circumstances. Can you imagine it?

But what of the righteous who are alive and have not died at the time of Christ's Second Coming? Many have thought that all who are righteous, both the living and the dead, will be resurrected at the time of His Second Coming. This clearly is not the case. Someone must remain mortal to continue to have posterity and raise them in righteousness during the Millennium when the Lord will reign on the earth for a thousand years.[312] We are told that the righteous who are alive upon the earth at Christ's return will not experience the resurrection at that time for, "he that liveth when the Lord shall come, and hath kept the faith, blessed is he; nevertheless, it is appointed to him to die at the age of man."[313] However, they will also be caught up to meet Him in the clouds at the Lord's return for, "the saints that are upon the earth, who are alive, shall be quickened and be caught up to meet him."[314] They will join those resurrected beings who have assembled in the heavens with their glorious Redeemer. This quickening of the righteous who are alive at His return is not the same as being resurrected since they are appointed to die "at the age of man." Rather, it is a quickening, or transformation of their bodies from their mortal telestial state to a mortal terrestrial state. This is so they can survive on the earth when it is transformed into a terrestrial orb as it receives its paradisiacal glory at the time the Lord returns,[315] paradisiacal meaning free from sin, a paradise, and belonging to God.

When those who live during the Millennium as transformed mortals who are now in a terrestrial mortal state die, they are changed from a mortal existence to an immortal existence in a twinkling of an eye. We read, "And when he dies he shall not sleep, that is to say in the earth, but shall be changed in the twinkling of an eye, and shall be caught up, and his rest shall be glorious."[316] During the Millennium, death for the righteous does not cease, but burial in the grave does. What a blessing for those who live during the Millennium to not be separated from their body, experience the sorrow of death and burial, or enter the spirit world to await a future resurrection. Their resurrection and rest shall be glorious. As Alma taught his son, "And then shall the righteous shine forth in the kingdom of God."[317]

The celestial resurrection is typified by the sun. Just as the sun eclipses everything else, those who receive this reward eclipse in glory and intelligence all those of a lower kingdom. Like the sun controls and gives life, light, and warmth to all, and is consistent, so too are those who are worthy of a celestial resurrection. Their presence brings life, light, truth, and warmth to all they encounter. They are superior in all things when compared with those of another kingdom. Those who receive celestial bodies have hearkened to celestial laws and have attuned their spirits to celestial things, so much so that they are resurrected by that same spirit, or glory. For, as the Lord taught through Joseph Smith, "your glory shall be that glory by which your bodies are quickened. Ye who are quickened by a portion of the celestial glory shall then receive of the same, even a fulness."[318] They receive a crown,[319] and their glory is one, unlike the telestial kingdom, which varies from person to person as the stars vary in the heavens.

Those resurrected in celestial glory have been baptized, have received the gift of the Holy Ghost, and have experienced the baptism of fire.[320] They have been forgiven of all their sins through repentance and the Atonement of Jesus Christ.[321] They have received all ordinances required to enter the celestial kingdom of our God. They enjoy the presence of the Father, the Son, and the Holy Ghost. They administer to those living in the terrestrial kingdom.[322] They will be found on God's and Christ's right hand in the day of judgment.[323] They will dwell on the earth eternally after the earth is resurrected.[324] Just as there are three degrees of glory celestial, terrestrial, and telestial, we are told that there are three different degrees of glory within the celestial kingdom itself.

Three Degrees within the Celestial Kingdom

Within the celestial kingdom are three degrees of glory.[325] Most of the revelation contained in the Doctrine and Covenants Section 76 concerning the celestial kingdom relates to the highest degree of glory within this kingdom. The revelation illustrates this fact by teaching that those who receive the highest degree are called gods, who overcame all things, and into whose hands God has given all things.[326] This description does not fit those who receive the lower two degrees of glory in the celestial kingdom. They are limited, they did not overcome all things, and are not able to enjoy eternal offspring.[327]

In addition to the blessings previously discussed, those who inherit the highest degree are the exalted faithful saints who become Kings and Priests, and Queens and Priestesses.[328] It is they who obtain eternal lives, and God's full salvation. They are the sons and daughters of God.[329] They are joint heirs with Jesus Christ.[330] They obtain all the Father has, and are eventually given all power.[331] They will be given a "White Stone" and a new name, which will be a personal Urim and Thummim that will reveal things of a higher order to them.[332] The earth in its resurrected state will become a giant Urim and Thummim, revealing all things pertaining to lower kingdoms to them.[333] These individuals are defined as a "spiritual body," and are said to receive their "natural body." We read, "For notwithstanding they die, they also shall rise again, a spiritual body. They who are of a celestial spirit shall receive the same body which was a natural body; even ye shall receive your bodies."[334] They are a "spiritual body" because they are filled with a fullness of glory and the spirit of Christ. They receive their natural bodies in the sense that all the abilities, functions, and capabilities of mortality are theirs, coupled with the increases gained through the process of resurrection, perfection, and exaltation.[335]

These come up to the Church of Enoch, the Church of the Firstborn, and the General Assembly.[336] "To come up" to is to be made equal with, or of an equivalent stature, and to commune with those exalted beings. The Church of Enoch includes the faithful exalted ancient followers of Jesus Christ in Enoch's day—those who established Zion.[337] Hence, they are held up as an example for all who are seeking to establish Zion. They are members of The Church of the Firstborn, or Christ's eternal Church, which comprises the faithful exalted saints in eternity who have received all that the Father has.[338] The "Firstborn" is a title for Jesus Christ,[339] thus making "The Church of the Firstborn" and "The Church of Jesus Christ" interchangeable titles for Christ's Church in the eternities. The Church of the Firstborn includes faithful, exalted, and perfected members of The Church of Jesus Christ of Latter-day Saints. Though not all members of The Church of Jesus Christ of Latter-day Saints will be members of The Church of the Firstborn. The General Assembly refers to the congregation of The Church of the Firstborn, which constitutes the exalted and faithful body of the saints from all ages.

Those who receive the highest degree of glory in the celestial kingdom have been sealed by the Holy Spirit of Promise,[340] and are recorded in the Book of the Sanctified.[341] They have been faithful in all things, obeyed the Gospel, had faith in Christ, received their temple ordinances, including the New and Everlasting Covenant of Marriage, endured to the end, and have proven themselves worthy of exaltation in the highest degree of the celestial kingdom.[342] The Prophet Joseph Smith once commented, "The question is frequently asked, "Can we not be saved without going through with all those [temple] ordinances? I would answer, No, not the fulness of salvation. Jesus said, There are many mansions in my Father's house, and I will go and prepare a place for you. House here named should have been translated kingdom; and any person who is exalted to the highest mansion has to abide a celestial law, and the whole law too."[343] For, "All men who become heirs of God and joint heirs with Jesus Christ will have to receive the fulness of the ordinances of his kingdom; and those who will not receive all the ordinances will come short of the fullness of that glory, if they do not lose the whole."[344]

It is clear that temple work will not be performed for everyone who has or will live upon the earth. The temple ordinances are meant to bring eternal glory to all those who will inherit the highest degree of the celestial kingdom of God. Joseph Fielding Smith spoke about this when he said, "I want to correct an idea that prevails very largely in the minds of many members of the Church...whether, or not the temple work will have to be performed for everybody upon the earth. I want to say to you no, absolutely no....All of the ordinances of the gospel—baptism, laying on of hands for the gift of the Holy Ghost, the work in the temples for the salvation of the living and the dead—these ordinances, everything else, all of the ordinances of the gospel pertain to the Celestial Kingdom of God."[345]

In addition, in regards to children we are told that, "all children who die before they arrive at the years of accountability are saved in the celestial kingdom of heaven."[346] Through God's and Christ's divine love and mercy, they will receive every blessing afforded the faithful, and obtain exaltation in the highest degree of the celestial kingdom. This is also true of those who suffer from diminished mental capacity.

The effort to obtain exaltation in the celestial kingdom can seem daunting. The path blazed by Jesus Christ shows the way and the requirements to that exaltation. For the faithful their weaknesses are made up by the saving grace of Christ, "for we know that it is by grace that we are saved, after all we can do."[347] Here is a doctrine of comfort and hope that we all can rely on. We can turn our hearts with full intent to Christ, do our best to follow Him, obey His laws and ordinances, and trust that in the end He can and will save us. His grace makes the impossible possible. We can point to Abraham as an example of one who overcame mortality and came forth following Christ's resurrection, and since has entered into his exaltation.[348] We read in the Doctrine and Covenants that, "Abraham received all things, whatsoever he received, by revelation and commandment, by my word, saith the Lord, and hath entered into his exaltation and sitteth upon his throne."[349] Others have succeeded in obtaining exaltation through the glorious Atonement and grace of Jesus Christ, and so can we!

The earth is the eternal place of residence for the exalted. We are told that the entrance to the celestial kingdom is like unto circling rings of fire,[350] and that angels are placed there to guard the way.[351] President David O. McKay saw a beautiful vision of the holy city—the reward of the saints. On May 10, 1921, as he approached Apia, Samoa, he recorded: "Towards evening, the reflection of the afterglow of a beautiful sunset was most splendid! The sky was tinged with pink, and the clouds lingering around the horizon were fringed with various hues of crimson and orange while the heavy cloud farther to the west was somber purple and black. These colors cast varying shadows on the peaceful surface of the water…I then fell asleep, and beheld in vison something infinitely sublime. In the distance I beheld a beautiful white city. Though it was far away, yet I seemed to realize that trees with luscious fruit, shrubbery with gorgeously tinted leaves, and flowers in perfect bloom abounded everywhere. The clear sky above seemed to reflect these beautiful shades of color. I then saw a great concourse of people approaching the city. Each one wore a white flowing robe and a white headdress. Instantly my attention seemed centered upon their leader, and though I could see only the profile of his features and his body, I recognized him at once as my Savior! The tint and radiance of his countenance were glorious to behold. There was a peace about him which seemed sublime—it was divine!

The city, I understood, was his. It was the City Eternal; and the people following him were to abide there in peace and eternal happiness."[352]

As President David O. McKay indicates, the celestial kingdom is a glorious city inhabited by the faithful followers of Christ. Have you ever met someone who is filled with the spirit of Jesus Christ? They are humble, kind, and patient. They seem imbued with a spirit of truth, peace, and love. When you are around them, it is easy to be good, they encourage a spirit of cooperation, and are easily entreated. I recall a friend of mine, Bob, who had these qualities. No, he was not perfect, but he was filled with Christ's spirit. All who met him felt a love and an admiration for him. His smile and handshake just warmed your heart. He was always quick to volunteer his time and resources and made any task easier by his presence. He loved the Lord and was eager to share his witness of the Gospel, and what it had done in his life. He had held many Church callings in his life and tried to excel in each. In later years, he served as a temple worker and was diligent in completing his ancestors' work. Despite his trials, he was upbeat and positive and always trusting in God. One day he said to me that he needed another bypass surgery but thought he would not wake up if he had it done. Sadly, his insight proved prophetic. His passage left a void and it seemed that a light went out in the world. To me, he epitomized what one might call a celestial spirit. One with the characteristics that we should all emulate and cultivate during our lives.

Those who inherit a degree of glory other than the highest degree in the celestial kingdom remain single and distinct throughout eternity. Of them the Lord indicated, "Therefore, when they are out of the world they neither marry nor are given in marriage; but are appointed angels in heaven, which angels are ministering servants, to minister for those who are worthy of a far more, and an exceeding, and an eternal weight of glory. For these angels did not abide my law; therefore, they cannot be enlarged, but remain separately and singly, without exaltation, in their saved condition, to all eternity; and from henceforth are not gods but are angels of God forever and ever."[353] In this role they carry out the purposes of God in bringing salvation to His children in the eternities. We read an example of the work they will do where God sent His angels, "to Joseph Smith, whom I did call upon by mine angels, my ministering servants, and by mine own voice out of the heavens, to bring forth my work."[354] Despite continuing to contribute to the work of salvation, their progression in the eternities is limited because they failed to obey all of God's laws.

We are not told much else about the lower two realms in the

celestial kingdom, and perhaps that is appropriate, for our goal should be to obtain all that the Father has prepared for those who love Him. I think the directions for obtaining the gifts of the spirit apply here also. We are told, "seek ye earnestly the best gifts, always remembering for what they are given; For verily I say unto you, they are given for the benefit of those who love me and keep all my commandments, and him that seeketh so to do."[355]

As mentioned as necessary to obtain the highest degree of the celestial kingdom, we must enter into the New and Everlasting Covenant of Marriage, or celestial marriage. Let us examine this next.

Celestial Marriage

In God's prospective, just being civilly married is not enough; covenants must be completed through God's authority and by His authorized servants to have validity beyond the grave.[356] Joseph Smith taught that a man and his wife must enter into the New and Everlasting Covenant of Marriage in this world, or they will have no claim on each other in the next world.[357] As with ordinances like baptism and the gift of the Holy Ghost, we must obtain the ordinance of eternal marriage in mortality. This ordinance can be done either personally in mortality, or for the dead vicariously by someone acting in another's behalf.

The scriptures emphasize the importance of receiving this ordinance of eternal marriage in order to obtain exaltation. They state, "Therefore, if a man marry him a wife in the world, and he marry her not by me nor by my word…they are not bound by any law when they are out of the world. Therefore, when they are out of the world they neither marry nor are given in marriage; but are appointed angels in heaven…For these angels did not abide my law; therefore, they cannot be enlarged, but remain separately and singly, without exaltation… And again, verily I say unto you…if that covenant is not by me, or by my word, which is my law, and is not sealed by the Holy Spirit of promise, through him whom I have anointed and appointed unto this power, then it is not valid neither of force when they are out of the world, because they are not joined by me, saith the Lord."[358] Marriage must be fulfilled by one holding the proper priesthood power to seal a couple together under God's authority.[359] Being sealed by the Holy Spirit of promise, means that the ordinance is ratified, or approved, by the Spirit of God, or the Holy Ghost. A person in mortality may be able to obtain this ordinance through false pretense, or be unworthy of it, but without the ratification of the Holy Ghost it is of no value. Circumstances of mortality sometimes preclude those worthy of celestial marriage in obtaining it. However, if one lives a life worthy of celestial marriage and endures faithfully all blessings that the Lord has promised will be theirs, whether in this life or the life to come. As the Lord said, "blessed are they who are faithful and endure, whether in life or in death, for they shall inherit eternal life," and eternal life encompasses celestial marriage.[360]

Despite the marvelous promises of God, humankind down through the centuries has sought to modify God's requirements to suit their needs, has set up their own idols to worship, or has rejected God and denied His existence. Even members of the church sometimes fail to understand the importance of eternal marriage. They are not willing to do what God requires to obtain it, or continually postpone preparing themselves to receive the New and Everlasting Covenant of Marriage. But this course will only lead to sorrow and regret. Failing to marry for eternity will result in our not being fully added upon when obtaining the celestial kingdom, just as those who failed to prepare and obtain God's blessings in their first estate were limited, and in that situation were denied their second estate. God's house is a house of order, a house of ordinances and covenants, and is governed through His priesthood. As the Lord taught Joseph Smith, "For whatsoever things remain are by me; and whatsoever things are not by me shall be shaken and destroyed."[361]

Some faithful members wonder if they would lose their temple marriage blessings due to their spouse's subsequent unfaithfulness. The answer is that they certainly will not. God is no respecter of persons and is, "merciful and gracious unto those who fear me, and delight to honor those who serve me in righteousness and in truth unto the end. Great shall be their reward and eternal shall be their glory."[362] They have claim to the promised blessings contained within the New and Everlasting Covenant of Marriage ordinance, having faithfully entered into it under the proper authority of the priesthood and according to God's mandate. An unfaithful spouse's actions cannot nullify those promised blessings in their spouse's life, only their own. As mentioned, within the highest degree of the celestial kingdom those who obtain it receive the blessing of eternal increase, or posterity.

Let's next examine the concept and blessing of celestial offspring.

Celestial Offspring

"This is eternal lives—to know the only wise and true God, and Jesus Christ, whom he hath sent."[363] In this simple statement, the Lord declares a stunning truth: that those who truly come to know and live with God will have the opportunity to enjoy eternal posterity, that is, "eternal lives." Here in mortality, our role as parents within the covenant of temple marriage—between a man and a woman—is a symbol of that which is to come in our third estate if we are faithful to and obey God's laws. There, in the highest degree of the celestial kingdom, the exalted saints can continue to propagate their families throughout eternity. Preparing and obtaining the power and privilege to have eternal increase after the resurrection is part of our second estate. Like all blessings that come from God, this one is predicated on obeying His laws.[364] The Lord stipulates that to obtain eternal increase, "a man must enter into this order of the priesthood [meaning the New and Everlasting Covenant of Marriage]; And if he does not, he cannot obtain it. He may enter into the other, but that is the end of his kingdom; he cannot have an increase."[365] Those who receive the New and Everlasting Covenant of Marriage, remain faithful, and who are sealed by the Holy Spirit of Promise will receive their exaltation, "which glory shall be a fulness and a continuation of the seeds forever and ever."[366] A "fullness and a continuation of the seeds," is to have eternal offspring. It is part of the Abrahamic Covenant. As the Lord explained by referring to Abraham, "and as touching Abraham and his seed, out of the world they should continue; both in the world and out of the world should they continue as innumerable as the stars; or, if ye were to count the sand upon the seashore ye could not number them."[367] I love the sentiment expressed by Parley P. Pratt towards his wife and his faith in eternal posterity. He wrote, "It was from [Joseph Smith] that I learned that the wife of my bosom might be secured to me for time and all eternity; and that the refined sympathies and affections which endeared us to each other emanated from the fountain of divine eternal love. It was from him that I learned that we might cultivate these affections, and grow and increase in the same to all eternity; while the result of our endless union would be an offspring as numerous as the stars of heaven, or the sands of the sea shore. I had loved before, but I knew not why. But now I loved—with a pureness—an intensity of elevated, exalted feeling, which would lift my soul from the transitory things of this grovelling sphere and expand it as the ocean. In short, I could now love with the spirit and with the understanding also."[368]

Elder Melvin J. Ballard helped expound on the doctrine of eternal increase when he said, "What do we mean by endless, or eternal increase? We mean that through the righteousness and faithfulness of men and women who keep the commandments of God they will come forth with celestial bodies, fitted and prepared to enter into their great, high and eternal glory in the celestial kingdom of God; and unto them, through their preparation, there will come children, who will be spirit children…When blood flows in the veins of the being, the offspring will be what blood produces, which is tangible flesh and bone, but when that which flows in the veins is spirit matter, a substance which is more refined and pure and glorious than blood, the offspring of such beings will be spirit children."[369] The ability to propagate one's eternal family is a gift from God to all who prove themselves worthy of it.

Those who inherit the highest degree of the celestial kingdom will not only have been sealed together as individual eternal families, but these families will be linked together, forming an unbroken lineage of exalted humankind.

A Great Welding Link

This linked chain of exalted humankind applies to the highest glory in the celestial kingdom. This is affirmed by the fact that it is only there that couples are sealed together with their children in the New and Everlasting Covenant of Marriage.[370] This family sealing is an antecedent to linking those sealed families together with their ancestors. If you are not sealed together as an exalted family, it follows that you will not be sealed together as part of the exalted chain of humankind. It is only in the highest degree of the celestial kingdom where total perfection, exaltation, and eternal family relationships are found.

As mentioned, there in the highest degree of the celestial kingdom, children will be sealed to their parents and those parents sealed to their parents. Like links in a great priesthood interconnected chain going back to our first parents, Adam and Eve. Unworthy links will be dropped and worthy families will be welded in.[371] Joseph Smith went on to say that in order to form this welding link, the saints needed to do vicarious ordinance work for their departed ancestors, "By building their temples, erecting their baptismal fonts, and going forth and receiving all the ordinances, baptisms, confirmations, washings, anointings ordinations and sealing powers upon their heads, in behalf of all their progenitors who are dead, and redeem them that they may come forth in the first resurrection and be exalted to thrones of glory with them; and herein is the chain that binds the hearts of the fathers to the children, and the children to the fathers, which fulfills the mission of Elijah."[372]

This is the reason the saints build temples. These sealing ordinances cannot be done outside of a place that has been dedicated and set aside for these purposes, whereas others, such as baptism, can. Brigham Young spoke to this: "The sealing ordinances can connect Adam's righteous posterity eternally through priesthood authority. There are many of the ordinances of the house of God that must be performed in a temple that is erected expressly for the purpose.[373] There are other ordinances that we can administer without a temple. You know that there are some which you have received—baptism, the laying on of hands for the gift of the Holy Ghost… and many blessings bestowed upon the people, we have the privilege of receiving without a temple. There are other blessings, that will not be received, and ordinances that will not be performed according to the law that the Lord has revealed, without their being done in a temple prepared for that purpose."[374]

How will we find our worthy ancestors whom we don't know, or where records do not exist, and identify them so we can be sealed together? Brigham Young said, "we will have revelations to know our forefathers clear back to Father Adam and Mother Eve, and we will enter into the temples of God and officiate for them. Then man will be sealed to man until the chain is made perfect back to Adam, so that there will be a perfect chain of priesthood from Adam to the winding-up scene."[375] The winding-up scene referred to here is the end of the earth. This is the part of the planned destiny of the earth: for exalted humankind to be sealed together under the power of God's priesthood.[376] As Joseph Smith taught, "For we without them cannot be made perfect; neither can they without us be made perfect."[377]

This concept of being sealed together brings to mind an experience I had. One of my sisters, though a member of the Church, was not active and did not believe in the afterlife. She felt that at death everything ended. She became ill and died from the effects of cancer. During her final months, members of my family would take turns caring for her. During one of these times when my wife and I were with her, our discussion turned to the spirit world and what she could expect there. She was skeptical but listened as we talked about life after death. Following her death, I began to have impressions that she wanted her temple work done. I knew there would be skepticism and possible opposition from family members. I prayed about it and said my deceased sister would need to soften her mother's and her husband's heart if she wanted her work done, and I would approach them in four weeks. If they gave their consent, I would submit her work to be done. Four weeks passed and I approached them both. They readily agreed that the temple work for my sister should be done. I was amazed and shortly thereafter my wife and I took her name to the temple and had her ordinance work done. Whatever she experienced in the world of spirits kindled in her a desire to have faith in Christ and obtain the ordinances He requires for exaltation. Those who pass on are aware of the ordinances we perform vicariously for them here on earth. Like my sister, they will be anxious to assist us in accomplishing this work of salvation. What joy it will bring to not only see our loved ones again after mortality, but also to rejoice in their having received the saving and exalting ordinances of the Gospel.

But will we be able to communicate with our loved ones who inherit another kingdom?

Communication Between Kingdoms

A friend once inquired if we would be allowed to visit family members who, because of their lack of faith and works, inherit a lower kingdom of glory. Many families have the situation where individuals have different levels of commitment to, or acceptance of the Gospel of Jesus Christ, which may lead to different consequences in eternity.

Despite these variances, we have all experienced the fact that distance, time, and circumstances do not negate the feelings we have for our family members, or loved ones, and the longing to see them. It would seem unfathomable that a God of love would deny His children who obtain exaltation the opportunity to continue to associate with family members and loved ones who may fall short of this blessing. Those who fall short may not receive all that God has made available to His children, but that does not diminish their inherent worth as children of our God. Nor does it extinguish our humanity. The ties that bind us—love, empathy, and concern, which exist in our hearts for loved ones—continue on after death and will have a claim on us.

All of God's realm are kingdoms of glory, and communication within and between them is a reality. We know that those of a celestial glory minister to those of a terrestrial kingdom. And those of the terrestrial glory minister to the telestial kingdom.[378] It would seem logical that those in the celestial glory could also visit those who inherit a telestial glory, although their role may not be one of divine administration, but more of an expression of their love, empathy, and concern. Elder Melvin J. Ballard affirmed this when he said, "We must not overlook the fact that those who attain to the higher glories may minister unto and visit and associate with those of the lesser kingdoms. While the lesser may not come up, they may still enjoy the companionship of their loved ones who are in higher stations."[379] Despite the truth that those of a lesser kingdom cannot come up to a higher one, since their resurrected bodies cannot endure the glory of higher kingdoms, a way is provided for our relationships with loved ones to continue, wherever they might be within God's realm. For God's children, that distance and different circumstances are surmounted in the face of sacred relationships is no surprise. We will continue to be able to visit and communicate with one another despite any differences.

With that in mind, now let's turn to the terrestrial resurrection.

Terrestrial Resurrection Timing and Nature

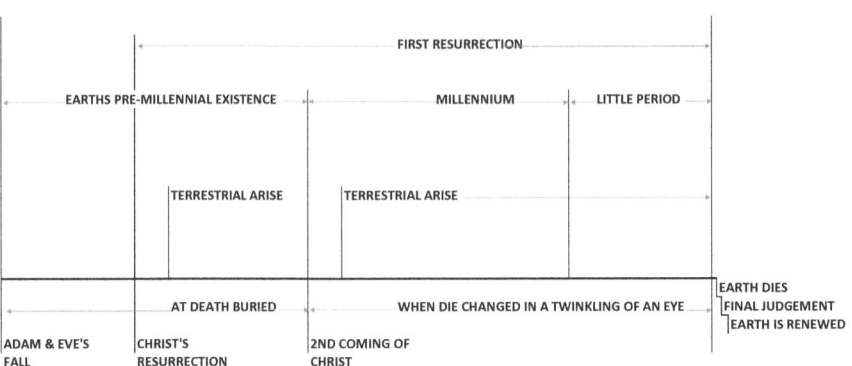

Illustration 7.4 Terrestrial Resurrection Timing

In discussing the terrestrial resurrection, it would be helpful to look back at the time of Christ's First Coming and the resurrection that occurred then. Let's review a chart of what Moses 7 teaches us about those resurrected following Christ's resurrection and then discuss it.

Moses 7	Celestial	Terrestrial	Telestial
V-38		Wicked Perish in the Great Flood	Also True
V-38		Put in Prison at Death	Also True
V-39		Christ Atones for Their Sins, Inasmuch as They Repent	These Suffer for Their Own Sins
V-39		Christ Pleads With God on Their Behalf	Does Not Apply
V-39		They Remain in Torment Until Christ Returns to God	Does Not Apply
V-55	Christ Lifted Up on the Cross		
V-56 & 57	The Saints Arise	Many of the Spirts in Prison Come Forth	Does Not Apply
V-56	Receive Crowns of Glory	Not True	Not True
V-56 & 57	Stand on Christ's Right Hand	Stand on Christ's Right Hand	Also True
V-57			Remainder Reserved in Chains of Darkness Until Great Day of Judgment

Note: *Italicized* words are authors comments

Illustration 7.5 Moses 7 Resurrection Teachings

Our inquiry begins in the Book of Moses where we read about those who lived before the flood in great wickedness. "But behold, these which thine eyes are upon shall perish in the floods; and behold, I will shut them up; a prison have I prepared for them."[380] The wicked were ushered into the spirit world and specifically a spirit prison, by the flood. We then read about Jesus Christ pleading their cause before God. God said, "And That which I have chosen hath pled before my face. Wherefore, he suffereth for their sins; inasmuch as they will repent in the day that my Chosen shall return unto me, and until that day they shall be in torment."[381] From this we learn they were to remain in that spirit prison until they repent and Jesus Christ, who plead their case, left God's presence and then returned to it. When Jesus Christ was born in mortality He left God's presence,[382] and we know Jesus Christ returned to the Father following His earthly ministry and resurrection. Of His return to God, to Mary Magdalene He said, "but go to my brethren, and say unto them, I ascend unto my Father, and your Father; and to my God, and your God."[383] Having now left and returned to God's presence the time had come for the release of those spirits held in Spirit Prison who were worthy of the First Resurrection.

Enoch records that at this time that, "he heard a loud voice; and the heavens were veiled; and all the creations of God mourned; and the earth groaned; and the rocks were rent; and the saints arose, and were crowned at the right hand of the Son of Man, with crowns of glory; And as many of the spirits as were in prison came forth, and stood on the right hand of God; and the remainder were reserved in chains of darkness until the judgment of the great day."[384] Creation mourned at the death of the Creator. The saints came forth from their graves and received a celestial resurrection and crowns of glory, but interestingly others spirits were resurrected, or came forth from their graves, and stood on the right hand of God. They did not receive crowns of glory and came from a prison. These were spirits held in spirit prison from the time of the flood, along with others in spirit prison who died after the flood, down until the time of Christ's mortal ministry. They had prepared themselves and were ready to be resurrected. Celestial and terrestrial beings arise during the First Resurrection, and celestial beings receive a crown of righteousness whereas terrestrial beings don't. Since they came forth in the First Resurrection separate from the saints who received celestial glory and crowns, we know they came forth as terrestrial beings. In addition, the celestial resurrection precedes the terrestrial resurrection. It seems that these events brought about the First Resurrection for all of humankind who had died, who were worthy, from Adam down until the time of Christ's resurrection. The exception is those who had died and would inherit a telestial resurrection. These last will remain in the spirit world "in chains of darkness" until after the Millennium.[385] They had not and were not prepared for the resurrection. Now let us focus on the future resurrection of terrestrial beings at Christ's Second Coming.

This resurrection of terrestrial beings is part of the First Resurrection, or resurrection of the "Just." It follows sometime shortly after Christ's Second Coming in the heavens. We learn that, "after this another angel shall sound, which is the second trump; and then cometh the redemption of those who are Christ's at his coming; who have received their part in that prison which is prepared for them, that they might receive the Gospel, and be judged according to men in the flesh."[386] Those worthy of a celestial glory have already been resurrected and now those worthy of a terrestrial glory come forth. This is a repeat of what happened at the time just following Jesus Christ's resurrection. But the remainder who have not prepared themselves for this resurrection will again remain in spirit prison. A repeat of the time following Christ's resurrection, and those who now remain in the spirit prison become part of the Second, or Last Resurrection.

During the Millennium, will some of humankind be changed in a twinkling of an eye be raised to a terrestrial glory? The prophet Zacharias records that those nations that previously fought against Jerusalem, and do not come up to worship the Savior during the millennium will be chastened. The Lord will cause no rain to fall upon them. He will send plagues upon them and smite them.[387] The result for some will be death as the Lord seeks to humble them during the millennium and bring them to worship Him. In their disbelieving state they are not worthy of a celestial glory, but a terrestrial one having survived the Lord's Second Coming. In addition, following the Lord's Second Coming we are told, "then shall the heathen nations be redeemed, and they that knew no law shall have part in the first resurrection; and it shall be tolerable for them."[388] Again indicating that some of humankind will merit a terrestrial resurrection during the millennium.

All these will be changed in a twinkling of an eye as the terrestrial resurrection continues until the end of the world.

The glory of the terrestrial resurrection is likened in the scriptures to the moon. Like the moon, which waxes and wanes, those who inherit this kingdom are wavering in the commitment to Christ and His Gospel. Like colors at night, where white is grey and grey is black, they see things only partially and unclearly. They do not have access to all truth and have no means to inquire into things of the kingdoms above, or below them unless it is made known by those who minister to them. They are eclipsed by those who are of the celestial kingdom just as the sun eclipses the moon when present. They are inferior in all things when compared to those of the celestial kingdom, but superior to those of the telestial kingdom. Although we are not told what differences there are in the bodies that come forth in this resurrection we do know they are not the same as those of the celestial kingdom either in makeup, or glory, and they cannot endure the conditions found there. Like the other kingdoms, "they who are quickened by a portion of the terrestrial glory shall then receive of the same, even a fulness."[389] Their glorious nature is one like the celestial kingdom, but differs in luminosity as the Moon's light does from the Sun.[390] Since the earth, in the eternities, is reserved for those who inherit a celestial glory the home of the terrestrial beings in the eternities will be on another world of a terrestrial nature.

Jesus Christ visits and governs here, but they are deprived of the presence of the Father.[391] These are a part of our Heavenly Father's realm and will be found on His right side in the day of final judgment. But a crown of glory is not theirs, and where God and Christ dwell they cannot come worlds without end. Like any saved in a kingdom of God they must repent of all their sins.[392] These include those who have died without the law of Christ, who were part of the spirit prison, and did not accept Jesus Christ until after mortality.[393] They are honorable men and women blinded by humankind's false beliefs who do not accept the Gospel,[394] but it also includes those who accepted the Gospel but are not valiant in their testimonies of Jesus Christ.[395] As the celestial ministers to the terrestrial, so the terrestrial ministers to the telestial kingdom.[396]

What constitutes a terrestrial nature? I am reminded of two different couples who were experiencing financial difficulty. Each had unique problems, but both lacked the means to meet their financial commitments. Neither paid their tithing. We looked for how we could support them and help them weather this financial storm. We talked about how they needed the blessings of tithing in their lives, and I challenged them to pay a faithful tithe. Both left my office to consider my challenge but were comforted that the Church would help them as they sought resolution to their problems. Both were wonderful couples, members of the Church, and upstanding members of the community. One couple returned and indicated that though they did not understand how it would work, but they would obey God's command to pay a full tithe, and trust in Christ to help them overcome their difficulties as they worked for a solution. The second couple wrote a scathing letter pointing out the foolishness of the counsel they had been given. They said they would not pay a tithe and remonstrated me for suggesting it. Although the actions of these two couples were not the final determination of their eternal reward I could not help but think it reflected where they were at that point in time. One had faith in Christ and his promises—the other not. One was willing to follow the commandments even in the face of financial risk—one was not. One was faithful to their testimonies of Christ—one was not. In the months that followed the couple who paid their tithing found solutions to their problems—the other did not. Perhaps the second couple in this story in a simple way illustrates the nature of a terrestrial spirit versus a celestial one. Their hearts, desires, and actions define them as good people, but not able to rise to a level of faith to valiantly follow Jesus Christ. At worst, those of a terrestrial nature hide their light under a basket, or at best close the blinds when darkness comes. What would others say about our actions? Are we valiant followers of Christ?

Let us now turn to the telestial resurrection.

Telestial Resurrection Timing and Nature

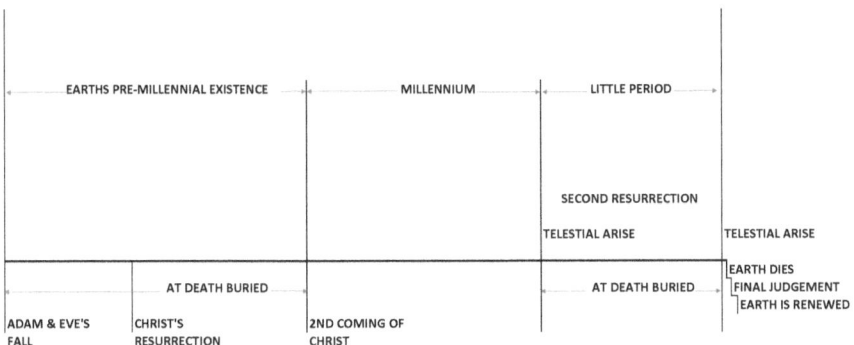

Illustration 7.6 Telestial Resurrection Timing

The resurrection of telestial beings is part of the Second Resurrection. It is the resurrection of "Damnation," or the "Unjust."[397] Second Peter indicates, "The Lord knoweth how to deliver the godly out of temptations, and to reserve the unjust unto the day of judgment to be punished."[398] As with all things in God's kingdom there is a logical pre-determined order to the resurrection. The "Unjust" arise after the "Just" children of our God have been resurrected. They are unjust because they have not accepted the Gospel and do not have a testimony of Jesus Christ. Yet even these will bend the knee before our great God and acknowledge that Jesus is the Christ.[399]

Unlike the celestial and terrestrial resurrection, which have occurred twice before and continue during the Millennium, the first group in the Second Resurrection occurs after the Millennium, which is why it is called the "Last."[400] The scriptures in speaking of them say, "And these are the rest of the dead; and they live not again until the thousand years are ended." For any who may die following the end of the Millennium that are of a telestial spirit, or who do not come forth at that time, they are not resurrected individually during the "Little Period" that follows the Millennium. Those who die during this time are buried and enter the spirit world to await their resurrection. They join the others that have remained in spirit prison and as the scriptures indicate arise, "neither again, until the end of the earth."[401] Concerning them, the Lord said, "These are they who are cast down to hell and suffer the wrath of Almighty God, until the fulness of times, when Christ shall have subdued all enemies under his feet, and shall have perfected his work."[402]

The telestial resurrection is likened to the stars.[403] Their glory and natures differs as one star differs from another. They are numberless and encompass all who are not worthy of a celestial, or terrestrial resurrection, and have languished in spirit prison during mankind's history. "But behold, and lo, we saw the glory and the inhabitants of the telestial world, that they were as innumerable as the stars in the firmament of heaven, or as the sand upon the seashore."[404] The Holy Ghost ministers here along with those of a terrestrial order.[405] Just as the sun and moon eclipse the stars they are inferior to the inhabitants of both the celestial and terrestrial kingdom in all ways. They have no access to knowledge of those kingdoms above them. Where God and Christ dwell they cannot come worlds without end.[406] However, it is a kingdom of glory, and they will be found on God's right hand in the day of final judgment.[407] They will be redeemed after suffering the wrath of a just God. Although we are not told what differences there are in the bodies that come forth in this resurrection we do know they are not the same as those of the celestial, or terrestrial kingdoms either in makeup or glory, and they cannot endure the conditions found in either. As in all of Gods kingdoms they must repent of all their sins.[408] Like the other kingdoms, "they who are quickened by a portion of the telestial glory shall then receive of the same, even a fulness."[409] Their eternal home is another world suited for telestial beings.

They have not denied the Holy Ghost but are thrust down to hell."[410] For these are they who are of Paul, and of Apollos, and of Cephas. These are they who say they are some of one and some of another, "some of Christ and some of John, and some of Moses, and some of Elias, and some of Esaias, and some of Isaiah, and some of Enoch."[411] They make up their own religion, ignoring truth by changing it into something they are more comfortable with and worship idols of their own making. "These are they who are liars, and sorcerers, and adulterers, and whoremongers, and whosoever loves and makes a lie."[412] A pretty rough description and too common in our world.

Wilford Woodruff had a vision of the resurrection shown to him by a heavenly messenger. He recorded, speaking of a heavenly messenger, "Then he showed me the resurrection of the dead — what is termed the first and second resurrection. In the first resurrection I saw no graves, nor anyone raised from the grave. I saw legions of celestial beings, men and women who had received the Gospel, all clothed in white robes. In the form they were presented to me, they had already been raised from the grave. After this, he showed me what is termed the second resurrection. Vast fields of graves were before me, and the spirit of God rested upon the earth like a shower of gentle rain, and when that fell upon the graves they were opened and an immense host of human beings came forth. They were just as diversified in their dress as we see here, or as they were laid down."[413]

Have you ever met someone who exhibits a telestial nature? I recall during business trips calling on customers to review their purchases and account activity. Later, I often went to dinner with the owner. On one such visit, while we ate dinner, the business owner talked of opportunities and how we could both make money. He asked me if I was willing to discount the monies he owed the company in exchange for some of the money saved. He called it a win-win. I think the surprise on my face was his first clue about how I felt. I was chagrinned that he thought he could ask me to do that. Later I found this customer had unaccounted for adjustments being made to the amount he owed the company through unauthorized computer entries. When I inquired into it with the accounts receivable manager, he appeared confused and denied any knowledge. A few weeks later the accounts receivable manager unexpectedly quit. I am not sure how these two individual lives eventually turned out, but I can say they loved and made a lie and seemed to epitomize those of a telestial spirit. Where are our hearts at? Do we speak and deal honestly with our fellowman? Do we espouse and follow pure and virtuous principles? If we desire to obtain all that God has, honesty and virtue will be part of our character.

Now let's review those who refuse to repent: the resurrection of the damned.

Sons of Perdition Resurrection Timing and Nature

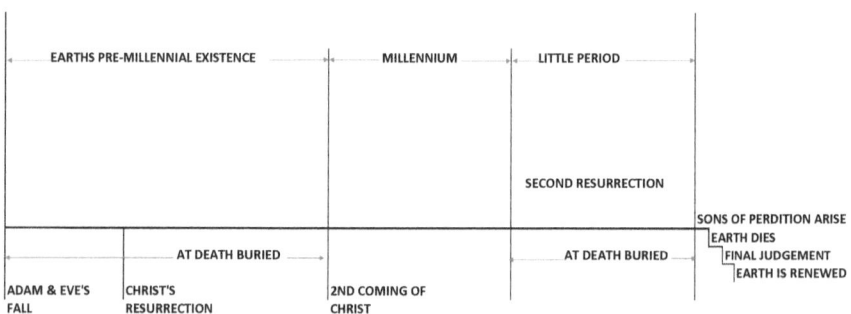

Illustration 7.7 Sons of Perdition Resurrection Timing

The resurrection of Sons of Perdition, or the damned is the other part of the Second Resurrection. They become part of Satan's kingdom of no glory. For any who may die following the Millennium, that become Sons of Perdition, they are not resurrected individually during the "Little Period" that follows the Millennium. They come forth with those of a telestial glory who have remained until the very end of the earth's existence. This final resurrection happens just before the end of the earth after the "Little Season," and just before the earth dies.[414] "Yea, even that great day when the earth shall be rolled together as a scroll, and the elements shall melt with fervent heat, yea, in that great day when ye shall be brought to stand before the Lamb of God."[415] They represent the ignominious part of the resurrection of damnation, or the unjust. The fourth trump declares their sad condition. The angel proclaims, "there are found among those who are to remain until that great and last day, even the end, [those] who shall remain filthy still."[416] They reject the Savior, His kingdom, and are found on God's left hand.[417] Where they are will be weeping, wailing, and gnashing of teeth.[418] These do not inherit a kingdom of our God, do not repent, and remain filthy still, slaves to their sins. They cannot be and will not be saved through the atonement of Christ.[419] For, "That which breaketh a law, and abideth not by law, but seeketh to become a law unto itself, and willeth to abide in sin, and altogether abideth in sin, cannot be sanctified by law, neither by mercy, justice, nor judgment. Therefore, they must remain filthy still."[420] They receive a resurrected body of no glory, and like the rest of humankind are brought back into God's presence for the final judgment at the end of the world, "And wo, wo, wo, is their doom."[421] They will join Satan, their father.[422] Along with those spirits who followed Satan in the pre-earth existence and were denied physical bodies. "These are they who shall go away into the lake of fire and brimstone, with the devil and his angels."[423] They will reside eternally together on a planet of no light, or glory, outside of God's realm. Never to return to God.

God's inescapable eternal justice claims the unrepentant sinner, and His judgment, wrath, and destruction follow. Like a person jumping off of a 10-story building is unavoidable crushed as they hit the ground due to the effects of gravity, so the unrepentant sinner reaps eternal destruction due to the effects of God's everlasting justice. As the Lord's haunting words declare, "Behold, and lo, there are none to deliver you; for ye obeyed not my voice when I called to you out of the heavens; ye believed not my servants, and when they were sent unto you ye received them not. Wherefore, they sealed up the testimony and bound up the law, and ye were delivered over unto darkness. These shall go away into outer darkness, where there is weeping, and wailing, and gnashing of teeth."[424] These are the only ones on whom the second death has any power.[425] However, their final end will not be known until the day of judgment, but awful is their fate.[426] Of those who inherit this kingdom of no glory it is said, "And wo be unto him that will not hearken unto the words of Jesus, and also to them whom he hath chosen and sent among them; for whoso receiveth not the words of Jesus and the words of those whom he hath sent receiveth not him; and therefore he will not receive them at the last day; And it would be better for them if they had not been born."[427]

These include those who commit the "Unpardonable Sin." These have had the light of the Gospel, experienced the presence of the Holy Ghost, and have a sure knowledge of their Redeemer. Like denying the sun in the heavens as it shines down upon them they crucify the Lord anew unto themselves through their denial of Him. "Thus saith the Lord concerning all those who know my power, and have been made partakers thereof, and suffered themselves through the power of the devil to be overcome, and to deny the truth and defy my power—They are they who are the sons of perdition."[428] Blasphemy against the Holy Ghost also falls into the category. The Lord has said, "Wherefore I say unto you, All manner of sin and blasphemy shall be forgiven unto men: but the blasphemy against the Holy Ghost shall not be forgiven unto men."[429] The Doctrine and Covenants defines what this means. It says, "The blasphemy against the Holy Ghost, which shall not be forgiven in the world nor out of the world, is in that ye commit murder wherein ye shed innocent blood, and assent unto my death, after ye have received my new and everlasting covenant, saith the Lord God; and he that abideth not this law can in nowise enter into my glory, but shall be damned, saith the Lord."[430] This also includes those who engage in pre-meditated murder or the deliberate and unjustified taking of another's life. We are told, "Thou shalt not kill; and he that kills shall not have forgiveness in this world, nor in the world to come."[431]

Some have speculated about who and how many of these poor, blighted, and damned individuals there will be. Suffice it to say there will be a number who refuse to repent of their sins, crucify Christ anew, murder, or sin against the Holy Ghost. Regardless of the number, Satan's reign of terror and destruction will end, "and thus we see that the devil will not support his children at the last day, but doth speedily drag them down to hell."⁴³² With Jesus Christ our Savior declaring that He has, "accomplished and finished the will of him whose I am, even the Father, concerning me—having done this that I might subdue all things unto myself—Retaining all power, even to the destroying of Satan and his works at the end of the world, and the last great day of judgment, which I shall pass upon the inhabitants thereof, judging every man according to his works and the deeds which he hath done."⁴³³

One might ask themselves why would someone not want to repent, and be cleansed of sin? There was a mobster who was known in the community. He was allegedly involved in prostitution, illegal gambling, and crime. When he was interviewed near the end of his life, he was asked if he was satisfied with his life and how he lived it. He replied, my life speaks for itself. Although we do not know all of what is in one's soul his life represented an attitude of unrepentant arrogance toward sin, and vice, which he was pleased with. This type of an unrepentant nature seems to reflect the attitude of one who will remain filthy still. The message for us is that we must all be careful not to justify our sins and refuse to repent.

Summary

The resurrection of celestial beings is part of the First Resurrection, which began with the resurrection of Jesus Christ, immediately followed by the ancient saints who had died, or were translated before that time. It occurs again at His Second Coming, and then continues till the end of the earth as the saints are changed in a twinkling of an eye. It is likened to the sun. They receive a crown of glory and their glory is one. Their presence brings life, light, truth, and warmth to all those they encounter, and they are eternal and dependable. They are superior in all things when compared with those of another kingdom. They are found on God's right hand in the day of judgment and inherit the earth. They minister to the terrestrial kingdom and communicate with those they hold dear in other kingdoms. Within the celestial kingdom are three degrees of glory. Only those obtaining the highest degree of the celestial kingdom having received all the ordinances of the Gospel, including the New and Everlasting Covenant of Marriage, will enjoy eternal increase and be sealed together as families as part of exalted humankind.

Those worthy of a terrestrial glory came forth after the celestial resurrection at the time of Christ's resurrection. The resurrection of terrestrial beings is part of the First Resurrection. It will occur again following Christ's return, and is signaled with the sounding of the second trump and then continues till the end of the earth as they are change in a twinkling of an eye. They inherit a world of a terrestrial nature. Terrestrial beings are likened to the moon. They do not receive a crown of glory but do not differ in glory one from another. They are eclipsed by those who are of the celestial kingdom just as the sun eclipses the moon when present. They are inferior in all things when compared to those of the celestial kingdom but superior to those of the telestial kingdom. They are found on God's right hand in the day of judgment. They minister to the telestial kingdom.

The resurrection of telestial beings is part of the Second, or Last Resurrection. It is also called the Resurrection of the Unjust and the Second Resurrection happens after the Millennium and once again after the "Little Period," just before the end of the earth. They are not individually resurrected between these two events. They inherit a world of a telestial nature. Just as the sun and moon eclipse the stars, those of a telestial glory are inferior to the inhabitants of both the celestial and terrestrial kingdom in all ways. Their glory differs as one star differs from another. They are found on God's right hand in the day of judgment.

The resurrection of the Sons of Perdition is the other part of the Second, or Last Resurrection. It happens after the "Little Period" just before the end of the earth when they come forth as a group. The fourth trump proclaims a sad ending for those who are a part of it. They are found on God's left hand. These do not inherit a kingdom of glory, do not repent, and remain filthy still, slaves to their sins. They inherit a world of no glory. They cannot and will not be saved through the Atonement of Christ. They are the only ones on whom the second death has any claim. They become part of Satan's dominion, and it would have been better if they had not been born.

Truly, a loving God grants to all His children the desires of their hearts and has prepared a place for them all. "For where your treasure is, there will your heart be also."[434]

CHAPTER 8

JESUS CHRIST'S RESURRECTION

Our Lord has written the promise of resurrection, not in books alone but in every leaf of springtime

~ Martin Luther

IN CONTEMPLATING THE Lord's resurrection, my mind is drawn to the powerful hymn, "He Is Risen" with words by Cecil Frances Alexander.

HE IS RISEN,

He is risen! He is risen!
Tell it out with joyful voice.
He has burst his three days' prison;
Let the whole wide earth rejoice.
Death is conquered; man is free.
Christ has won the victory.

Let us see what insights we can gain about His victory as we turn to the timing of Jesus Christ's birth, death and resurrection, fulfillment of the law of witnesses, events around His death and resurrection, and some Jewish traditions surrounding this sacred event.

Dating Christ's Birth, Death, and Resurrection

In examining the date of Jesus Christ's resurrection, perhaps it would be beneficial to start by answering the questions of when He was born, when He died, and when was He in the tomb, which will lead us to the date of His resurrection.

There have been different dates suggested by member and non-members alike for His birth.[435] Through the years, many in the Church have referred to Doctrine and Covenants Section 20, verse one, for support that Christ was born in 1 A.D. But the meaning of the statement, "being one thousand eight hundred and thirty years since the coming of our Lord and Savior Jesus Christ in the flesh," could more accurately refer to anytime in Christ's lifespan, and not specifically His birth. In addition, the section begins with a third-person review of the founding of the Church, and a brief history of Joseph Smith. It focuses on establishing the date of the organization of the Church, rather than determining the birth date of Christ. It is not the first-person voice of God declaring His will, indicating that the opening remarks came from man, not God.

In determining the date of Jesus Christ's birth: first is the date of Herod the Great's well documented death in early 4 B.C. who was alive at the birth of Christ.[436] So Christ had to be born prior to early 4 B.C. This is then tied to Herod's killing of the children in Bethlehem who were two years old or younger in an effort to negate a supposed threat to his reign. Together these two events show Christ was born somewhere between 6–5 B.C. in order for these two events recorded at His birth to take place. Jeffery R. Chadwick has taken this further and put together a convincing analysis that points to Christ's birth being in late December of 5 B.C.[437]

With His estimated birth year in mind, let's next review His death date. The Book of Mormon shows us Jesus Christ lived a full 33 years and not 34 years. It says that thirty-three years after the sign of Jesus's birth, a great storm occurred with destruction and three days of darkness marking the day on which Jesus Christ died.[438] Also with this terrible sign of Jesus's death, Mormon wrote that, "the thirty and third year had passed away," and that the storm hit, "in the thirty and fourth year, in the first month, on the fourth day of the month."[439] The record in 3 Nephi shows that Jesus lived thirty-three full years. He died on the 14th of Nissan (April 6th), based on the Gospels' account of His death.[440] There is only one year that the 14th of Nissan falls on that could support the Gospels' narration of Christ arising on the first day of the week, and that He lived a full 33 years, which is 30 A.D. Using this as the year of Christ's death, Chadwick more specifically determined that Christ died on Thursday, April 6th, 30 A.D, the 14th day of Nissan.[441] Again Chadwick determined Christ's death[442] based on those and other facts and then working back from that date, he arrived at a birth month of December in 5 B.C, as Jesus Christ's birth year.[443]

Next let's look at the time Jesus Christ spent in the tomb based on Chadwick's findings and his published study of the date of Christ's death. In doing so, it is important to know that the Jewish day ended at sunset. In addition, Jewish tradition was that the spirit hovered over the body for three days—another reason Christ was in the tomb for three days was to assure the Jews that He died. The following is a chart summarizing the dates of when Christ was in the tomb.

Day of Week	Date	Day Ends at Sundown	Next Day Starts after Sundown
Thursday	Dies 3:00pm April 6th (14th Nissan) Christ is buried prior to Sunset		Night one
Friday	April 7th (15th Nissan)	Day one	Night Two
Saturday	April 8th (16th Nissan)	Day two	Night Three
Sunday	April 9th (17th Nissan)	Day three	

Illustration 8.1 Jesus Christ's Time in the Tomb

As you can see, Thursday, April 6th, thru Saturday, April 8th, comprises three nights in the tomb. Friday, April 7th, thru Sunday, April 9th, makes up the three days in the tomb. He arose early Sunday morning, April 9th, 30 A.D. Thus fulfilling His prophecy that the wicked generation of Pharisees and Sadducees would only receive the sign of Jonas (Jonah) as a witness of His divinity.[444]

As mentioned at the time of His resurrection, He was the Firstfruits, or the first one resurrected in the history of humankind. Hence, as the scriptures affirm, God raised Him up by giving Him the power to arise. And having given His life for humankind, performed the Atonement, and arisen from the dead, He received the keys of the resurrection. As Joseph Fielding Smith said, "So Jesus Christ did for us something that we could not do for ourselves, through his infinite atonement. On the third day after the crucifixion he took up his body and gained the keys of the resurrection, and thus has power to open the graves for all mankind, but this he could not do until he had first passed through death himself and conquered."[445] The debate surrounding Christ's exact birth and death date will surely continue, however the critical point is that these events occurred. His subsequent resurrection was a crucial pivotal event that sent a tidal wave of rejoicing through the eternities.

It was also attested to under the law of witnesses, which requires two or more witnesses to authenticate a circumstance.

The Law of Witnesses and the Resurrection

The law of witnesses was a part of God's law in ancient times. We read in the Old Testament, "At the mouth of two witnesses, or three witnesses, shall he that is worthy of death be put to death; but at the mouth of one witness he shall not be put to death."[446] And again in the New Testament, "that in the mouth of two, or three witnesses every word may be established."[447] This law of multiple witnesses was fulfilled in the life events surrounding Jesus Christ. We find that at least two women were witnesses in mortality of His conception, birth, death, and resurrection. Mary, the mother of Jesus, was first to witness Christ's conception, followed by her cousin Elizabeth.[448] When Christ was born, it was Mary, His mother, and her midwife, who is not spoken of, who were the two mortal witnesses.[449] When He died, we find women mourning and watching His death, "Among which was Mary Magdalene, and Mary the mother of James and Joses, and the mother of Zebedee's children."[450] Following His resurrection, the women of Galilee, Mary Magdalene, Mary the mother of James and Salome, along with others, witnessed the empty tomb.[451] Then the women beheld Christ Himself.[452] Further, we are told He first appeared to Mary Magdalene,[453] then to the other women. All of these events fulfill the law of witnesses. It is of interest that at conception, and for each of the three gateways of mortality, birth, death, and the resurrection, that women were the first witnesses for humankind. We also know that many others witnessed these events or became later witnesses for the events surrounding Christ.

Now let's examine the day of Christ's death and resurrection.

Christ's Death and Resurrection Day

Jesus Christ had control over His death and voluntarily gave His life in completing His Atonement. He said, "No man taketh it from me, but I lay it down of myself. I have power to lay it down, and I have power to take it again. This commandment have I received of my Father."[454] He orchestrated events so that He fulfilled God's commandments, the prophets' declarations, and the Jewish traditions concerning His death and resurrection.

At Christ's death, we read, "when he had cried again with a loud voice, yielded up the ghost. And, behold, the veil of the Temple was rent in twain from the top to the bottom; and the earth did quake, and the rocks rent."[455] In the New World, the cataclysmic events at Christ's death were even greater: "And there was also a great and terrible tempest; and there was terrible thunder, insomuch that it did shake the whole earth as if it was about to divide asunder. And there were exceedingly sharp lightnings, such as never had been known in all the land."[456] Some cities caught fire, while others were sunk in the sea or buried in the earth. Still others were demolished by whirlwinds or shaken and destroyed. As 3 Nephi 8 reports, "And thus the face of the whole earth became deformed, because of the tempests, and the thunderings, and the lightnings, and the quaking of the earth."[457] These tragedies helped fulfill the prophecy that, "many of the kings of the isles of the sea shall be wrought upon by the Spirit of God, to exclaim: The God of nature suffers."[458]

Following His death, "When the even was come, there came a rich man of Arimathaea, named Joseph, who also himself was Jesus' disciple: He went to Pilate, and begged the body of Jesus. Then Pilate commanded the body to be delivered. And when Joseph had taken the body, he wrapped it in a clean linen cloth, And laid it in a new tomb, which had hewn out in the rock: and rolled a great stone to the door of the sepulchre, and departed."[459] This burial was hastily done because the Jewish day ended at sunset, and the next day was the Sabbath, a day sacred to the Jews.

We know that the Jewish leaders understood the prophecies concerning Jesus Christ. They went to Pilate and asked him to make the sepulchre secure indicating to Pilate that Christ said He would rise again in three days. And, "Pilate said unto them, Ye have a watch: go your way, make it as sure as ye can. So they went, and made the sepulchre sure, sealing the stone, and setting a watch."[460] To seal the stone, in the presence of the guards, a rope was probably stretched across the stone, and then fastened on the stone face and rock at either side of the sepulchre by the means of wax or sealing clay. The wax or sealing clay would have been broken if the stone were moved. A signet ring may also have been impressed in the wax or sealing clay for additional security.[461] Another view is that a large cork–shaped blocking stone was placed in the opening of the tomb and was sealed with wax or sealing clay.[462] This, along with the number of Roman guards at the tomb, would ensure there was no tampering with the tomb in which Christ was laid.[463]

The Roman guards set to watch the tomb were the first to see an angel of God and, "For fear of him the keepers did shake, and became as dead men."[464] Then, "some of the watch came into the city, and shewed unto the chief priests all the things that were done. And when they were assembled with the elders, and had taken counsel, they gave large money unto the soldiers, Saying, Say ye, His disciples came by night, and stole him away while we slept. And if this come to the governor's ears, we will persuade him, and secure you. So they took the money, and did as they were taught: and this saying is commonly reported among the Jews until this day."[465] The soldiers did this because the Roman penalty for abandoning one's post was to be deported and to lose one's Roman citizenship. To fall asleep during a watch was punishable by death.[466] By siding with the Jewish leaders, the guards garnered their support and could convince Pilate not to punish them. They received money, too. But humankind's puny attempts to thwart the works of God failed. The seal representing man's authority could not prevent Jesus from fulfilling His divine destiny. Likewise, the tomb, representing death's claim on humankind, could not hold Him, and the Roman guards representing humankind's strength, could not stop Him.

Following the Jewish Sabbath, we read about the women who came with spices to prepare Christ's body for burial: "And very early in the morning the first day of the week, they came unto the sepulchre at the rising of the sun. And they said among themselves, Who shall roll us away the stone from the door of the sepulchre? And when they looked, they saw that the stone was rolled away: for it was very great."[467] They arrived at the tomb and found it empty, whereupon an angel met them and they inquired as to where Christ was laid. "And the angel answered and said unto the women, "Fear not ye: for I know that ye seek Jesus, which was crucified. He is not here: for he is risen, as he said. Come, see the place where the Lord lay. And go quickly, and tell his disciples that he is risen from the dead; and, behold, he goeth before you into Galilee; there shall ye see him: lo, I have told you. And they departed quickly from the sepulchre with fear and great joy; and did run to bring his disciples word." [468]

The women on their way to find the disciples met Simon Peter and John the Beloved. We know that Christ has not yet appeared to the women, for Mary Magdalene said to them, "they have taken away the Lord out of the sepulchre, and we know not where they have laid him."[469] Like others, the realization that Jesus Christ had risen had not penetrated their unbelief. Peter and John, upon hearing the news, ran to the tomb. John gets there first and looks into the tomb, but does not enter, perhaps out of respect for Peter's role as chief Apostle. Simon Peter then arrives, goes into the tomb, and finds the linen clothes lying folded up neatly in a pile. John then enters, and the scriptures say, "and he saw, and believed.[470] The two then surprisingly return to their own homes.[471]

It appears Mary Magdalene returned to the tomb either with them, or shortly after, and remained after the two left, for we read, "But Mary stood without at the sepulchre weeping: and as she wept, she stooped down, and looked into the sepulchre, And seeth two angels in white sitting, the one at the head, and the other at the feet, where the body of Jesus had lain. And they say unto her, Woman, why weepest thou? She saith unto them, Because they have taken away my

Lord, and I know not where they have laid him. And when she had thus said, she turned herself back, and saw Jesus standing, and knew not that it was Jesus. Jesus saith unto her, Woman, why weepest thou? whom seekest thou? She, supposing him to be the gardener, saith unto him, Sir, if thou have borne him hence, tell me where thou hast laid him, and I will take him away. Jesus saith unto her, Mary. She turned herself, and saith unto him, Rabboni; which is to say, Master."[472] What a poignant moment. She experienced her intense pain turned to unspeakable joy—night changed into day at the realization that Christ had indeed risen. That she returned to the tomb and had a visitation separate from the other women is supported by the fact that Mark tells us Jesus Christ, "appeared first to Mary Magdalene."[473] Much has been written about Christ's admonition at that time to Mary: "Touch me not." A clearer translation might be, "Do not cling to Me [do not hold Me]."[474] She embraced her Lord in adoration, but He had more to accomplish, "for I am not yet ascended to my Father," and He needed to be about his Father's business.[475]

Meanwhile, the other women continued on to find the remaining disciples, Mary joining them at some point. "And as they went to tell his disciples, behold, Jesus met them, saying, All hail. And they came and held him by the feet, and worshipped him. Then said Jesus unto them, Be not afraid: go tell my brethren that they go into Galilee, and there shall they see me."[476] These disciples upon hearing the glorious news doubted the women's story, including Mary Magdalene's. Later we see this same doubt reappear. We read, "Then the eleven disciples went away into Galilee, into a mountain where Jesus had appointed them. And when they saw him, they worshipped him: but some doubted. And Jesus came and spake unto them, saying, All power is given unto me in heaven and in earth."[477] The veil of unbelief and doubt reasserting itself, yet turning again into belief through Christ's many appearances. Humankind's efforts to halt the work of God and stop Jesus Christ from rising were brought to naught. Jesus Christ had risen, and in doing so became the Firstfruits of the dead. It was an event for the ages, and all of Christ's creations here on earth and in the starry heavens are the recipients of its eternal blessings.

He also fulfilled Jewish traditions through the events surrounding His Atonement. Let's examine two of these traditions.

Feast of Unleavened Bread

Traditionally, the Jews celebrated the exodus from Egypt. Since there was not time for bread to rise when the Jews fled Egypt, the Lord memorialized this event by commanding the Jews to only eat unleavened bread for seven days. "Thou shalt eat no leavened bread with it; seven days shalt thou eat unleavened bread therewith, even the bread of affliction; for thou camest forth out of the land of Egypt in haste: that thou mayest remember the day when thou camest forth out of the land of Egypt all the days of thy life."[478]

The timeframe for eating unleavened bread seems to have been compressed by the time of Jesus's birth. The Last Supper occurred when Jesus Christ and His disciples were meeting in the upper room in Jerusalem to observe the Passover early. During this meal, they ate unleavened bread. Leaven is the symbol of death and decay, which is the natural result of fermentation. Its removal from the bread symbolized the removal of the impurities in their lives. Unleavened bread was also called "lechem oni" by the Jews, meaning the "bread of humiliation," or as it says in the Old Testament, the "bread of affliction." As Jesus Christ partook of and shared the unleavened bread with His disciples, He was symbolically indicating that through His suffering and humiliation, He was bringing life to His disciples, and purging them of death and decay. As Isaiah said, "Surely he hath borne our griefs, and carried our sorrows: yet we did esteem him stricken, smitten of God, and afflicted. But he was wounded for our transgressions, he was bruised for our iniquities: the chastisement of our peace was upon him; and with his stripes we are healed."[479]

At this time, Christ could have also set aside the afikomen, which is part of the unleavened bread that is broken off, wrapped in a cloth, hidden, and reserved until the end of the meal.[480] The term afikomen is a Greek word meaning "The Coming One," a clear reference to the Messiah. The afikomen is the last thing eaten at the Passover meal. It was often hidden for the family's children to find. When Jesus celebrated the Passover in the upper room, after the meal, He would have brought out the afikomen, which came from the unleavened bread. He then broke and shared it with His disciples, and in doing so, He instituted the sacrament. "And when he had given thanks, he brake it, and said, Take, eat: this is my body, which is broken for you: this do in remembrance of me."[481]

Thus, Jesus Christ fulfills the Passover with powerful symbolism. He was the pure unleavened bread of the afikomen, hidden from the sight of the Jews, to be sought for, and wrapped in a cloth, symbolic of His burial. Just as He came forth from the tomb, the afikomen is taken out of hiding and brought to light again, to be received just as He gave the afikomen to His disciples, who consumed it, thus making it part of their being. That through His suffering and humility, He would bring them life, being the bread of life, purging their lives of all impurities and death, just as the afikomen was free of decay and death. As Jesus rightly testified to the Jews, "I am that bread [afikomen] of life."[482]

Having explored how Christ fulfilled the Feast of Unleavened Bread, next let's look at the tradition of the Feast of Firstfruits.

Feast of Firstfruits

The Feast of Firstfruits occurs on the first day of the week following the Passover which, based on the chart of His time in the tomb, would be the 17th of Nissan, our Sunday.[483] It is called *Shavuot* or Pentecost. The Jews would bring the firstfruits of their barley harvest to the temple and give them to the High Priest. The High Priest would ask God to acknowledge their offering by waving the sheaves of barley before God from side to side and to the four points of the compass.[484] Interestingly, on the day before the Jewish Sabbath or the 16th of Nissan, the High Priest would have read from the Torah in Ezekiel 37, where in speaking of the field of bones, the Lord says, "Thus saith the Lord God unto these bones; Behold, I will cause breath to enter into you, and ye shall live."[485] Here, Christ clearly fulfilled the Feast of Firstfruits. While He lay in the tomb on Saturday, Israel's High Priest in the temple at Jerusalem was reading aloud Israel's hope that God would bring life and raise up His people from the dead. Then on the first day of the week, when the Jews brought their firstfruits of barley, and the High Priest was seeking a blessings and acknowledgment before God for their offering of the firstfruits of the field, Christ arose as the Firstfruits or as the bread of life bringing salvation from death to His people in acknowledgment of their request.

Following His resurrection, can you picture the rumors of an empty tomb and claims that Jesus Christ had appeared to His disciples, spreading around Jerusalem? While the dead saints now resurrected appeared to others and the traditional rituals of the Jews, unbeknownst to them, proclaim His victory. Yet He rises not to produce speculation and rumors but to complete His divine mandate and in doing so fulfilled their laws, traditions, and pleas.

Summary

Historical records point to Christ's birth occurring in late December of 5 B.C. He subsequently died on Thursday, April 6th, 30 A.D. He arose early Sunday morning, April 9th. This crucial event sent a tidal wave of rejoicing through the eternities and was attested to under the law of witnesses. He was in control of His death and orchestrated the events so that He fulfilled His divine mission, the prophets' declarations, and Jewish traditions concerning His death and resurrection. Humankind's efforts to halt the work of God and stop Jesus Christ from rising were brought to naught. Jesus Christ had risen and in doing so became the Firstfruits of the dead. In the process, He fulfilled the Feast of Unleavened Bread. Through His suffering and humility, He brought humankind life, being the bread of life. And in rising during the Feast of Firstfruits, He fulfilled Israel's High Priest's plea to God to raise up the dead, bringing salvation to Israel.

CHAPTER 9

THEORIES DENYING THE RESURRECTION

*The truth may be stretched thin, but it never breaks, and
it always surfaces above lies, as oil floats on water.*

~ Miguel De Cervantes Saavedra

DOWN THROUGH THE ages, beginning at Christ's resurrection, theories have been promulgated to discredit this divine event. Instead of embracing it and the wondrous miracle it represents, much of humankind has sought to reject it, preferring falsehood rather than truth, darkness rather than light, and sorrow rather than hope. The following is a few of the more prevalent ideas that seek to discredit His resurrection, and the arguments their assumptions present.

Disciples Stole Him Away

It began with the Roman guards who, having failed to protect the tomb and after collusion with the Chief Priests, said, "his disciples came by night, and stole him away while we slept."[486] Although on the surface this seems like a credible claim, one must ask: if they were sleeping, how did they know the disciples had stolen His body: Also, the tomb had a large stone placed in front of it and had been officially sealed. Any attempt to remove the large stone and break the seal would have awoken the purported sleeping guards and would have been seen by them, and the armed guards would have prevented any attempt to remove the body. Additionally, the penalty for a Roman guard falling asleep while at their post was death. The facts indicate it was not the disciples of Christ who were the source of the hoax, but those who had previously refuted the resurrection.

Another claim is that someone other than the disciples stole the body.

Others Stole Him Away

Some may argue that someone else, other than His disciples, stole Christ's body. Some suggest it could have been the gardener, the Sanhedrin, Pilate, the Sadducees, or someone else. Yet when the reports began to circulate that Christ's disciples had seen Him again, risen from the dead, one would assume that whoever stole the body would immediately produce it or explain what happened and deny that He had risen. No such denial or explanation was made. This also suggests that the Roman guards were not part of the hoax. If they were, why did they go to the Chief Priests seeking support to avoid punishment, and why did they receive money to claim that Christ's disciples stole Him away while they slept? This attempt to explain what occurred is not credible.

The Tomb was not Empty

In this theory the critics seek to dismiss the resurrection by claiming the tomb was not empty. One suggestion is that the disciples were mistaken as to Christ's tomb whereabouts, and that He was buried in another tomb and remained there. This is contrary to the gospels account that several individuals went to visit the tomb after the Sabbath day, which presupposes they knew where it was. It also disregards Mary's statement, "they have taken away my Lord, and I know not where they have laid him."[487] She knew where Christ was buried and that He was now missing. Also, all they would have to do is ask the Romans or others where He was buried. His burial was a public fact. Joseph of Arimathea was not the only one involved. If He had not risen when the apostles and disciples began to tell others that He was resurrected, all the Romans would need to do is say, no, He is right here in this tomb. They never suggested this. The Roman and Jewish leadership's premise from the start was—Jesus is gone from His tomb. Their weak explanation, "His disciples came by night, and stole him away while we slept," demonstrates they knew He was gone.[488] Also, if He had not risen from the tomb, when the followers of Jesus began to establish His church in Jerusalem, where this all occurred, the inhabitants would have said wait a minute, Jesus was buried and is still there! Their efforts to establish the Church would have failed and certainly multitudes would not have been willing to give their life for a dead unrisen savior. The facts and accounts surrounding His burial and resurrection repudiate their allegations. The empty tomb is a great rock upon which the sophistry of the critics continues to be shattered.

Unconscious When Removed from Cross

Another assertion called the "Swoon" has circulated arguing that Jesus merely fainted or lapsed into unconsciousness while on the cross. But if this were the case, why would a living person be taken by Joseph of Arimathea and buried in his tomb? Also, why would Pilate release His body to Joseph if He was not dead? On the day of the resurrection, He was seen walking the road to Emmaus. Does it seem logical that a person with a wound in his side, having been scourged and his feet nailed to a cross, would be making that journey three days after their crucifixion? William D. Edwards, MD, succinctly addresses the issue of whether Jesus Christ died on the cross from a medical standpoint. He wrote, "Clearly, the weight of historical and medical evidence indicates that Jesus was dead before the wound to his side was inflicted and supports the traditional view that the spear, thrust between his right ribs, probably perforated not only the right lung but also the pericardium and heart and thereby ensured his death. Accordingly, interpretations based on the assumption that Jesus did not die on the cross appear to be at odds with modern medical knowledge."[489] In addition, if Jesus Christ had by some means survived crucifixion–His woeful state would have never inspired His followers to face persecution and death to proclaim that He had triumphed over death and that they would have a resurrected body like His. The facts surrounding Christ's death and resurrection disproves their assertion.

Vision Hypothesis

Then there is the hypothesis that Christ's appearances were only visions. In this, critics maintain that the Apostles really believed in the resurrection, but that this belief was a result of merely visions of Christ. These visions they had were apparently caused by an excited state of mind, or conjecture. The objection to this is that such visions demonstrate an earlier expectation of the resurrection. This is opposite to the scriptural accounts, which clearly show the Apostles did not believe in the resurrection beforehand. When Mary and the other women who had seen the Lord told the Apostles of it, Luke records, "And their words seemed to them as idle tales, and they believed them not."[490] To believe this theory, we have to ignore numerous unexplained facts: the events at the empty tomb, His command after His resurrection that they handle Him so as to convince them of His corporal nature, His eating with the disciples, His appearance to over five-hundred brethren at once, etc. The events recorded in Luke by themselves make the vision hypothesis impossible.[491]

Discrepancies in Gospel Accounts

Critics then turn to Bible discrepancies seeking to use them to discredit Christ arising from the tomb. Some point to discrepancies between the various Gospel accounts, as if different authors writing at different times to different audiences, and perhaps using different sources, would not report some points differently. They often point to the fact that the Gospels differ on how many angels were present at the tomb. The question of whether there was one, or two angels present when Mary Magdalene came to the empty tomb does not change what she reported—that He had risen.[492] Other critics point to the names of those who were recorded as present at the tomb in the early morning and note the differences between the gospel accounts and conclude the gospels cannot be relied on.[493] Yet, no author of the gospels indicated they were giving a complete list of those present at the tomb on resurrection day. In reality there were probably a number of people present, including some not even reported. Jesus' crucifixion, and His prophecy about His resurrection, was well known among those who followed Him. Certainly, they gathered to witness this event. The key is, despite secondary discrepancies, the core truths that He was crucified, Joseph of Arimathea took His body and placed it in the tomb, the tomb was visited by a small group of followers, they found the tomb empty, and they saw angels testifying that He arose, is consistent among all the gospels. The secondary discrepancies have little impact to the overarching and undergirding truth that the resurrection was real.

A variation of this is that the original writers did not record events near the time they occurred, or when they did at a much later date, it led them to inaccurately record or embellish the truth. We often forget that theirs was an oral society and rabbis would often commit the entire Old Testament to memory. Also, writings were kept on papyrus or animal skins, which would have been available to the early apostles and others to record the sayings and teaching of Christ. Examples of early records are the Chester Beatty Biblical Papyri discovered in about 1930. Papyrus number one contains portions of the four gospels and Acts, which date to about the third century. Papyrus number two contains portions of the letters of Paul dating from about 200 A.D.[494] In the Rylands Library, Papyrus 52 is a fragment of the gospel of John which dates to about 100–150 A.D., found in Egypt far from Ephesus in Asia Minor where the original gospel probably was written.[495]

Paul's statement of the ancient church's creed found in 1 Corinthians is believed by many to have been written just a few years after the death of Jesus Christ.[496] There are literally thousands of early copies of the New Testament, some dating back to the third century, in many languages such as Armenian, Ethiopic, Greek, and Slavic that are surprisingly similar. There is little doubt that the scriptures we have were written at a time fairly close to the Savior's ministry and essentially are as they were originally written.[497]

Failing this, critics attempt to discredit the entire Bible.

The Bible Is Fabricated

Perhaps the most absurd of all is the claim by some that Jesus Christ did not exist and that the entire record of the Bible is a hoax. Yet the reality of Jesus Christ is one of the most attested-to facts in history. To dismiss it is to fly in the face of historical events that were corroborated and taught down through the ages. He is mentioned by Flavius Josephus, a famous Jewish historian who was born in Jerusalem a few years after Jesus Christ's death.[498] Another source about Jesus Christ and early Christians is found in the letters of the Younger to Trajan, a Roman emperor, which is dated around 112 A.D. He asks advice about how to proceed with legal action against those accused of being Christians. He does this because of the great number of every class, race, sex, and age who are accused of being Christians. He writes, "They were in the habit of meeting on a certain fixed day before it was light, when they sang in alternate verses a hymn to Christ, as to a god, and bound themselves by a solemn oath, not to any wicked deeds, but never to commit any fraud, theft, or adultery, never to falsify their word, nor deny a trust when they should be called upon to deliver it up: after; which it was their custom to separate, and then reassemble to partake of food–but food of an ordinary and innocent kind." This demonstrates the presence of early Christian's and their worship of Christ in roman times.[499]

As mentioned, we have the writings of Paul and the First Epistle of Peter, that clearly bear witness to the reality of Jesus Christ, His divine parentage, and the resurrection. John tells us, "And there are also many other things which Jesus did, the which, if they should be written every one, I suppose that even the world itself could not contain the books that should be written."[500] Luke's opening remarks indicate that there were many accounts written of the Savior's ministry, which John alludes to. Luke, in his opening verse says, "many have taken in hand to set forth in order a declaration of those things which are most surely believed among us."[501] Some of these declarations we have, and others we do not.[502]

In addition to the Bible witnesses, we also have the testimony of the Book of Mormon which states unequivocally that Jesus is the Christ, and that He appeared as a resurrected person to thousands in the New World.[503] We also have the modern-day witnesses found in the Doctrine and Covenants that testify Jesus Christ lives and is the Son of God.[504] The claim that Christ did not exist and the Bible is a sham is like Don Quixote tilting at windmills; it is not credible.

Summary

A dead Christ might have been a great teacher and wonder-worker, remembered and loved. But only a risen and living Christ could be the Son of God, our Savior and Redeemer, and the Light and Life of our world. The absence of a reasonable counter explanation to Christ having risen from the dead is not in and of itself a verification of this fact. However, the testimonies of both ancient and modern scriptures and competent ancient and modern witnesses, clearly point to one conclusion. The birth, death, and resurrection of Jesus Christ is a historical fact. He came, He suffered, He conquered, and rose again on the third day. He lives!

CHAPTER 10

ANCIENT WITNESSES OF CHRIST'S RESURRECTION

He hath risen again, whereby he hath gained the victory over the grave

~ Mormon 7:5

THE UNPRECEDENTED EVENT of Jesus Christ's resurrection is attested to by numerous ancient witnesses. God would not orchestrate such an important event in the history of the eternities without leaving an abundance of proof for it. Many accounts exist of the Lord's post-resurrection appearances. In addition, the saints who arose from the dead and who appeared to many in Jerusalem following Christ's resurrection, would have also testified that He had risen. Let's turn to the scriptures and examine the accounts of the Lord's appearances following His resurrection, and those who witnessed it.

Jesus Post Mortal Appearances	References	Day / Time
Two Angels at the Tomb	JST Matt 28:1–3 ; Mark 16:5 ; Luke 24:4–6 ; John 20:11–13	Sunday a.m.
Mary Magdalene	Mark 16:9–11 ; John 20:10–18	Sunday a.m.
Mary the Mother of Joses, Joanna, Salome, and the Other Women	Matt. 28:1–10	Sunday a.m.
Simon Peter	Luke 24:34 ; 1 Cor. 15:5	Sunday afternoon
Cleopas and Another Disciple on the Road to Emmaus	Luke 24:13–35 ; Mark 16:12–13	Sunday afternoon
Ten Apostles and Disciples (not including Thomas)	John 20:19–25 ; Luke 24: 36–49	Sunday night
Eleven Apostles and Disciples in Jerusalem (including Thomas)	John 20:26–28 ; Mark 16:14	A week later
Seven Apostles at the Sea of Tiberius	John 21:1–14	Within 40 days
Eleven Apostles on the Mountain in Galilee	Matt. 28:16–20 ; Mark 16:15–18	Within 40 days
Five Hundred Brethren	1 Cor. 15:6	Within 40 days
James the Apostle	1 Cor. 15:7	Within 40 days
Eleven Apostles on the Mount of Olives	Luke 24:50–52 ; Acts 1:4–9 ; Mark 16:19	Within 40 days
Paul on the Road to Damascus	1 Cor. 9:1, 15:8 ; Acts 9:1–6, 22:3–16 , 26:12–18	After the 1st 40 days
Stephen's Stoning	Acts 7:55–56	A.D. 36
John on the Isle of Patmos	Revelation 1:13–18	Approx. A.D. 65–66
Christ's Appearances at the Temple in the New World	3 Nephi 11:8–11 3 Nephi 19:15	A.D. 34 A.D. 34
Lost Ten Tribes	3 Nephi 16:1–4, 17:4	A.D. 34
The Nephite Twelve	3 Nephi 27:1–2	A.D. 34–35
Other Book of Mormon Prophets Mormon Moroni	Mormon 1:15 Ether 12:39	Approx. A.D. 310–315 Prior to A.D. 421

Illustration 10.1 Christ's Post Mortal Appearances in the Bible and Book of Mormon

Two Angels at the Tomb

The first witnesses that we have record of are the two angels at the tomb of Christ. No record exists of what happened when Christ returned from the spirit world to the cold sepulchre, to take up His body once again. Did Jesus Christ just not speak of this event to His disciples, did they fail to record it, or was it so sacred that it was not to be spoken of? The Gospels are silent on this point. The key point is that He arose, and angels were present to witness it. In the Bible, it refers to one angel[505] being present at Christ's tomb, and in another place, there are two angels.[506] The Joseph Smith Translation clarifies that it was two angels, not one.[507] We read that the women who came on Sunday morning with spices to further prepare Christ's body for His interment found the great stone rolled away. "And it came to pass, as they were much perplexed thereabout, behold, two men stood by them in shining garments: And as they were afraid, and bowed down their faces to the earth, they said unto them, Why seek ye the living among the dead? He is not here, but is risen."[508] What an appropriate salutation: why are you seeking the living God here in a sepulchre? What Christ foretold had occurred! Who the angels were, we are not told, but they became the first heavenly witnesses that we have record of to the glorious resurrection of the Lord.

Next, we turn to Mary Magdalene's experience.

Mary Magdalene

Mary Magdalene becomes the first mortal to witness Christ's resurrection. Having left and then returned to the tomb, she again inquires of the angels where they have taken Jesus Christ's body. Upon being told again that He had risen, she turns and finds the Lord standing before her. Mark records, "Now when Jesus was risen early the first day of the week, he appeared first to Mary Magdalene, out of whom he had cast seven devils. And she went and told them that had been with him, as they mourned and wept. And they, when they had heard that he was alive, and had been seen of her, believed not."[509] Despite what must have been her outspoken declaration along with others, that He had risen, the disciples could not yet believe the report. The veil of disbelief and doubt continued to cloud their vision, just as it does for much of mankind today.

Following His appearance to Mary Magdalene, and before she reports her experience to the disciples, He appears to the other women.

Mary the Mother of Joses, Joanna, Salome, and the Other Women

Mary the mother of Joses, Joanna, and Salome, the mother of John and James, along with other women, then see the risen Lord, sometime shortly after Mary Magdalene. The angels at the tomb send them to tell the disciples that He had risen. On the way, the women meet Christ, and then go to tell the disciples the glorious truth, not only that He had risen, but that they had seen Him. "And as they went to tell his disciples, behold, Jesus met them, saying, All hail. And they came and held him by the feet, and worshipped him. Then said Jesus unto them, Be not afraid: go tell my brethren that they go into Galilee, and there shall they see me."[510] This event bespeaks a joyous reunion, and at the wonder of His appearing, they fall at His feet, hold them, and worship Him. From a soul-wrenching crucifixion that wrought utter despair and heartache, they are brought full circle. In a brief moment, their pain is turned to jubilance and reverential worship.

Luke records that they followed the Lord's direction and went to the eleven Apostles to bear witness that He had risen. "And [the women] returned from the sepulchre, and told all these things unto the eleven, and to all the rest. It was Mary Magdalene [who now had joined them], and Joanna, and Mary the mother of James, and other women that were with them, which told these things unto the Apostles. And their words seemed to them as idle tales, and they believed them not."[511] Women are often more sensitive to spiritual things. Have we finally learned to heed their witnesses of the truth, or their impressions of spiritual things?

Following Christ's appearance to Mary and the other women, He seems to have appeared to Peter.

Simon Peter

We read that Cleopas and his companion came to share their news with the disciples that they had seen the Christ. They found the disciples saying, "The Lord is risen indeed, and hath appeared to Simon,"[512] thus indicating that Peter's visitation occurs after Mary's and the other women, and seemingly before the two disciples on the road to Emmaus, although Christ's appearance to Peter could have been after the two disciples on the road to Emmaus. No account exists of what transpired between the Lord and Peter, but it is clear that the visitation of Jesus left no doubt in Peter's mind that He had arisen. Perhaps it was too sacred of an event to record, or maybe the Lord's instructions were for Peter only. Regardless, the disciple's unbelief gave way to the sublime truth that Christ had indeed risen, as He had foretold. What of our hearts, are they open to the sublime truth that He has risen?

Next, Christ appears to the two disciples on the road to Emmaus.

Cleopas and Another on the Road to Emmaus

The village of Emmaus has been identified by modern scholars as being near Moza, about three and one-half miles from Jerusalem. We know that Cleopas was one of the two disciples, but we are not told who the other was.[513] The scriptures record, "And it came to pass, that, while they communed together and reasoned, Jesus himself drew near, and went with them. But their eyes were holden that they should not know him. And he said unto them, What manner of communications are these that ye have one to another, as ye walk, and are sad? And the one of them, whose name was Cleopas, answering said unto him, Art thou only a stranger in Jerusalem, and hast not known the things which are come to pass there in these days? And he said unto them, What things? And they said unto him, Concerning Jesus of Nazareth, which was a prophet mighty in deed and word before God and all the people: And how the chief priests and our rulers delivered him to be condemned to death, and have crucified him. But we trusted that it had been he which should have redeemed Israel: and beside all this, to day is the third day since these things were done."[514]

Here, these two are walking with our Lord and reciting the events as they had either witnessed or heard of them. They go on to explain that the women, who are among those who believe, went and found the sepulchre empty, and then saw a vision of angels and the risen Lord. Then others went and saw the tomb empty, but they did not see the risen Lord. Jesus's response is classic: "Then he said unto them, O fools, and slow of heart to believe all that the prophets have spoken: Ought not Christ to have suffered these things, and to enter into his glory?"[515] Jesus continues to their village, explaining the scriptures to them. When they arrive they ask Him to stay and eat with them. He accepts their invitation and takes bread, blesses it, and gives it to them. "And their eyes were opened, and they knew him; and he vanished out of their sight. And they said one to another, Did not our heart burn within us, while he talked with us by the way, and while he opened to us the scriptures?"[516] They go to where the other disciples are gathered to share their witness, and they find the disciples rehearsing events surrounding Christ's resurrection. What an amazing event that must have been, to spend hours with the risen Lord being taught concerning His mission and the prophecies surrounding it. His rebuke, "Oh fools," is a challenge to each of us not to be so foolish as to disbelieve our Lord has risen and fulfilled His divine mission.

Ten Apostles and Disciples at Jerusalem

That same night, Sunday evening in Jerusalem, the ten Apostles were gathered along with other disciples. Thomas was absent. The reason for his absence is unknown. But as the other ten Apostles and other disciples are discussing the events of the day, Jesus comes and appears in their midst: "And as they thus spake, Jesus himself stood in the midst of them, and saith unto them, Peace be unto you. But they were terrified and affrighted, and supposed that they had seen a spirit. And he said unto them, Why are ye troubled? and why do thoughts arise in your hearts?

Behold my hands and my feet, that it is I myself: handle me, and see; for a spirit hath not flesh and bones, as ye see me have. And when he had thus spoken, he shewed them his hands and his feet. And while they yet believed not for joy, and wondered, he said unto them, Have ye here any meat? And they gave him a piece of a broiled fish, and of an honeycomb. And he took it, and did eat before them."[517] Unbelief had again reasserted itself, but upon His appearance, it became belief, then sure knowledge with His invitation to come, see, and feel, followed by Christ eating before them. He stands in their midst and rehearses the scriptures to them about His mission and resurrection, and declares to them, "And ye are witnesses of these things."[518] How many disciples there were we are not told, but it was probably dozens. From time to time, disbelief may re-assert itself in our lives, but like the disciples of old, we must remember what we once knew, and turn our hearts from doubt to belief.

Jesus also appears to the eleven Apostles, which now includes Thomas, who was absent from the initial appearance to the ten Apostles.

The Eleven Apostles and Disciples in Jerusalem

Eight days later, Christ appears to the eleven Apostles, which now includes Thomas. Thomas, in doubting the corporeal nature of Christ's resurrection, is no different than the others. Some have condensed this visit with the earlier visit to the ten at Jerusalem, but John makes it clear they were two separate events: "But Thomas, one of the twelve, called Didymus, was not with them when Jesus came. The other disciples therefore said unto him, We have seen the Lord. But he said unto them, Except I shall see in his hands the print of the nails, and put my finger into the print of the nails, and thrust my hand into his side, I will not believe. And after eight days again his disciples were within, and Thomas with them: then came Jesus, the doors being shut, and stood in the midst, and said, Peace be unto you. Then saith he to Thomas, Reach hither thy finger, and behold my hands; and reach hither thy hand, and thrust it into my side: and be not faithless, but believing. And Thomas answered and said unto him, My Lord and my God. Jesus saith unto him, Thomas, because thou hast seen me, thou hast believed: blessed are they that have not seen, and yet have believed."[519] Some have suggested that we don't know if Thomas felt the wounds in His side and feet, but can one really imagine not doing as the Lord directs? Clearly Thomas's veil of unbelief is finally overcome, and he stands as a bold witness that Jesus is the Christ. His experience reminds us that although we may not see the risen Lord, we are blessed for having the faith to believe that which we have not personally seen.

Jesus then appears on the Sea of Tiberius.

Seven Apostles at the Sea of Tiberius

This was the third time Christ had shown Himself to His Apostles as a group. Interestingly, earlier, Simon Peter decides he is going fishing, and others follow him. We read, "There were together Simon Peter, and Thomas called Didymus, and Nathanael of Cana in Galilee, and the sons of Zebedee, and two other of his disciples. Simon Peter saith unto them, I go a fishing. They say unto him, We also go with thee. They went forth, and entered into a ship immediately; and that night they caught nothing."[520] The fact that they caught nothing would shortly work into a lesson on how they are to be fishers of men, not catchers of fish. Soon they see a figure standing on the shore who they at first don't recognize. "Then Jesus saith unto them, Children, have ye any meat? They answered him, No. And he said unto them, Cast the net on the right side of the ship, and ye shall find. They cast therefore, and now they were not able to draw it for the multitude of fishes. Therefore that disciple whom Jesus loved saith unto Peter, It is the Lord. Now when Simon Peter heard that it was the Lord, he girt his fisher's coat unto him, (for he was naked,) and did cast himself into the sea."[521] Peter recognizes that this has happened before: when they were first called by Jesus to follow him.[522] His reaction is immediate and unreserved. He puts on his clothes and dives into the sea to reach his Lord. The ship then arrives with their nets full of fish, and they find a fire of coals, with fish and bread laid on them. They gather in their huge catch of fish, and the Lord invites them to dine with Him.

Ever the perfect teacher, the Lord shows them in simple terms that He can care for their physical needs, as well as their spiritual. He demonstrates a trait of true leadership—he that is greatest is the servant of all. Christ, an exalted and glorified God, in humility prepares a meal for His hungry and tired Apostles. In wonder, they eat, not daring to ask who He is, but knowing it is the Lord. Having eaten, an exchange between Jesus and Peter occurs that is both interesting and instructive. Earlier at the time of Christ's betrayal, Peter had denied Him three times.[523] Now the Savior, in love, gives Peter three chances to confirm his love for Him. "So when they had dined, Jesus saith to Simon Peter, Simon, son of Jonas, lovest thou me more than these? He saith unto him, Yea, Lord; thou knowest that I love thee. He saith unto him, Feed my lambs. He saith to him again the second time, Simon, son of Jonas, lovest thou me? He saith unto him, Yea, Lord; thou knowest that I love thee. He saith unto him, Feed my sheep. He saith unto him the third time, Simon, son of Jonas, lovest thou me? Peter was grieved because he said unto him the third time, Lovest thou me? And he said unto him, Lord, thou knowest all things; thou knowest that I love thee. Jesus saith unto him, Feed my sheep."[524] Jesus, through this exchange, sends important messages. If you follow me and do what I say, you will be successful. Forget about fishing, I can provide all you need. Like me, you need to be about our Father's business. Humility and servitude are essential for leadership. The vigilant Peter, along with the others, understood this time, and they did not return to their fishing nets. How are we doing in feeding the Lord's sheep? Have we learned that by following Him we will find success? Do we trust that He can provided for our needs? Do we lead with servitude and humility?

Next, Christ appears to the eleven Apostles on a mountain in Galilee.

Eleven Apostles on the Mountain in Galilee

Of this event, it is recorded that, "Then the eleven disciples went away into Galilee, into a mountain where Jesus had appointed them. And when they saw him, they worshipped him: but some doubted. And Jesus came and spake unto them, saying, All power is given unto me in heaven and in earth. Go ye therefore, and teach all nations, baptizing them in the name of the Father, and of the Son, and of the Holy Ghost: Teaching them to observe all things whatsoever I have commanded you: and, lo, I am with you alway, even unto the end of the world. Amen."[525] Having proved Himself the faithful Son, Christ had overcome all things, and had been given all power by the Father, including the keys of the resurrection. The Savior continues to teach them, and charges them to convert and teach others. The Gospel message continues to be about rescuing all of God's children and bringing them back into His presence, a message for all of us today.

Next, He expands the number of witnesses of His resurrection to include many of the disciples who followed Him.

Five Hundred Brethren

Sometime during the time of Jesus's post-resurrection ministry, we have a record that He was, "seen of above five hundred brethren at once; of whom the greater part remain unto this present, but some are fallen asleep."[526] By "falling asleep," the scriptures mean they had died. Those that saw him were probably made up of His leadership and of other disciples who had followed Him through His earthly ministry. I assume the women who He ministered to and who supported Him were also present.

We see here a great expansion of the number of witnesses of His resurrection. There was to be no doubt as to the reality of His role as Redeemer and Savior, and of His literal resurrection. It also shows Christ is no respecter of persons and loves us all but loves and wishes to manifest Himself to all those who follow Him including us today.

James the Apostle

James the Apostle also had a personal visitation by the Lord. We only have a brief mention of this event in Acts, where Paul records that, "he was seen of James."⁵²⁷ The timing of this visit is unknown. Like the appearance to Peter, no record currently exists of what was said. James was Christ's cousin, along with John, and given his role in the leadership of the Church, the fact that Christ appeared to him is not surprising. Was the conversation so sacred or personal that no record exists, or was it, like so many things, lost over time?

Eleven Apostles on the Mount of Olives

Christ's final recorded biblical appearance, before His ascension, happens on the Mount of Olives. Even as the Savior leaves His little flock, He gathers and instructs them, and they then witness His ascension. "And he led them out as far as to Bethany, and he lifted up his hands, and blessed them. And it came to pass, while he blessed them, he was parted from them, and carried up into heaven. And they worshipped him, and returned to Jerusalem with great joy."⁵²⁸ Of this event, in the book of Acts we find written, "When they therefore were come together, they asked of him, saying, Lord, wilt thou at this time restore again the kingdom to Israel? And he said unto them, It is not for you to know the times, or the seasons, which the Father hath put in his own power. But ye shall receive power, after that the Holy Ghost is come upon you: and ye shall be witnesses unto me both in Jerusalem, and in all Judaea, and in Samaria, and unto the uttermost part of the earth. And when he had spoken these things, while they beheld, he was taken up; and a cloud received him out of their sight. And while they looked steadfastly toward heaven as he went up, behold, two men stood by them in white apparel; Which also said, Ye men of Galilee, why stand ye gazing up into heaven? this same Jesus, which is taken up from you into heaven, shall so come in like manner as ye have seen him go into heaven. Then returned they unto Jerusalem from the mount called Olivet, which is from Jerusalem a sabbath day's journey."⁵²⁹

Now we turn to Stephen, a disciple who was stoned in Jerusalem and saw the Lord after His ascension into heaven.

Stephen's Stoning

Stephen was reviled of the Jews and he testified to them about Jesus Christ. For this supposed blasphemy, the Jews cast him out of the city. And the mob who followed stoned him in their frenzy, although it was against Roman law for them to do so. During this tragedy, the book of Acts relates, "He being full of the Holy Ghost, looked up steadfastly into heaven, and saw the glory of God, and Jesus standing on the right hand of God, And said, Behold, I see the heavens opened, and the Son of man standing on the right hand of God."[530] The hatred and zeal of the Pharisees and Sadducees, and their continual stirring up the people against Christ and His disciples, continued well after the Savior's death. Persecution has always followed the declaration of the truth. Following Christ's ascension and earlier appearances, which probably includes numerous unrecorded appearances during His forty days post-resurrection ministry,[531] we know He appeared to Paul.

Paul on the Road to Damascus

Paul later becomes a witness to the resurrected Christ. Paul, who was first known as Saul of Tarsus, witnessed the Lord as he went on his way to persecute the Saints. Although Paul did not initially say he saw the Lord, he said he saw a light and heard a voice, but later indicated that he saw the Lord. He wrote, "As also the high priest doth bear me witness, and all the estate of the elders: from whom also I received letters unto the brethren, and went to Damascus, to bring them which were there bound unto Jerusalem, for to be punished. And it came to pass, that, as I made my journey, and was come nigh unto Damascus about noon, suddenly there shone from heaven a great light round about me. And I fell unto the ground, and heard a voice saying unto me, Saul, Saul, why persecutest thou me? And I answered, Who art thou, Lord? And he said unto me, I am Jesus of Nazareth, whom thou persecutest. And they that were with me saw indeed the light, and were afraid; but they heard not the voice of him that spake to me. And I said, What shall I do, Lord?

And the Lord said unto me, Arise, and go into Damascus; and there it shall be told thee of all things which are appointed for thee to do."[532] Later he declares, "And last of all he was seen of me also, as of one born out of due time,"[533] making him a clear witness of the Lord.

John on the Isle of Patmos

The final appearance of Christ in the Old World fell on John the Beloved, who later experienced another visitation by the resurrected Christ. The Lord, years after His ascension, appeared to John the Beloved on the Isle of Patmos, where John had been exiled. John records, "His head and his hairs were white like wool, as white as snow; and his eyes were as a flame of fire; And his feet like unto fine brass, as if they burned in a furnace; and his voice as the sound of many waters. And he had in his right hand seven stars: and out of his mouth went a sharp twoedged sword: and his countenance was as the sun shineth in his strength. And when I saw him, I fell at his feet as dead. And he laid his right hand upon me, saying unto me, Fear not; I am the first and the last: I am he that liveth, and was dead; and, behold, I am alive for evermore, Amen."[534]

Next, let's turn from Christ's appearances in the Old World to Christ's appearances in the New World.

Christ's Appearances at the Temple in the New World

In the New World, the people were gathered at the temple in the land Bountiful. They were talking about all the destruction and the signs of Christ's death that had been given. As they were conversing, they heard a voice from heaven and looked up, "and behold, they saw a Man descending out of heaven; and he was clothed in a white robe; and he came down and stood in the midst of them...And it came to pass that he stretched forth his hand and spake unto the people, saying: Behold, I am Jesus Christ, whom the prophets testified shall come into the world."[535] Then the Savior challenged them to feel the wounds in His side, hands, and feet. "Arise and come forth unto me, that ye may thrust your hands into my side, and also that ye may feel the prints of the nails in my hands and in my feet, that ye may know that I am the God of Israel, and the God of the whole earth, and have been slain for the sins of the world. And it came to pass that the multitude went forth, and thrust their hands into his side, and did feel the prints of the nails in his hands and in my feet…and did know of a surety and did bear record, that it was he, of whom it was written by the prophets, that should come."[536] Christ appears and teaches them for three days, and afterwards He appears to them often and breaks bread with them.[537] A second witness has now occurred, not in terms of an individual, but in terms of a people and nation, illustrating that Christ is the God of the whole world.

Later, Christ appeared separately to the twelve Nephite disciples.

The Nephite Twelve

Next, we have the appearance of the Lord to the twelve Nephite disciples as a group in the New World. Of this account we read, "And it came to pass that as the disciples of Jesus were journeying and were preaching the things which they had both heard and seen, and were baptizing in the name of Jesus, it came to pass that the disciples were gathered together and were united in mighty prayer and fasting. And Jesus again showed himself unto them, for they were praying unto the Father in his name; and Jesus came and stood in the midst of them."[538] The purpose of his appearance was to answer their question about what they should call His church, because there had been disagreements over this among the Nephites. His direction is appropriate for our day as well as theirs. He said, "Therefore whatsoever ye shall do, ye shall do it in my name; therefore ye shall call the church in my name…And how be it my church save it be called in my name? For if a church be called in Moses' name then it be Moses' church;, or if it be called in the name of a man then it be the church of a man; but if it be called in my name then it is my church, if it so be that they are built upon my gospel."[539] Christ's Church must bear His name, and must be built upon His Gospel. No other church or system of religion is acceptable to Him, emphasizing again that God's house is a house of order.

Christ goes on to expound upon His mission as Redeemer and Savior, emphasize His Gospel, command all to be baptized and receive the Holy Ghost, and to pattern their lives after His, proving once again that He is the same yesterday, today, and forever.

Lost Ten Tribes

Although we do not have a firsthand account of Jesus Christ visiting the Lost Ten Tribes, we do have Christ's declaration that He will visit them. He said, "But I have received a commandment of the Father that I shall go unto them, and that they shall hear my voice, and shall be numbered among my sheep, that there may be one fold and one shepherd; therefore I go to show myself unto them."[540]

Other Book of Mormon Prophets

We have two other accounts of the Lord appearing as a resurrected being in the Book of Mormon. First to the great prophet Mormon, who compiled the Book of Mormon. Of this event, Mormon said, "And I, being fifteen years of age and being somewhat of a sober mind, therefore I was visited of the Lord, and tasted and knew of the goodness of Jesus."[541] The second is to Mormon's son, Moroni, who upon writing some concluding remarks to the Book of Ether, said, "And then shall ye know that I have seen Jesus, and that he hath talked with me face to face."[542] Clearly Christ's appearances as a resurrected being were not only reserved for those of the Old World, but spans across all of God's children.

Summary

Prior to the resurrection of Christ, a belief in this doctrine struggled under a twofold difficulty. First, it was something to look forward to, not look back upon. No one had yet risen from the grave as an immortal, glorified person. The marvelous realization of Christ's resurrection from the dead, with its accompanying witnesses, had not yet occurred, and was not clearly understood or clearly anticipated by society.

Secondly, the religious sects were teaching doctrines contrary to the simple truth that humankind would rise again. The Sadducees did not believe in the resurrection and taught that any teachings in the Torah regarding the resurrection, to the contrary, were to be understood spiritually. They demanded proof from the letter of the law, mocking those who believed. The Pharisees believed in the resurrection, but exploited the law for their doctrinal inferences, which they alone could derive. Confusing debates of nonsensical proportions surrounded the resurrection and only obscured the truths about it.

Christ's own disciples doubted and found it difficult to believe in the corporeal resurrection, even though they had walked and talked with the Savior and had heard Him declare that He would raise His body up again. In this challenging milieu, the Lord, undeterred, became the Firstfruits of those who slept. Then He witnessed the glorious truth to His initial unbelieving disciples, and to others who, once converted, became unflinching, competent witnesses to this awe-inspiring eternal truth. To their testimonies were added those of the New World when Christ visited His people there, and who also felt the wounds in His hands, side, and feet. He has risen, and so shall we.

CHAPTER 11

MODERN DAY WITNESSES OF CHRIST

The entire plan for the future has its key in the resurrection

~ Billy Graham

THERE HAVE BEEN numerous modern-day witnesses of the reality of God the Father, and Jesus Christ His Son. We are told, "he is the same God yesterday, today, and forever."[543] This being the case, if the Lord appeared to the prophets and saints anciently, He should appear to them in modern times as well—and He has. Some of these appearances have been open visions, dreams, and others are testimonies tied to personal knowledge. The Apostles in 2000 issued a statement concerning their witness of the living Christ[544] and a number of general authorities have related their witness of Jesus Christ in general conferences.[545] Also, here are a few other modern-day accounts that confirm that Jesus Christ is our Savior, and that He lives.

Alexander Neibaur's Vision

Alexander Neibaur, a Jewish convert from England and a dental surgeon by profession was asked by his son shortly before his death, "'Father, you have been telling us of your long and hard experience, and we have listened with intense affection and interest, but let me ask you, is it worth it all? Is the Gospel worth all this sacrifice?' "The glow of testimony and truth lighted the torches in the dimming eyes of that ancient Hebrew prophet and poet and he lifted his voice in firm and lofty assurance as he said:

"Yes! Yes! and more! I have seen my Savior. I have seen the prints in his hands! I know that Jesus is the Son of God, and I know that this work is true and that Joseph Smith was a prophet of God. I would suffer it all and more, far more than I have ever suffered for that knowledge even to the laying down of my body on the plains for the wolves to devour.'"[546]

Alfred Douglas Young's Vision

Alfred Douglas Young, an early convert to the Church, was conversing with his brother on the morning of September 17, 1841, about the principles of the Gospel when he was constrained by the Spirit to go to some secret place. Out into the woods some distance from his brother's house, he was beckoned in vision by an angelic personage to "Follow thou me." The story continues:

"He ascended upward in the direction from whence he came and I followed him. He took me into the presence of God the Father and his Son Jesus Christ. There was a rail between us; but I saw them seated on a throne. I had in my hands many sheaves of wheat of the purest white.

There was an altar on my left hand and also one directly in front of me. The one on my left appeared to be about three feet in height, the one in front about eighteen inches. I laid the sheaves of wheat that were in my hands on the altar to my left as an offering to the Lord. I bowed myself on my knees on the altar in front of me which was also in front of the throne.

I prayed God the Father in the name of his Son Jesus Christ to accept the offering I had laid upon the altar. While I prayed the rail was removed and I stood upon my feet. Jesus arose and stepped from the side of his Father and came near where I stood. I was in their Presence and I gazed upon their glory.

Jesus then said to me, 'Your offering is accepted, and wouldest thou know the interpretation thereof?' I replied, 'Yes, Lord.' The angel, my conductor, said, 'Look,' and I saw as it were an innumerable company that had come up from all nations, kindreds, tongues, and peoples around the throne of God, and they fell down and worshipped Him and gave glory to Him. Jesus then said, 'These are they thou shalt be the means of bringing into my Father's Kingdom and this is the interpretation of the offering thou hast laid upon the altar.'"[547]

Frederick G. William's Vision

Elder George A. Smith stated in a discourse: "On the first day of the [Kirtland Temple] dedication, President Frederick G. Williams, one of the Council of the Prophet, and who occupied the upper pulpit, bore testimony that the Savior, dressed in his vesture without seam, came into the stand and accepted of the dedication of the house; that he saw him, and gave a description of his clothing and all things pertaining to it. That evening there was a collection of Elders, Priests, Teachers, and Deacons, etc., amounting to four hundred and sixteen, gathered in the house; there were great manifestations of power, such as speaking in tongues, seeing visions, administration of angels. Many individuals bore testimony that they saw angels, and David Whitmer bore testimony that he saw three angels passing up the south aisle, and there came a shock on the house like the sound of a mighty rushing wind, and almost every man in the house arose, and hundreds of them were speaking in tongues, prophecying, or declaring visions, almost with one voice."[548]

Joseph Smith's Vision in the Grove

Joseph Smith, early in the Spring of 1820, went into a grove of trees to inquire into which church was right and had the following experience: "I saw a pillar of light exactly over my head, above the brightness of the sun, which descended gradually until it fell upon me. It no sooner appeared than I found myself delivered from the enemy which held me bound. When the light rested upon me I saw two Personages, whose brightness and glory defy all description, standing above me in the air. One of them spake unto me, calling me by name and said, pointing to the other—This is My Beloved Son. Hear Him!"[549] This visitation of the Father and the Son ushered in the Latter-day restoration of the Gospel of Jesus Christ.

Joseph Smith and Oliver Cowdery's Vision

A week after the dedication of the Kirtland Temple, the Prophet Joseph Smith, with Oliver Cowdery, the Council of the Twelve, and others partook of the sacrament. Afterwards, Joseph and Oliver retired to the pulpit on the west side of the room, and the veils that separated the brethren were dropped. The two men then offered silent prayers. After rising from prayer, they saw the following vision:

"The veil was taken from our minds, and the eyes of our understanding were opened. We saw the Lord standing upon the breastwork of the pulpit, before us; and under his feet was a paved work of pure gold, in color like amber. His eyes were as a flame of fire; the hair of his head was white like the pure snow; his countenance shone above the brightness of the sun; and his voice was as the sound of the rushing of great waters, even the voice of Jehovah, saying: I am the first and the last; I am he who liveth, I am he who was slain; I am your advocate with the Father."[550]

Joseph Smith and Sidney Rigdon's Vision

In a remarkable, open vision at Father Johnson's farm, Joseph Smith and Sidney Rigdon received D&C 76, or what is commonly known as the Three Degrees of Glory, in which they wrote that they, "saw the holy angels, and them who are sanctified before his throne, worshiping God, and the Lamb, who worship him forever and ever. And now, after the many testimonies which have been given of him, this is the testimony, last of all, which we give of him: That he lives! For we saw him, even on the right hand of God; and we heard the voice bearing record that he is the Only Begotten of the Father—That by him, and through him, and of him, the worlds are and were created, and the inhabitants thereof are begotten sons and daughters unto God."[551]

Of this event, Philo Dibble said, "On a subsequent visit to Hiram I arrived at Father Johnson's just as Joseph and Sidney were coming out of the vision alluded to in the book of Doctrine and Covenant, in which mention is made of the three glories. Joseph wore black clothes but at this time seemed to be dressed in an element of glorious white, and his face shown as if it were transparent, but I did not see the same glory attending Sidney. Joseph appeared as strong as a lion but Sidney seemed as weak as water, and Joseph noticing his condition smiled and said: "Brother Sidney is not as used to it as I am."[552]

Lorenzo Snow's Vision

President Snow's vision was recounted by LeRoi C. Snow, President Snow's son. He wrote, "Upon learning of the death of President Wilford Woodruff, President Snow dressed in his holy Temple robes, retired to the sacred altar in the Salt Lake Temple, and poured out his heart to the Lord. He reminded the Lord how he had pleaded that President Woodruff outlive him, that he might not be called to bear the heavy burdens and responsibilities of Church leadership. 'Nevertheless,' he prayed, 'Thy will be done. I have not sought this responsibility, but if it be Thy will I will present myself before thee for Thy guidance and instruction. I ask that Thou show me what Thou wouldst have me do.'

After finishing the prayer, he expected a reply, some special manifestation from the Lord. He waited—and waited—and waited. There was no reply, no voice, no manifestation. He left the room in deep disappointment, passed through the celestial room and out into the large corridor leading to his own room, where a most glorious manifestation was given him. One of the most beautiful accounts of this experience is given by his granddaughter, Allie Young Pond. One day she and

President Snow were walking in the Salt Lake Temple, and she tells of the following conversation:

'One evening while I was visiting Grandpa Snow in his room in the Salt Lake Temple, I remained until the door keepers had gone and the night watchmen had not yet come in, so grandpa said he would take me to the main front entrance and let me out that way.... After we left his room and while we were still in the large corridor leading into the celestial room, I was walking several steps ahead of Grandpa when he stopped me and said: 'Wait a moment, Allie, I want to tell you something. It was right here that the Lord Jesus Christ appeared to me at the time of the death of President Woodruff. He instructed me to go right ahead and reorganize the First Presidency of the Church at once and not wait as had been done after the death of the previous presidents, and that I was to succeed President Woodruff.' Then Grandpa came a step nearer and held out his left hand and said: 'He stood right here, about three feet above the floor. It looked as though He stood on a plate of solid gold.' Grandpa told what a glorious personage the Savior is and described His hands, feet, countenance, and beautiful white robes, all of which were of such a glory of whiteness and brightness that he could hardly gaze upon Him. Then he came another step nearer and put his right hand on my head and said: 'Now, Granddaughter, I want you to remember that this is the testimony of your grandfather, that he told you with his own lips that he actually saw the Savior, here in the Temple, and talked with Him face to face.'"[553]

Lyman Wight's Vision

Lyman Wight was an early leader of the Church and was ordained a High Priest on the fourth of June, 1831, by Joseph Smith. This occurred near Isaac Morley's home at the school house. The building was built of logs and filled with slab benches. The record of this event is as follows, "After he [Joseph Smith] had prophesied he laid his hands upon Lyman Wight [and ordained him] to the High Priesthood after the Holy Order of God. And the spirit fell upon Lyman, and he prophesied, concerning the coming of Christ, he said that there were some in the congregation that should live until the Savior should descend from heaven, with a Shout, with all the holy angels with him. He said the coming of the Savior should be like; the sun rising in the east, and will cover the whole earth, so with the coming of the Son of man he, yea, he will appear in his brightness and consume all before him. And the hills will be laid low, and the valies [sic] be exalted; and the crooked be made straight; and the rough Smooth. And some of my brethren Shall suffer marterdom [sic] for the sake of the religion of Jesus Christ, and seal the testimony of Jesus with their blood. He saw the heavens opened, and the Son of man sitting on the right hand of the Father. Making intercession for his brethren, the Saints. He said that God would work a work in these last days that tongue cannot express, and the mind is not capable to conceive. The glory of the Lord shone around."[554]

Meeting of the High Priests 1833

A meeting of the High Priests was held on March 8, 1833, in the upper room of the Newell K. Whitney store. The records of the meeting show, "Doctor Hurlburt was ordained an Elder; after which Elder Rigdon expressed a desire that himself and Brother Frederick G. Williams should be ordained to the offices to which they had been called, viz., those of Presidents of the High Priesthood, and to be equal in holding the keys of the kingdom with Brother Joseph Smith, Jun., according to the revelation given on the 8th of March, 1833. Accordingly I laid my hands on Brothers Sidney and Frederick, and ordained them to take part with me in holding the keys of this last kingdom, and to assist in the Presidency of the High Priesthood, as my Counselors; after which I exhorted the brethren to faithfulness and diligence in keeping the commandments of God, and gave much instruction for the benefit of the Saints, with a promise that the pure in heart should see a heavenly vision; and after remaining a short time in secret prayer, the promise was verified; for many present had the eyes of their understanding opened by the Spirit of God, so as to behold many things. I then blessed the bread and wine, and distributed a portion to each. Many of the brethren saw a heavenly vision of the Savior, and concourses of angels, and many other things, of which each one has a record of what he saw."[555]

Melvin J. Ballard's Dream

Melvin J. Ballard was ordained an Apostle on January 7, 1919. He recorded the following dream, testifying of Jesus Christ: "I found myself one evening in the dreams of the night, in that sacred building, the Temple. After a season of prayer and rejoicing, I was informed that I should have the privilege of entering into one of those rooms, to meet a glorious personage, and as I entered the door, I saw, seated on a raised platform, the most glorious Being my eyes have ever beheld, or that I ever conceived existed in all the eternal worlds. As I approached to be introduced, he arose and stepped towards me with extended arms, and he smiled as he softly spoke my name. If I shall live to be a million years old, I shall never forget that smile. He took me into his arms and kissed me, pressed me to His bosom, and blessed me, until the marrow of my bones seemed to melt! When He had finished, I fell at His feet, and as I bathed them with my tears and kisses, I saw the prints of the nails in the feet of the Redeemer of the world. The feeling that I had in the presence of Him who hath all things in His hands, to have His love, His affection, and His blessings was such that if I ever can receive that of which I had but a foretaste, I would give all that I am, all that I ever hope to be, to feel what I then felt."[556]

Orson F. Whitney's Dream

Orson F. Whitney was ordained an Apostle in 1906. He records the following dream of the Savior: "One night I dreamed…that I was in the Garden of Gethsemane, a witness of the Savior's agony.…I stood behind a tree in the foreground.… Jesus, with Peter, James, and John, came through a little wicket gate at my right. Leaving the three Apostles there, after telling them to kneel and pray, He passed over to the other side, where He also knelt and prayed: 'Oh my Father, if it be possible, let this cup pass from me; nevertheless not as I will but as Thou wilt.' As He prayed the tears streamed down His face, which was [turned] toward me. I was so moved at the sight that I wept also, out of pure sympathy with His great sorrow. My whole heart went out to Him. I loved Him with all my soul and longed to be with Him as I longed for nothing else. Presently He arose and walked to where those Apostles were kneeling—fast asleep! He shook them gently, awoke them, and in a tone of tender reproach, untinctured by the least show of anger, or scolding, asked them if they could not watch with Him one hour....Returning to His place, He prayed again and then went back and found them again sleeping. Again He awoke them, admonished them, and returned and prayed as before. Three times this happened, until I was perfectly familiar with His appearance—face, form, and movements. He was of noble stature and of majestic mien...the very God that He was and is, yet as meek and lowly as a little child. All at once the circumstance seemed to change....Instead of before, it was after the Crucifixion, and the Savior, with those three Apostles, now stood together in a class at my left. They were about to depart and ascend into heaven. I could endure it no longer. I ran from behind the tree, fell at His feet, clasped Him around the knees, and begged Him to take me with Him. I shall never forget the kind and gentle manner in which He stooped and raised me up and embraced me. It was so vivid, so real that I felt the very warmth of His bosom against which I rested. Then He said: 'No, my son; these have finished their work, and they may go with me; but you must stay and finish yours.' Still I clung to Him. Gazing up into His face—for He was taller than I—I besought Him most earnestly: 'Well, promise me that I will come to You at the last.' He smiled sweetly and tenderly and replied: 'That will depend entirely upon yourself.' I awoke with a sob in my throat, and it was morning."[557]

Rebecca Bean's Dream

Rebecca Bean was the wife of Willard Bean. In early 1915, they received a mission call and moved to Palmyra, New York, in the spring of 1915, where they occupied the Joseph Smith farm. In 1964 at a fireside she related the following experience that occurred while they were there, "I decided to pick up a few things and make things easier for me in the morning. But I was so weary and so tired that I was crying a little as I straightening things around. Everybody was in bed and asleep but me. I looked at the clock and it was 11:00, and I can remember so well that I said, "I better call it a day." I went into my room and my husband and my baby were sound asleep. It was peaceful and quiet. I got myself ready for bed and I was crying a little. I said my prayers and got into bed and I was crying on my pillow. Then this dream or vision came to me. I thought it was another day. It had been a wonderful morning. I had prepared breakfast for my visitors. My children were happily playing around. I had done my work and cared for the baby and he was contented and happy. Then I prepared lunch. I called our visitors into lunch and we were all seated around the table, my little baby in his high chair, and everything was just peaceful, wonderfully and sweet. There was a knock at the front door. I went in and opened it and there was a very handsome young man standing there. I just took it for granted that he was just another new missionary that had come to see us. I said, "You're here just in time for lunch. Come with me."

As he walked through the little hall into the dining room, I noticed he put some pamphlets down on the little table there. We walked into the dining room and I introduced him around and then I said, "Now, you sit right here by Dr. Talmage and I'll set a plate for you." I thought, of course, he was strange to all of us and yet he and Dr. Talmage seemed so happy to see each other. They talked about such wonderful things while we were eating. Some of them we could hardly understand. The spirit and mood that was there was so peaceful and nice, and everyone seemed so happy to be together. After the meal was over, Dr. Talmage said to the missionary, "Now let's go outside and just be alone and enjoy the spirit of this wonderful place because" he said, "you'll soon have to leave."

I put my baby to bed and the other little ones went out to play, and then I was alone with the young man. He thanked me for having him to dinner and told me how much it meant for him to be there. He told me that he thought that the children were so sweet and well-trained and I felt so happy about that. And then we walked in the hall together and he said, "I have far to go so I must be on my way." I turned from him for just a moment to pick up the little pamphlets that he had put on the table, and when I turned back to him it was the Savior who stood before me and He was in His glory. I could not tell you the love and the sweetness that He had in His face and in His eyes. Lovingly He laid His hands on my shoulders, and He looked down into my face with the kindest face that I had ever seen. And this is what He said to me: "Sister Bean, this day hasn't been too hard for you, has it?" And I said, "Oh no, I have been so happy with my work and everything has gone on so well." Then He said, "I promise you if you will go about your work every day as you have done it this day, you will be equal to it. For remember these missionaries represent me on this earth and all that you do unto them, you give unto me."

And I know I was crying as we walked to the hall out onto the porch. He repeated the same thing: "these missionaries represent me on earth, and all you do unto them, you do unto me." Then He started upward. The roof of the porch was no obstruction for Him to go through, nor for me to see through. He went upward, and upward, and upward. I wondered and wondered how I could see Him so far away. And then all at once He disappeared and I was crying on my pillow like I was when I went to bed."[558]

School of the Prophets Kirtland

The School of the Prophets was held in the upper room of the Newel K. Whitney store. At one of its meetings, it was recorded that, "As some brethren were being introduced into the School of the Prophets, Zebedee Coltrin spoke and, referring to the original school in Kirtland, said: 'While sitting in Council a personage passed through the room dressed in usual clothing. Joseph said That was the Savior. Soon another personage passed through the house clothed in fire; his features and feet were visible, but his body was wrapped in flames. Joseph said That was God the Father.'"[559]

Summary

Today we look back upon the resurrection of Christ in hope and faith, and we look forward to our own resurrection in trust and love. Here in the latter-days, God is gathering all things into one, and He has opened the heavens once again. Like in times of old, many have seen, heard, and become witnesses to the reality that God and Christ live. These worthy modern-day witnesses, combined with those from the time of Christ's resurrection, become a bulwark of truth for the pure in heart upon which the voices of disbelief collide without effect. Knowing that God lives and that Jesus is the Christ and was resurrected, reaffirms the divine truth taught in the scriptures that through the Atonement of Jesus Christ all humankind may be saved. The scriptures indicate that in the mouth of two or three witnesses shall every word be established. For this supernal event God has provided dozens of witnesses, which all declare the same eternal truth, He has risen!

CHAPTER 12

PREPARING FOR THE RESURRECTION

Hearken to my voice, lest death overtake you ...
and the harvest ended, and your souls not saved

~ D&C 45:2

IN OUR FAST-PACED society, instant gratification feeds the hunger of an ever increasing and demanding desire to have everything now. The internet has become what some feel is the sum of all wisdom, with knowledge available at the click of a mouse. You can have groceries placed in your refrigerator without going to a grocery store. Online retailers are touting "twelve-hour" delivery service. But obtaining perfection and our exaltation is a process that takes focus, time, and effort.

Just as Rome was not built in a day, our exaltation is not obtained in a day. In order to obtain the full blessings that God has in store for the faithful, we must continually progress toward perfection. Our learning, spiritual development, and perfection will take time. We learn that the Savior, "received not of the fulness at first, but continued from grace to grace, until he received a fullness."[560] Like our Savior, we grow line upon line, going from one spiritual improvement to another, and increasing our Christlike traits in all aspects of our lives until one day we find ourselves resurrected, perfected, and exalted in the kingdom of our God and Savior.

Benjamin Franklin realized that self-improvement was a process. He decided on thirteen traits that, if mastered, would lead to perfection. They were: temperance, silence, order, resolution, frugality, industry, sincerity, justice, moderation, cleanliness, tranquility, chastity, and humility. He reasoned, "My intention being to acquire the habitude of all these virtues, I judg'd it would be well not to distract my attention by attempting the whole at once, but to fix it on one of them at a time; and, when I should be master of that, then to proceed to another, and so on, till I should have gone thro' the thirteen."[561] He determined that as he gained one characteristic, it made acquiring the next easier. He made a little book and lined it with seven columns for the seven days in a week, and with thirteen lines, one for each virtue. He put the first letter of the virtue he was working on that week on the top line and made a black dot each day when he felt he had accomplished that virtue. He would go through all the virtues in thirteen weeks and would repeat this process four times in a year. He put some quotes in his book to inspire him and solicited God's help in accomplishing his goal.

As he embarked on his plan, he was surprised to find himself much fuller of faults than he had imagined. Then, to his chagrin, he found that as he mastered the first few virtues and went on to the next, he found himself going backwards on the first few virtues he thought he had mastered. Doesn't that sound just like life; two steps forward, and then one back? The key in our lives is to accept that perfection is a process, and during that process we will have successes and failures. That is our human nature and the reality of mortality. We will not gain full perfection until after the resurrection. As someone wisely said, it is not the number of times you fall down that counts, but the number of times you get back up. So keep on trying!

This journey of personal change determines what we will become in our journey back to God as eternal beings, and reminds me of a poem by Ella Wheeler Wilcox:

THERE IS NO DEATH, THERE ARE NO DEAD, BY ELLA WHEELER WILCOX

'There is no death, there are no dead.'
From zone to zone, from sphere to sphere,
The souls of all who pass from here
By hosts of living thoughts are led;
And dark or bright, those souls must tread
The paths they fashioned year on year.
For hells are built of hate or fear,
And heavens of love our lives have shed.

Across unatlassed worlds of space,
And through God's mighty universe,
With thoughts that bless or thoughts that curse,
Each journeys to his rightful place.
Oh, greater truth no man has said,
'There is no death, there are no dead.'

It lifts the mourner from the sod,
And bids him cast away the reed
Of some uncomforting poor creed,
And walk with Knowledge for a rod.
It bids the doubter seek the broad
Vast fields, where living facts will feed
All those whose patience proves their need
Of these immortal truths of God.

> It brings before the eyes of faith
> Those realms of radiance, tier on tier,
> Where our beloved 'dead' appear,
> More beautiful because of 'death.'
> It speaks to grief: 'Be comforted;
> There is no death, there are no dead.'

We are all on an eternal journey of change. Let us examine concepts that will help us along our path towards perfection.

Concepts that Help Us Prepare

These concepts are general ideas, or approaches, that can help in our preparation for the resurrection and our desire to obtain exaltation. Their applications are broad and may cover many principles. Yet, at the same time, they provide specific direction and a defined approach to the process of perfection. Let's examine six concepts that can help focus our efforts in preparing for the resurrection and for exaltation.

Shekhinah, or God's Presence

Western society seems to invoke a sense of isolation in many. We feel alone, like strangers who do not acknowledge one another, and we often ignore and in turn are ignored by those around us. These feelings are often reflected in our attitude toward God who is envisioned as absent or uninvolved. Contrary to society's view, God is intimately involved and aware of us individually and as a society. King David wrote, "Whither shall I go from thy spirit? or whither shall I flee from thy presence? If I ascend up into heaven, thou art there: if I make my bed in hell, behold, thou art there. If I take the wings of the morning, and dwell in the uttermost parts of the sea; Even there shall thy hand lead me, and thy right hand shall hold me."[562] We are always in God's presence and He is aware of our thoughts and actions. As an old proverb says, "The eyes of the Lord are in every place, beholding the evil and the good."[563] Not only are we always in His presence, but our actual lives are recorded in heaven for, "behold, all things are written by the Father."[564]

The Jews have a word for the presence of God: *shekhinah*, pronounced (shee-kie-na). It is used to signify the presence or dwelling place of God. In a real sense, God's dwelling place and presence is here and now. As the scriptures testify, we are always before His face. Our lives, like a textbook are open before Him. We cannot hide or flee from His presence. How would our actions change if we truly understood that we are neither alone or isolated from Him? How would we act differently if we comprehended God's *shekhinah*? When we see a wallet or a purse sitting on a park bench unattended, perhaps some would be less inclined to open the wallet or purse and check it for money and more inclined to seek to reunite it with its owner. When another person is distressed or in need perhaps, those around them would be more open to stopping to offer comfort and helping rather than leaving it for someone else to respond? For thy, "Father which seeth in secret shall reward thee openly."[565]

This can be a powerful tool in helping us shape our lives, to become more like our God, always reminding us that a loving and intimately interested Heavenly Father is ever-present and concerned about our welfare and preparation for the resurrection.

Preparation and The Five "Ps"

In teaching the youth, one of my sayings was "Prior Planning Prevents Poor Performance." It was named the five "Ps" and as a class we memorized it and talked about what it meant. The youth soon made up their own words for the acronym. It was "Papa Please Pass (the) Peas Por favor." They thought they were hilarious and looking back now I see more of the humor. Regardless, preparing for our resurrection is a process, and the extent to which we can preemptively plan will help us avoid a poor performance or an unfavorable outcome.

Part of that preparation is gaining a greater knowledge concerning the resurrection. As mentioned in the preface, knowledge is power because it not only gives us more choices, but it also helps us focus our efforts to achieve the most favorable outcome. It gives us power to more accurately determine what we can become. It focuses our strengths, faith, and actions. It illuminates our potential and provides a stimulus for the endeavor of life, while also providing great hope and solace.

With knowledge of the resurrection we can expand our goals for righteous living, and then work to achieve them. Those goals which are identified, articulated, written down, and measured have a greater chance of being realized. Planning ahead by setting actionable spiritual goals will always produce greater results than just thinking about them. We should ask ourselves what goals will help us act upon the increased knowledge of the resurrection we have obtained, and then go through the process of writing them down with a way to measure them.

These goals may include specific objectives within the principles of obedience, such as keeping the commandments, sacrificing, consecrating our lives, loving God and our fellowman, or some combination of them, or other areas. We should list specific points under these goals that more narrowly define them. For example, if one of our goals fell under keeping the commandments, a more narrowly defined goal might be keeping the Sabbath day holy. A specific measurable action item under that heading might be not watching non-religious TV shows on Sunday. At the end of the Sabbath day, we would make a notation of our results. Based on the results, we might modify, change, or keep the original goal. Once we felt we had achieved our goal, we could add another one and begin the process anew or focus on another goal we were working on. Each individual's approaches and goals will be different. But the process of identifying goals, articulating them, writing them down, and measuring them is the same. If you act now, a rich harvest of spiritual growth awaits you.

In considering the concept of prior planning, an experience comes to mind. At one point in my career I working for a subsidiary of a Japanese parent company. I traveled to Japan to meet with the Shacho.

Shacho is an honorary title and referred to the head of the company. He had purchased a vessel with which he planned to test the electronic equipment that his company sold. When I spoke with others in the company, they explained that Shacho had the Shinto priest come and bless the vessel. Then he had the Buddhist monk do the same. I asked why he had them both bless the vessel, and was told, "one of them might be right." He was planning ahead, seeking to avoid a disaster in the future by soliciting divine help now. His efforts, however, were not based on faith, but on trying to shift the odds in his favor.

Sometimes people plan ahead, but they have no real faith or belief behind their actions. Eventually, one must come to believe by exercising faith and trusting in Christ if their efforts are to produce results of eternal value. As the Savior declared, "I know thy works, that thou art neither cold nor hot: I would thou wert cold, or hot. So then because thou art lukewarm, and neither cold nor hot, I will spue thee out of my mouth."[566] Like Shacho, if our actions are not based in faith, our prior planning and efforts to achieve exaltation will result in failure. We must become converted if we are to properly prepare to gain salvation. For, "the Lord hath sought him a [person] after his own heart."[567]

Next, let's consider the concept of raising our sights to a higher law, so that we do not miss the mark, the target we are aiming for.

Chaata'ah, or Missing the Mark

The Hebrew word most often translated for sin in our Bible is *chata'ah* pronounced (khat-aw-aw'), meaning to miss the mark or target. This is a great description for sin. We come close, but do not achieve the desired results. We shoot but miss the target. The Sermon on the Mount can be used to illustrate this concept. If we view the Sermon on the Mount as a call to live a higher law, rather than a list of dos or don'ts, we catch the spirit of what Jesus was trying to infuse in His disciples. It becomes more about raising our aspirations higher so as not to miss the mark and to simultaneously free ourselves from the minutia of trying to live every jot and tittle of the commandments.[568]

For example, think of Christ's teachings on giving. He said, "Take heed that ye do not your alms before men, to be seen of them: otherwise ye have no reward of your Father which is in heaven."[569] The act of giving is important, but only if you have the right attitude. You should not do it to be seen of others, or to garner the praise of men. You do it, "That thine alms may be in secret: and thy Father which seeth in secret himself shall reward thee openly."[570] You love the Lord and your fellowman, you want to help those in need, and you want to build the kingdom of God. If you do it for praise or glory, you *Chaata'ah*, or miss the mark.

Consider another example: "Ye have heard that it was said by them of old time, Thou shalt not commit adultery: But I say unto you, That whosoever looketh on a woman to lust after her hath committed adultery with her already in his heart."[571] Adultery is a grievous sin, but it begins as a matter of the heart. Those who look upon a woman in lust have committed sin in their heart. They *Chata'ah* or miss the mark. Christ was asking us to look to a higher ideal. Our hearts should be pure and untainted by the base lusts of the flesh. With this purified mind set, the prospects of committing fornication or adultery are greatly diminished.

Christ also taught, "Ye have heard that it hath been said, An eye for an eye, and a tooth for a tooth: But I say unto you, That ye resist not evil: but whosoever shall smite thee on thy right cheek, turn to him the other also."[572] Again, look to higher ground. He is not asking us to be doormats that people walk over, but He is asking us not to get caught up in revenge. Revenge is like drinking poison and thinking someone else will die. Rather, be patient, humble, and seek to be reconciled with those who offend you. As Jesus told the Nephites, "For verily, verily I say unto you, he that hath the spirit of contention is not of me, but is of the devil, who is the father of contention, and he stirreth up the hearts of men to contend with anger, one with another. Behold, this is not my doctrine, to stir up the hearts of men with anger, one against another; but this is my doctrine, that such things should be done away."⁵⁷³ Those who react in anger *Chata'ah*. Those who are the peacemakers are the children of God.

In our lives, if we can raise our sights and try to live on a higher spiritual and charitable plane in our day-to-day thoughts and activities, we will find the mark of perfection easier to hit. Questions about the minutia involved in living the commandments will cease. We don't need a sage to interpret Christ's laws in our life. We just need His spirit, and to develop loving kindness for God and one another.

Hasidut, or Piety and Loving Kindness

On our path to perfection we must look for ways to become more loving and kind. We need to root out our old hard hearts and replace them with new, loving ones. As we develop Christlike attributes, we are becoming *hasidut* pronounced (ha-see-DOOT). *Hasidut* is Hebrew for the concept of piety—it comes from *hesed*, meaning loving kindness. The scriptures talk about this as obtaining the "pure love of Christ." Mormon helped us understand the pure love of Christ when he defined it as charity. He wrote, "And charity suffereth long, and is kind, and envieth not, and is not puffed up, seeketh not her own, is not easily provoked, thinketh no evil, and rejoiceth not in iniquity but rejoiceth in the truth, beareth all things, believeth all things, hopeth all things, endureth all things. Wherefore, my beloved brethren, if ye have not charity, ye are nothing, for charity never faileth. Wherefore, cleave unto charity, which is the greatest of all, for all things must fail—But charity is the pure love of Christ, and it endureth forever; and whoso is found possessed of it at the last day, it shall be well with him."⁵⁷⁴ Think of these powerful Godlike traits he outlines as helping one move to a more *hasidut* life. When confronted by a request from one's Bishop for fast offerings to help the needy, one's attitude is one of rejoicing at the opportunity to bless others. It frees us from worrying about how little can we give and focuses us on how much we can help. When a tragedy comes into our lives, we move from anger and how could God allow this to happen to us, to asking the Lord to help us pass through this tragedy with grace and hope in Christ, and His atoning sacrifice. When someone offends us, which occurs to all, instead of angrily thinking of how to repay the slight, or crying over the pain one feels, we bear the slight with patience and turn our hearts to Christ asking God to help us forgive and forget the offense. This is a powerful and liberating concept. One of becoming more *hasidut*, or pious and loving, that will help engender the faith and attributes required for a glorious resurrection and a desire to serve others. We reap what we sow.

Law of the Harvest: You Reap What You Sow

The fourth concept I call of the "Law of the Harvest." Simply put, it means that what you sow in your life is what you reap. How can we use this concept? By directing our thoughts along with our hearts' desires, we can in a great measure determine what our personal characteristics will be, or we can change them. First, we should identify those Christlike attitudes that we wish to develop in our lives. Then we should focus our thoughts and hearts on developing them. If we wish to be a patient person, we consider how a patient person reacts. We imagine ourselves responding in a gentle manner, and then we conform our actions to reflect that attribute. We seek entertainment that is not violent. We listen to peaceful music and read books reflecting a calm demeanor. We associate with those who exemplify this character trait, and we ask God to help us become more serene. We write our goal down, including how we intend to achieve it, and we measure our progress. Over time, with repetition of calm actions, we will develop into a patient person. We harvest the type of character we sow. Yes, sometimes we may become impatient, but instead of giving up, we persevere in our efforts. "Sow to yourselves in righteousness, reap in mercy; break up your fallow ground: for it is time to seek the Lord, till he come and rain righteousness upon you."[575]

For some reason, many think they are exempt from becoming what they sow, and they harbor ill thoughts, or they seek after vain and frivolous things, or they coast through life changing with whatever way the wind is blowing. They are sowing a weak and meandering attitude that will negatively shape their character and their lives. If you sow doubt, fear, or distrust in your thoughts, conversations, and actions, you will become what those things engender: a doubting, fearful, distrusting person. If you constantly reflect upon these negative things, read about them, seek entertainment with a core message that embraces them, you will find these a part of your life. The Lord put it this way, "For they that are after the flesh do mind the things of the flesh; but they that are after the Spirit the things of the Spirit. For to be carnally minded is death; but to be spiritually minded is life and peace."576

Each of us has the ability to control, change, and direct our thoughts. For, "All truth is independent in that sphere in which God has placed it, to act for itself, as all intelligence also; otherwise there is no existence."577 As fertile soil, our minds will bring forth a harvest. What kind of harvest depends upon us.

Law of Proliferation

The last preparatory law we will discuss is an important concept that impacts our preparation for the resurrection and is what I call the "Law of Proliferation." Have you ever noticed that if you plant a garden, and then ignore it, weeds take over in an unprecedented manner? They will fill the unplanted spot in your garden and eventually choke out the planted areas.

One year we decided we would plant a garden. We dug up a portion of the lawn in our backyard and turned the soil to prepare it for planting. We happily put lettuce, beans, peas, tomatoes, and peppers in our garden space, anticipating the future harvest. Work and life soon drew our attention away from our garden space. Around this time, my wife's parents came up for a visit from California. My father in-law is an avid gardener and he quickly located my garden plot. But what had become of my efforts? Everywhere weeds choked the vegetables and the plants were spindly and weak. The weeds had seemingly proliferated without any effort on my part. In disgust, he weeded the garden and placed manure around the plants, watering them all frequently. In time, the vegetables rebounded and we had a lovely garden filled with produce. I marveled at the difference, and when they left to return home, my father-in-law admonished me to keep my garden clear of weeds, watered and fertilized, or I would lose the harvest.

As with my garden, so it is with our minds. They will bring forth an increase of what we plant and tend, or in the absence of our conscious efforts to cultivate them, our minds will bring forth proliferating weeds. This is the law of increase. Just like the earth around us, our minds are created to bring forth a harvest. If we ignore our fertile minds, weeds will spring up with little effort on our part. The weeds that spring up seemingly unaided will be hatred, greed, jealousy, and base desires, to name a few. They will enter our minds, and like the weeds in a garden, they will soon crowd out beneficial plants and we are in danger of losing our harvest of exaltation. What can we do? First, like a garden when we notice these weeds, we pull them out, and put productive plants in their place. Then we need to fertilize these plants with positive influences to help them grow. We must give them the life-enhancing water of faith and good works. For example, if the weed of anger enters our thoughts, we stop and pull it out by not dwelling on that feeling. Emotions unfed will die. They cannot sustain themselves without us giving them strength. Then we need to put in their place a productive plant, like peace. We give strength to that emotion by feeding it with good influences, and by watering it with faith and good works. As our peace grows, we reinforce it with other productive plants such as love, patience, or charity. We select things that exhibit these traits and bring their influences into our lives. Some examples of such influences are good music, worship of God, and uplifting entertainment. When base lustful thoughts and feelings come into our minds, we pull them up and replace them with pure and virtuous feelings. We avoid influences and inappropriate media that reinforce them, and we cease to give them strength.

Do you see the process? We are actively working the garden of our minds, removing unwanted weeds, or flaws, and replacing them with beneficial plants, or strengths, and fertilizing them with positive influences. As we do so, there is less and less space for the weeds. We should also be proactive and seek to select and plant good seeds in the fertile ground of our minds before weeds appear. We act rather than be acted upon. For example, we can develop the trait of selflessness by focusing on selfless acts of service. We direct our thoughts to the needs of others. We seek entertainment that promotes and displays the benefits of serving others. We lend these emotions strength by feeding them with thoughts of charity and kindness. The Lord's admonition to cleanse the gardens of our minds now has application, "prepare yourselves, and sanctify yourselves; yea, purify your hearts, and cleanse your hands and your feet before me, that I may make you clean."[578]

Now let us turn to other principles that also help us develop into Christlike disciples.

Principles that Develop Christlike Qualities

Just as there are concepts that can help us obtain exaltation, there are principles that when lived will help us prepare for the resurrection. Although there are many that could be touched on, we will limit our discussion to the following eight principles signifying a new beginning. They are: obedience, keeping the commandments, repentance, forgiveness, loving all, serving others, sacrifice, and consecration. Let us discuss each of them in turn.

Obedience

First, obedience. How can one love God and serve Him without being obedient to Him? Over time, our actions betray the actual intent of our hearts. Through a person's overall actions, we can discern between those whose words are only a façade of faith and those whose statements are a manifestation of their faith. We all make mistakes and fall short, but over time, a pattern of obedience or disobedience emerges. Obedience is the gold standard by which all are judged. Bruce R. McConkie highlighted this when he said, "Obedience is the first law of heaven, the cornerstone upon which all righteousness and progression rest. It consists in compliance with divine law, in conformity to the mind and will of Deity, in complete subjection to God and his commands."[579]

Obedience is not forced or a result of guilt or fear. It springs from voluntary acts founded in love. One may not begin with this as the basis for their actions, but over time it should become the motivating force. Whatever the motivation for one's obedience to God's commandments, the key is to watch what occurs as we obey or disobey. As we do this we will discover that obedience to God brings," "the fruit of the Spirit [which] is love, joy, peace, longsuffering, gentleness, goodness, faith, meekness, temperance."[580] When we are obedient, we avoid the consequences that come with sin, and instead reap the blessings that come with conforming to God's will. If we choose disobedience, we will learn that sorrow and pain accompany noncompliant choices, setting us on a tough path. However, as we comply with God's commandments and continue this process of obedience and observation of the results, our motivation will transform into faith and love. One then finds that the commandments become guidelines for happiness, not constraints on our choices. Rather than rules we must comply with, commandments become adages of wisdom to be respected. If we do this, we will find in our own lives that mighty change of heart that Alma the Younger speaks of when we put our faith in God and remain faithful to the end.[581]

Joseph F. Smith spoke to the motivation for obedience when he said, "Obedience must be voluntary; it must not be forced; there must be no coercion. Men must not be constrained against their will to obey the will of God; they must obey it because they know it to be right, because they desire to do it, and because it is their pleasure to do it. God delights in the willing heart."[582] Wherever you are, whatever your motivation for obeying God and Christ, continue on. Over time, the process of obedience and observation of the results will change one's heart as one recognizes the blessings that come from it. Through obedience, Isaiah's prophecy to Israel will also apply to us, "And I will give them one heart, and I will put a new spirit within you; and I will take the stony heart out of their flesh, and will give them an heart of flesh: That they may walk in my statutes, and keep mine ordinances, and do them: and they shall be my people, and I will be their God."[583] Not only will our hearts be changed, but God will prosper us. For, "the willing and obedient shall eat the good of the land of Zion in these last days."[584]

Keeping the commandments is central to the principle of obedience to God.

Keeping God's Commandments

One cannot prepare for the resurrection without keeping the commandments of God. King Benjamin declared that humankind, "should be diligent in keeping his [God's] commandments, and continue in the faith even unto the end of his life…this is the man who receiveth salvation."[585] The commandments are, in a sense, guideposts for living. They bring us into harmony with eternal principles and the cosmos. They put us in a position to reap the rewards that accompany obedience to them. By them we are purified, sanctified, and prepared to gain our exaltation. Hence, when we go contrary to the commandments, we forfeit the benefits that obedience to them engenders. As a wise person said, "you don't break the commandments, you break yourself against them." Christ Himself did nothing but what God commanded Him, and in all ways kept the commandments.[586] So likewise, we should seek to do God's will and obey His commandments. You cannot obtain all power from God without living His commandments. Satan is a prime example of one who lost all through disobedience. He once held a premier role in Gods kingdom, but he forfeited all through disobedience and rebellion.

The commandments are like exercise. As we exercise our bodies, our muscles increase in strength. Tasks that were once hard become easier. Likewise, as we obey the commandments, we gain strength, and what was once a hard principle to live becomes easier. For, "if they humble themselves before me, and have faith in me, then will I make weak things become strong unto them."[587] Thus, we improve our obedience by going from one grace to another until we arrive at perfection. "For if you keep my commandments you shall receive of his fulness, and be glorified in me as I am in the Father; therefore, I say unto you, you shall receive grace for grace."[588] The key is not so much a matter of where we are in the process, but that we are always moving forward and refining ourselves.

Chastity is a good example of a commandment that both purifies and sanctifies us. As we are obedient to the law of chastity, the natural man is brought into submission. Licentious behavior that steals the soul and makes it unfit for God's kingdom is left behind or avoided. Lust leaves our hearts, and we find our thoughts and motivations more circumspect and Christlike. Our desires become more refined and our actions purified. We do not dwell on base desires, but we are motivated by respect, kindness, and caring. In effect, we are motivated by the pure love of Christ. The bond of sexuality becomes a sacred and ennobling relationship based in godliness. In reflecting upon eternity, one must ask themselves how can one hold a position of trust in eternity if they cannot be faithful to their spouse in mortality? Yes, repentance allows us to right our wrongs, but becoming chaste and virtuous is a process that is delayed and made more difficult by moral transgressions. A person who has walked the path of chastity finds themselves at peace and filled with joy, thanksgiving, and love: the fruits of the spirit.

I recall a man who asked his employer for a substantial loan to meet his financial obligations, which his employer mercifully granted. The man promised to repay the loan. It was well-known in the company that the man was having an affair with another married associate, and they would meet after work to pursue their relationship. Later on, he left the company and refused to repay the loan. The seeds of dishonesty were evident in his moral actions that later played out in his fiscal obligations. His dishonesty with his wife affected his other commitments.

Our character is not made up of separate boxes that are isolated from one another. If we are dishonest in our marriage vows, we are likely to be dishonest in other aspects of our lives. What we do profoundly affects our being. We must ever be diligent in keeping ourselves morally clean and deal honestly with our fellow man. We must all be careful not to rationalize disobedience or fool ourselves into believing there won't be consequences. What we do in secret will not remain secret, but will follow us wherever we go. In preparing for the resurrection, keeping the commandments is essential to our salvation. "And in nothing doth man offend God, or against none is his wrath kindled, save those who confess not his hand in all things, and obey not his commandments."[589]

Although we may desire and often are obedient, we do make mistakes. Given this human condition, it is important in our preparation to practice the principle of repentance while walking the road to perfection.

Repentance

Repentance is a great gift from a loving Heavenly Father. Repentance is like a hoe that allows us to clear the weeds of sin and the base desires from the infested ground of our minds and hearts. Like hoeing weeds from a garden prepares the garden to bear fruit, repentance prepares the ground of our souls for beneficial character traits. However, like a garden overrun by weeds, it takes time and effort to remove them and prepare the soil anew for beneficial plants. Likewise, repentance takes time and effort to remove the unwanted sins and traits from our hearts and minds. We take up our hoes of repentance by forsaking our sins, confessing them to God and, if grievous, to proper Priesthood authority. "By this ye may know if a man repenteth of his sins—behold, he will confess them and forsake them."[590] We must feel real Godly sorrow, which humbles us and causes our hearts to mourn over our trespasses.

Where appropriate, we also need to make restitution to those we have sinned against. In order to offset the demands of the law of restoration in our life, for harm we have done others, we must restore or repair the damage we have done to the extent possible. By doing so, we qualify for the Atonement of Jesus Christ, which places us in a position to receive mercy rather than the justice the law of restoration requires. If we fail to make a proper effort, like stubborn dandelions, vestiges of the weeds remain to re-sprout. If we allow them to re-infest our hearts and minds and grow again, it will require the weeding, or repentance process, to be done anew. As the scriptures say, "go your ways and sin no more; but unto that soul who sinneth shall the former sins return, saith the Lord your God."[591] But it is more than this. With true repentance, we experience the mighty change of heart where we no longer feel a desire to commit sin. It is a change of heart such that, like Nephi, we would ask the Lord, "wilt thou make me that I may shake at the appearance of sin?"[592]

Developing the principle of repentance in our lives is critical in our efforts toward achieving perfection. If we fail to clear out the weeds of sin in our lives, they will consume us. Eventually they will be exhibited to others through our daily actions and communications. "Let such beware and repent speedily, lest judgment shall come upon them as a snare, and their folly shall be made manifest, and their works shall follow them in the eyes of the people."[593] The consequence in our lives of whether we repent or not eventually brings about a reckoning that will produce in us eternal joy or eternal misery. Only the truly repentant inherit a kingdom of God.

In the process of perfection, we must also employ the principle of forgiveness in our lives.

Forgiveness

Forgiveness applies to both ourselves and to others. In regards to ourselves, we must be willing to forgive ourselves despite our errors and trespasses. I recall a friend who, after repenting and sincerely doing all they could to set their life aright, telling me they could not be forgiven of their sins. As we talked, I said, "this may sound strange, but you need to repent and have faith in Jesus Christ. You have imagined up for yourself a god who is not the God we serve. Our God is a forgiving Father who sent His son Jesus Christ to pay the price of sin for all God's children if they repent." The Lord said, "For behold, I, God, have suffered these things for all, that they might not suffer if they would repent."[594] As Christ also said, "be ye kind one to another, tenderhearted, forgiving one another, even as God for Christ's sake hath forgiven you."[595] Like my friend, having repented, we must remember that God has forgiven us, and that we must find the faith and strength to forgive ourselves of our trespasses.

As we are seeking to repent, forgive, and be forgiven ourselves, we must also forgive others. "Wherefore, I say unto you, that ye ought to forgive one another; for he that forgiveth not his brother his trespasses standeth condemned before the Lord; for there remaineth in him the greater sin. I, the Lord, will forgive whom I will forgive, but of you it is required to forgive all men."[596] As we forgive, we come to understand that it is a healing balm that removes the canker of loathing, jealousy, and self-conflagration from our lives. It allows us, and others, to move forward and not look back, improving and perfecting our lives. "Behold, he who has repented of his sins, the same is forgiven, and I, the Lord, remember them no more."[597]

As we are obedient and keep the commandments, while repenting of our sins and forgiving ourselves and those around us, we will find a fertile ground to develop a love for God and all humankind.

Loving All

In Christ's day, the Jews had a burning question: What was the one great law, or commandment? His reply to the lawyer's question about the greatest commandment was not only the response to this burning question of His day, but it also suggested a pattern for celestial living. "Jesus said unto him, Thou shalt love the Lord thy God with all thy heart, and with all thy soul, and with all thy mind. This is the first and great commandment. And the second is like unto it, Thou shalt love thy neighbour as thyself. On these two commandments hang all the law and the prophets."[598] We must love God and seek to do His will. Motivation that is based on rewards, consequences, guilt, or fear will not produce the lasting obedience and homage for God that leads to exaltation. All motivation except love will eventually fail and potentially cause us to fall short of salvation.[599]

If we cannot love God, how can we fully love His children? The lack of true love for God and an understanding of the fatherhood of all mankind can lead to the bigotry and cultural divisiveness that is so prevalent today. When motivated by love of God and humankind, all other considerations and human fragilities fall by the wayside. Rather than seeing one ethnic group as better than another, or odd, we see them as equals and appreciate the diversity they bring. Rather than judging, we accept people for who they are. Rather than seeking to aggrandize ourselves at the cost of others, we seek their best welfare. Rather than viewing others with hate or vengeance, we look to them with a patient and a forgiving heart. Rather than taking advantage of others, we seek to bless and promote their welfare. Reflecting on this concept I like the Amplified Version of Romans 13:8–9, it reads, "Let no debt remain outstanding, except the continuing debt to love one another, for whoever loves others has fulfilled the law. The commandments, "You shall not commit adultery," "You shall not murder," "You shall not steal," "You shall not covet,"[a] and whatever other command there may be, are summed up in this one command: "Love your neighbor as yourself."

Encapsulated in this teaching of Christ is the idea that we should love ourselves, which is quite a contrast to the self-starvation, mutilation, and debasing some people and religions practice. On the surface this concept of loving one's self seems at odds with the Christian concepts of selflessness and humility. Like all characteristics, one can over-indulge in loving one's self, becoming indulgent, self-centered, and vain. But if we are bereft of a healthy love of self, we will be insecure, self-conscious, and continually looking outside ourselves for personal gratification and affirmation. We will be like a three-wheel wagon rolling down the street, perpetually unbalanced and ready to crash. Yes, we may love others and God on some level without loving ourselves, but we will lack the peace, inner strength, and self-confidence that loving ourselves provides and is required to find a fullness of joy.

We should acknowledge our failures and seek to benefit from the wisdom they impart while avoiding the paralyzing nature of extreme self-criticism. As we draw nearer to God, keep His ordinances and statutes, and serve others, we will find ourselves more in sync with our divine nature and our internal conflicts will decrease. In addition, God will fill us with love for Him, all humankind, and ourselves.[600] We call this the true love of Christ. As it says in the Amplified Bible 1 Timothy, "Whereas the object and purpose of our instruction and charge is love, which springs from a pure heart, and a good (clear) conscience and sincere (unfeigned) faith."[601] Again, Jesus Christ's emphasis was to move to a higher law, cease to focus on minutia, but rather look to God, your fellowman, and self, in love and live.

As we develop this love for all a desire to serve others will be fostered in our hearts and lives.

Service

Another aspect of preparing for the resurrection is focusing one's life on serving others and becoming close to God by developing a selfless attitude. Our focus should be on what God wants of us, and how to best use our talents and abilities to serve Him. We look for ways to fulfill God's purposes and we anticipate His will. Our sole focus is not building our own estates here on earth; "For whosoever will save his life shall lose it: and whosoever will lose his life for my sake shall find it. For what is a man profited, if he shall gain the whole world, and lose his own soul, or what shall a man give in exchange for his soul?"[602] We must be willing to turn our lives over to God, who can make so much more of us than we can of ourselves.

As we turn our thoughts to serving Him and our fellowman, the process of perfection is accelerated. We are freed from wondering how much money we make or have, which will never be enough, to how can we use our lives and resources in the service of our God and others. When it comes time for senior missions, it won't be a question of *will* we go, but *when can* we go. When the Elder's Quorum President, Relief Society President, or Primary President ask for help, it won't be "let's wait and let others raise their hands first." It becomes how quickly can we raise our hand to help. Again, it is moving to a higher plane of living and giving, by focusing and living outside ourselves and serving others. "Pure religion and undefiled before God and the Father is this, To visit the fatherless and widows in their affliction."[603] Can you imagine a world where humanity's actions are based in serving others? When doing this, we fulfill Christ's message concerning the two great commandments.

As we love and serve others we will find an inherent desire growing within us to sacrifice of our time, talents, and resources to build God's kingdom.

Sacrifice

In ancient times, the law of sacrifice included the shedding of blood. In the meridian of time, Christ became the ultimate and final blood sacrifice.[604] Today we offer a sacrifice of a broken heart and a contrite spirit.[605] A broken heart in this scriptural sense does not mean that we are sad, but rather that we are humble and that we submit to God's will. To be contrite is to show sorrow or remorse for our sins and shortcomings. To sacrifice is to give up something we value for a better cause. It is to put something better above one's desires, wants, or needs. It is also the offering of something to deity in propitiation, or homage. It stems from the unselfish motivations that compete against a desire to serve oneself. It is an essential characteristic of the exalted in eternity.

One cannot be selfish and self-centered and be granted all power and all things in eternity. Why? Because they will eventually act in accordance with their own desires contrary to the good of others. Is this not what we have seen down through the history of mankind with the despots and unrighteous rulers? In the eternities, having all means you are the servant of all, and others' welfare is paramount to your own.[606] Christ is the ultimate example of selflessness and sacrifice, as He illustrated through His Atonement. Though He was the Son of God, the great I Am, "the Lord your Redeemer suffered death in the flesh; wherefore he suffered the pain of all men, that all men might repent and come unto him."[607]

As saints, we are often called upon to sacrifice our time, talents, and resources to build the kingdom of God. In this effort, balance is the key. For example, if we lose our employment due to overzealous religious efforts, we harm our ability to provide for our families, and also weaken our ability to contribute to the kingdom. On the other hand, if we so focus on our employment that we become estranged from God, or lack time for God, we fail to serve in the kingdom. Between the two extremes is the golden mean. Through self-examination, prayer, and the promptings of the spirit, we can find the right balance of sacrifice in our lives.

We should all be ready and willing to make sacrifices to help build the kingdom, however small or great they may be. If we have not mastered these characteristics through sacrificing for the kingdom, we will not be prepared for exaltation. You cannot be prepared for the resurrection, to become a joint-heir with Christ, and not be willing to sacrifice for the kingdom, and for others. We should be willing and ready to sacrifice all we have and lead a consecrated life dedicated to God.

Consecration

Here we find a principle of eternity that is somewhat foreign to humankind in our "me" society. It is diametrically opposed to what the world hails as our essential right and entitlement—to live only for self. In God's realm, consecration is an eternal principle and embraces the concept of living for others, and a cause greater than ourselves. It is not a law of material nature, but it is a matter of the heart. Our hearts must be turned to God, His kingdom, and we should treasure His purposes and presence. To consecrate is to set aside something in a religious rite as a dedication to God. In this sense, Latter-day Saints consecrate churches, temples, and sacred items for use in the service of God. In a similar vein, we consecrate ourselves to the service of God and His kingdom. In doing so, we give our time, talents, and resources in the service of others, and to the worship of deity.

Consecration is intertwined with the principles of obedience and sacrifice to God. One can only consecrate themselves to God by being obedient and by sacrificing. How can one hope to receive all that God has without in turn pledging all that one has? Joseph Smith taught that, "a religion that does not require the sacrifice of all things never has the power sufficient to produce the faith necessary unto life and salvation."[608] In the eternal perspective, the blessings received by sacrificing are greater than anything that is given up.

When one has consecrated their resources and life to the kingdom of God, all they are and do goes to build up Zion in one form or another. Their daily actions reflect as a light upon the hill, inviting all to come and enjoy the blessings of the kingdom.[609] Their careers build Zion through the payment of tithing, fast offerings, and other donations. It provides the means for them to participate in Church service by providing for their daily needs, allowing them to worship without the burden of want. Their education becomes the vehicle for them to be gainfully employed and to increase in knowledge, which in turn allows them to bring their talents to bear in building the Church. The raising of righteous children provides an increase of faithful and devoted followers of God, who themselves reap the rewards of lives well lived, and in turn, with the passage of time, join and eventually assume the role of their parents in building God's kingdom.

Some set aside their worldly concerns to fully dedicate their daily lives to building the kingdom, such as the First Presidency, the Twelve Apostles, and other general authorities of the Church. Some set aside their daily pursuits to serve full-time missions as young adults, adults, or seniors in various capacities for a season. This we must do with a willing heart if it is to be fully recognized by God.[610] In a real sense, nothing we have is our own. All has come through the grace of God. A life of consecration is simply returning to God what is already His, for which He in turn blesses us with the riches of eternity. A friend of mine, when giving of his time and resources to the Church, would often say, "it is all God's anyway."

Consecration will refine each of us and help us prepare to inherit all God has by purifying our desires and focusing them on things of eternal value. We are all the beneficiary of those who lived before us and consecrated their lives to God. The Protestant reformers Martin Luther, John Wycliffe, William Tyndale, and many others gave themselves and sometimes their lives for God's work. In the restoration, Joseph Smith, a martyr; Brigham Young; Wilford Woodruff; and many others consecrated their lives that we might enjoy the blessings of the Gospel. In our day, the Prophet, his Counselors, the Twelve Apostles, regional and local leaders, parents, and many others have consecrated their lives to God that we might enjoy the blessings of God's kingdom. Perhaps we may never be required to give our all, but our willingness to give all is a witness to God of our desire to submit to His will. A consecrated life is a good life filled with good work. It is an attitude and commitment that prepares us for the resurrection and exaltation.

Summary

Remembering God's *shekhinah*, or that we are always in the presence of God, can help us control our actions and submit too His will. We can plan ahead and prevent poor performance as we seek to live by the higher law of love for God and humankind, and as we avoid getting caught up in performing the minimum acceptable actions or behaviors. We can seek to avoid *chata'ah*, or missing the mark, by having a clear, Christlike objective and by striving to excel. We can develop *hasidut*, or piety, and loving kindness towards our fellowman and God, and continue to grow in divine attributes. With the Law of the Harvest, or by reaping what we sow, we can focus on the best gifts that bring salvation. By understanding the Law of Proliferation, we can direct the harvest of character that comes from our hearts and minds toward spiritual things. As we serve others, we will become outwardly focused and less fixated with our own selves.

We can draw closer to our Savior by incorporating the principles of obedience, keeping the commandments, repenting, forgiving, loving God and humankind, serving others, sacrificing, and consecrating our lives to refine ourselves. Through obedience, which is the first law of heaven, we warrant God's blessings. Through repentance, we can be forgiven and reclaim the areas of our lives where we have made mistakes or gone astray. Through the principle of forgiveness, we can actively move forward in our efforts to perfect ourselves, and to help others do the same. As we serve others, we will grow in our love of God and humankind. By keeping the commandments, we become sanctified, prepare to sacrifice for the kingdom, and live a life of consecration to God. Finally, love is the real motivation that will endure and lead to exaltation. This process of perfection will eventually bring us to a glorious resurrection, while providing peace, safety, and a Christlike walk in this life.

CHAPTER 13

SYMBOLS OF THE GOSPEL AND THE RESURRECTION

All things testify of Christ

A SYMBOL IS SOMETHING that represents something else by association, resemblance, or convention. Some Gospel symbols are related to ordinances, like baptism. Others are more abstract, like colors or numbers. They can be powerful teaching tools to help fire the imagination, and they can convey more than what the words themselves denote. It is beyond the scope of this book to do a comprehensive and exhaustive examination of all Gospel symbols. However, in studying the resurrection, a basic understanding of some of these symbols will help us find more meaning by adding depth and insight to our studies.[611]

Animals

Animals are used by the scriptures to represent divinity, people, classes, attitudes, and attributes. Some that have ties to the resurrection are:

Lambs. These peaceful creatures have been a symbol for Christ throughout the ages. He was the lamb slain from the foundation of the earth.[612] From the time of Adam, the sacrifice of a lamb without blemish, along with the shedding of its blood, was a symbol for the great sacrifice of Christ and His shedding of blood in the meridian of time.[613] Thus, it can represent the resurrection, newness of life, faithfulness, and so on.

Sheep. These animals are used symbolically to represent the flock of God and of Christ. They are pure, white, and of high value. Christ spoke of being the Shepherd to His sheep.[614] He also spoke of gathering them in and seeking those that were lost.[615] They can represent innocence, purity, discipleship, gentleness, and meekness. To Peter, Christ emphasized three times the importance of feeding His sheep.[616] Through the resurrection and atonement of Jesus Christ the faithful saints or sheep, are gathered back into the sheep hold or presence of God.

Goats. These animals can either be a positive or negative symbol. In terms of the resurrection, they are usually seen as negative.[617] They can represent Satan, rebellion, willfulness, evil, stubbornness, or the damned.

Fish. Fish are mentioned throughout the scriptures, though the type of fish is not usually identified. They often represent humankind, as in casting one's net to catch souls.[618] Some can also be bad, such as those fish which are tossed to and froe by the sophistry of the world unprepared for the resurrection.

Baptism

Baptism is a strong Gospel symbol of the resurrection. Paul, in Romans, says, "Therefore we are buried with him by baptism into death: that like as Christ was raised up from the dead by the glory of the Father, even so we also should walk in newness of life."[619] The ordinance of baptism, instituted by our Heavenly Father for our salvation, also shows us how to return to Him. By being buried in water, baptism reflects our mortal death and burial in the earth. Our coming up out of the water represents the resurrection and walking in the newness of a righteous life, just as our future glorified, eternal, and perfected bodies will allow us to enter God's kingdom and walk with Him in a newness of life.

Baptism is also a symbol of the vicarious work we do in behalf of the dead. The Prophet Joseph Smith taught, "Herein is glory and honor, and immortality and eternal life—The ordinance of baptism by water, to be immersed therein in order to answer to the likeness of the dead, that one principle might accord with the other; to be immersed in the water and come forth out of the water is in the likeness of the resurrection of the dead in coming forth out of their graves; hence, this ordinance was instituted to form a relationship with the ordinance of baptism for the dead, being in likeness of the dead."[620]

Each member of the Church has been baptized, symbolically putting off the old person of sin, and has been raised a new person in the likeness of the resurrection. Each time this ordinance is performed, we are reinforcing our faith in the resurrection and in the Savior. He is the source, the power, and the exemplar of this transformational gateway to eternal life.

Birth and Death

Birth and Death are both symbols of the resurrection. As discussed, they represent gateways between planes of existence. They are two parts of the three transitionary, interconnected gateways of mortality. Birth, the first transitionary gateway, represents a newness of life, and it is filled with hope and future possibilities, like the promise of the resurrection, which is also filled with eternal hope and possibilities.

Death, which is intrinsically tied to birth, is the second transitionary gateway, and it shows the movement between mortality toward eternity. It reminds us that our lives are ephemeral in nature. It forces us to face our future, contemplate our mortality, and the hope of immortality. Those who have been laid down in death will be raised up by the third transitional gateway of the resurrection, which awaits all of humankind.

Body Parts

The arm is a symbol of divine power, as illustrated in such phrases as "The arm of the Lord." It can represent strength, submission, commitment, and prayer when raised up. It represents the power of judgment and ensuing destruction when "The arm of the Lord" falls upon the nations.[621] It also can represent mercy and compassion when "The arm of the Lord" is stretched out, or made bare to humankind.[622]

Blood represents the cleansing Atonement, forgiveness, mortality, humanity, war, and death, which are all part of our journey to immortality. In relationship to the Atonement, Jesus Christ has washed and cleansed us of our sins by His own blood in preparation for the resurrection.[623]

The eye is a representation of light, truth, and desires, such as your eye being single to the glory of God.[624] It can also represent God's ability to know all our thoughts and doings.[625]

The head is a symbol for what rules the body, and when crowned, it represents royalty, authority, and exaltation:[626] as in a crown of eternal glory upon one's head for those worthy of exaltation.[627]

The heart represents a person's commitment, feelings, receipt of revelation, and desires.[628] As we refine our hearts we are sanctified and prepared to receive a celestial resurrection through living celestial laws. Where your heart is, there will your treasure be also.[629]

The knee is a symbol that represents one's station in regards to another. For example, the bended knee can mean acceptance of Christ or the Gospel. At the day of judgment, every knee shall bend and every tongue shall confess that Jesus is the Christ.[630]

Colors

Darkness is technically not a color but a shade of color. However, it can represent spiritual ignorance and those who lack spirituality are described as, "walking in darkness at noon-day."[631] It is the absence of truth and light for, "that which doth not edify is not of God, and is darkness."[632] We are encouraged to cast off the works of darkness and to have no fellowship with them.[633] Those whose works are evil, whom the devil takes possession of, are cast into outer darkness.[634] It describes Satan's domain.[635] Darkness is also associated with great destruction.[636]

Scripturally, green represents life, and hence the resurrection. John the Beloved saw a vision of Christ and His heavenly throne surrounded by a green rainbow. He wrote, "And immediately I was in the spirit: and, behold, a throne was set in heaven, and one sat on the throne. And he that sat was to look upon like a jasper and a sardine stone: and there was a rainbow round about the throne, in sight like unto an emerald."[637] The rainbow around the throne was the color of emerald, or green. It symbolizes that Christ, as a resurrected being, abounds in life and is the source of life. The rainbow also hearkened back to His promise that the earth would never again be destroyed by water, thereby representing the promise of life's continuance and the resurrection.[638]

Gold represents wealth, power, or worldliness. It can also imply the celestial glory, the reward of the faithful, such as in crowns of gold, or godliness for the resurrected exalted saints.[639]

Red can mean cleansing through the Atonement and Christ's blood, or war and death. We read about cleansing in the Book of Mormon, "Therefore they were called after this holy order, and were sanctified, and their garments were washed white through the blood of the Lamb."[640] An example of war and death is found in the Book of Revelation, where we read, "And there went out another horse that was red: and power was given to him that sat thereon to take peace from the earth, and that they should kill one another: and there was given unto him a great sword."[641]

White embodies purity, worthiness, and righteousness. As John wrote, "He that overcometh, the same shall be clothed in white raiment."[642] And the saints are, "arrayed in fine linen, clean and white: for the fine linen is the righteousness of saints."[643] Messengers from God appear in white, a symbol of their worthiness.[644] The resurrected saints will be clothed in white.[645] It can also represent a state of preparedness as in, "the field is white already to harvest."[646]

Heavenly Orbs

The heavenly stars and planets remind us of the resurrection. The sun sets and rises, the moon waxes and wanes. The stars come out at night, and then once again fade with the rising sun. Their organization, obedience to laws, and orderliness bespeaks a divine influence and power. "The earth rolls upon her wings, and the sun giveth his light by day, and the moon giveth her light by night, and the stars also give their light, as they roll upon their wings in their glory, in the midst of the power of God."[647] Each in their turn testify of Jesus Christ as their Creator and Redeemer and confirms the reality of the resurrection. As the Psalmist witnessed, "The heavens declare the glory of God; and the firmament sheweth his handywork."[648]

Nature

Nature is a symbol that represents the resurrection, like plants that unfurl their colorful flowers, and then seemingly die, only to re-emerge again next spring renewed and invigorated to repeat the cycle once more. My daffodils pop up each spring and unfurl their yellow caps in a colorful display of beauty. However, they fade all too quickly, as the once brilliant display of flowers wilts to a brown, earthy tone, soon to pass from existence until spring calls them forth from the earth once more. How like our life this is: we are born into life at the spring of our existence, only to fade as the winter of our lives comes. We pass from mortality until Jesus Christ, through resurrection's embrace, calls us forth once again. It reminds me of the poem titled "Flowers," by Henry Wadsworth Longfellow:

FLOWERS, BY HENRY WADSWORTH LONGFELLOW

In all places, then, and in all seasons,
Flowers expand their light and soul-like wings,
Teaching us, by most persuasive reasons,
How akin they are to human things.

And with childlike, credulous affection
We behold their tender buds expand;
Emblems of our own great resurrection,
Emblems of the bright and better land.

Numbers

Our lives are governed by numbers. Important events of our lives are recorded in numeric values. The day we are born, married, and later die are examples. Numbers affect when we can vote, drive, or engage in events. They define certain groups like seniors when they turn sixty-five, teenagers when their thirteenth birthday arrives, or classmates, which are based on age groups. Numbers are also used frequently as Gospel symbols in the scriptures and are related to humankind's journey. Let us examine some of the more prominent ones, and what they symbolize.

One represents perfection, just as God is perfection. Likewise, Jesus Christ, the First and the Last, represents the Perfect One. "But to us there is but one God, the Father, of whom are all things, and we in him; and one Lord Jesus Christ, by whom are all things, and we by him."[649] Just as God and Christ are perfect, we are instructed to become perfect.[650] And it is through the Atonement of Jesus Christ, our faith, good works, repentance, and the resurrection that we obtain perfection.

Two represents separation, or division into distinct parts. It is a juxtaposition, which emphasizes opposing views, outcomes, or situations that highlight their differences. A good example would be the day of judgment, and the separation of nations onto the right and left hand of the Lord. Those on the right hand comprise the righteous, and those on the left hand the wicked.[651]

Three represents divine oversight, direction, purpose, and involvement. It is a numeric representation of the Godhead: the Father, Son, and Holy Ghost. We also see this divine influence in the three areas of the law of restoration, three gateways of mortality, three degrees of glory, three degrees within the celestial kingdom, three members in a presidency, and so on. Also, Jesus Christ was three days and nights in the earth, after which God raised Him up, again showing divine purpose.[652]

Three and one/half represents an arrestment, or halting of a process, or event before it finds fulfillment. It can also mean the restarting of a process or event that has been interrupted. A good example is the two prophets who will be slain in Jerusalem after preaching three and one-half years, and then arise again in three and one-half days.[653]

Four represents an entirety, or the whole earth, as in the four quarters of the earth, or the four angels holding power over the elements of the earth.[654] It reflects the idea of before, behind, and from each side. It shows a completeness of the geography covered, or the limits by which humankind is bound. We see this in the Lord's gathering of Israel from the four quarters of the earth,[655] which emphasizes the comprehensive nature of the gathering and can also be applied to the all-encompassing nature of the resurrection.

Six represents incompleteness, to fall short, or to be imperfect. Perhaps the number 666 in Revelation is the perfect representation of Satan who will forever fall short of realizing the resurrection.[656]

Seven represents perfection. For in seven days, God finished his work of creation.[657] We are asked to forgive not just seven times, but seventy times seven, multiplying the sense of perfect forgiveness that we should show humankind.[658] As discussed earlier, it also reflects the perfect nature of the resurrection through the seven distinct periods or times the resurrection occurs during mankind's history.[659]

Eight represents the resurrection, regeneration, and a new beginning. Eight is seven plus one, and since it comes just after seven, its progression signifies an end to something and a new beginning.[660] In the Book of Mormon, we read about Lehi and his family that they, "did sojourn for the space of many years, yea, even eight years in the wilderness,"[661] before coming to the land Bountiful, which was a new beginning. At eight years old, children become accountable before the Lord for their actions, are baptized, receive the Gift of the Holy Ghost, and participate in the doctrine of repentance, signaling a new beginning.[662] Their baptism is a new era in their life, a new beginning that foreshadows the resurrection. So, eight itself is associated with the beginning of a new era, or a new order, which the resurrection is. Jesus Christ arose on the first day of the week following His crucifixion. It was the eighth day, and God chose for Him to arise in the newness of eternal life.[663] This is the penultimate new era, and a new beginning.

Twelve represents a fullness of priesthood and the right to govern. As exemplified in the twelve tribes of Israel, or the Twelve Apostles.[664] In Revelation, the 144,000 High Priests, 12,000 from each tribe is multiplication of priesthood perfection (12,000 X 12).[665]

Seasons

The seasons symbolize life's journey. Summer is thought of as the prime of life. Fall represents the passage of time, and aging. Winter is associated with death. Springtime represents the resurrection.

Spring is the time of year when nature re-awakens and the earth brings forth new life. The death and starkness of winter is overcome once again, and natures bursts forth in a colorful display. What once appeared barren and forsaken now spreads it leafy vegetation for all to witness its rebirth. And we find our own burdens lighter, our countenance brighter, and our energy higher as we experience the newness of springtime. This cycle has been repeated for millennia, and like the phoenix rising from the ashes, the seasons reflect humankind's ultimate triumph over death and the hope of a brighter future. A poem which encapsulates this thought is "The Seed Shop," by Muriel Stuart:

THE SEED SHOP, BY MURIEL STUART

HERE in a quiet and dusty room they lie,
Faded as crumbled stone and shifting sand,
Forlorn as ashes, shrivelled, scentless, dry—
Meadows and gardens running through my hand.

Dead that shall quicken at the voice of spring,
Sleepers to wake beneath June's tempest kiss;
Though birds pass over, unremembering,
And no bee find here roses that were his.

In this brown husk a dale of hawthorn dreams;
A cedar in this narrow cell is thrust
That shall drink deeply at a century's streams;
These lilies shall make summer on my dust.

Here in their safe and simple house of death,
Sealed in their shells, a million roses leap;
Here I can stir a garden with my breath,
And in my hand a forest lies asleep.

The Sacrament

The sacrament also has reference to the resurrection. In it, we take upon us the name of Christ, commit to always remember Him and keep His commandments, that we may have His spirit to be with us. When we partake of the bread and water in remembrance of His body and blood, we are drawn to reflect on His sacrifice and Atonement. In the New World, when He appeared to the Nephites, He instituted His sacrament. He appeared to them with His resurrected and immortal body and said, "And this shall ye do in remembrance of my body, which I have shown unto you. And it shall be a testimony unto the Father that ye do always remember me. And if ye do always remember me ye shall have my Spirit to be with you."[666] Clearly, He wants us to remember Him in His resurrected and perfected state, foreshadowing what awaits us all. We can remember Him each time we partake of the sacrament, and in solemnity reflect upon His Atonement and resurrection.

Vicarious Work

Members of the Church are engaged in bringing the saving ordinances of the Gospel to their departed ancestors. By doing genealogy work, they identify individuals, and the key dates and events in their lives. Next, members take their names to the temples and perform vicarious ceremonies in their behalf, such as baptism and receiving the Gift of the Holy Ghost. This allows their deceased ancestors to have the saving ordinances of the Gospel available to them and allows them the opportunity to accept or reject them. When Paul posed the question to the ancient saints, "Else what shall they do which are baptized for the dead, if the dead rise not at all? why are they then baptized for the dead?"[667] he was asking them why be baptized vicariously for your departed ancestors, if they did not rise in the resurrection, showing that vicarious work for the dead was a practice anciently, and that it also foreshadowed the resurrection.

Joseph Smith had similar thoughts in mind when he wrote, "Consequently, the baptismal font was instituted as a similitude of the grave, and was commanded to be in a place underneath where the living are wont to assemble, to show forth the living and the dead, and that all things may have their likeness, and that they may accord one with another—that which is earthly conforming to that which is heavenly."[668] The ordinance of baptism teaches us about the need to bring salvation to our departed ancestors who likewise will take part in the resurrection. It also teaches them about the work we are doing in their behalf, and binds us together in the work of salvation, all symbolically pointing to the day of all humankind's eventual resurrection.

Summary

All things testify of Christ, whether it is ordinances, nature, life, numbers, colors, ourselves, the starry heavens, or vicarious work for the dead. As Jacob testified, "All things denote there is a God; yea, even the earth, all things that are upon the face of it, yea, and its motion, yea, and also all the planets which move in their regular form do witness that there is a Supreme Creator."[669] As we view those witnesses and experience their reality, we have our faith reinforced. These witnesses compound the hope of our own glorious resurrection, which burns brighter and brighter until the perfect day when we shall arise in the newness of life. For they, "that sleep in the dust of the earth shall awake, some to everlasting life, and some to shame and everlasting contempt. And they that be wise shall shine as the brightness of the firmament; and they that turn many to righteousness as the stars for ever and ever."[670]

CHAPTER 14

PARABLES APPLICABLE TO THE RESURRECTION

Everything is either symbol or parable

~ Paul Claudel

THE SAVIOR BEGAN His ministry teaching the word in plainness and showing forth miracles as proof of His divinity and mission. The Pharisaic party claimed His teachings and miracles were of a Satanic origin, which lie turned many against Him.[671] As opposition and unreceptiveness grew, He turned to teaching in parables, an approach that allowed Christ to continue His ministry in the face of intense opposition until it came time for His crucifixion. This change in method of teaching surprised His disciples, and they asked Him why He did this. He told them that for them it was given to know the mysteries of the kingdom, but for the hard of heart, those that rejected Him, it was not.[672]

Yet despite the lack of plainness, we can gain insights through the parables He taught. Parables allowed the Lord to continue to teach truths using analogies that reinforced those truths. They added additional color and understanding that went beyond the words themselves. Parables can often be applied to many different situations and each can convey a different meaning without destroying the character of the analogy. They are not meant to be a detailed comparison that remains consistent when one drills down to the minutia, but are often to be viewed at a top level. They also are easily recalled since the analogies represent things that people were familiar with, and that were present in daily life. They can trigger other thoughts and insights. They also can keep eternal truths from those who are unprepared, unable, or unwilling to receive them. In looking at the parables that Jesus Christ taught, many have an element that correlates to the resurrection and can be used to reinforce truths surrounding it. Let's examine some of these and how they could be associated with the resurrection.

Cloth and Wineskins

These two parables are similar and make the same point. The new doctrine of Christ cannot be mixed with the old doctrine of the Pharisees and Sadducees, or any other religion. You don't put new cloth in an old garment, and you don't put new wine in an old wineskin. It was a warning to His disciples to be wary of the doctrine of the Pharisees and Sadducees. These two parables are found in all three of the synoptic Gospels.

"No man also seweth a piece of new cloth on an old garment: else the new piece that filled it up taketh away from the old, and the rent is made worse. And no man putteth new wine into old [wineskins]: else the new wine doth burst the [wineskins], and the wine is spilled, and the [wineskins] will be marred: but new wine must be put into new [wineskins]."[673]

Those in Christ's time generally used wineskins instead of bottles to store and carry wine. The proper translation of the Greek for this parable is not bottles, but wineskins.[674] Over time, wineskins became brittle. New wine ferments and expands, and if put in an old brittle wineskin, the skin will burst. A new wineskin, however, is flexible and will expand with the fermenting wine.

The focus of this parable is on our inward motivation and thoughts. Just as wine, when imbibed, influences one's behavior, the Gospel of Christ, when consumed, should influence our thoughts, motivation, and actions, making one more Christlike. You can't mix the old traditions of religion with the new faith taught by Jesus Christ. Our old brittle ways will not be able to expand and change to accept the true doctrine of Christ. It just doesn't work. You must make a clean break with the past and accept the Gospel truths in their purity. We need to be flexible enough to reject the traditions of our fathers and accept the teachings of Jesus Christ. As we do so, our hearts and motivation will turn more to the Savior and His salvation.

When you put new cloth in an old garment and wash it, the new cloth shrinks and pulls away from the old cloth, which had previously been shrunk. Mixing new cloth with old results in an unfit garment. The new cloth illustrates the outward, or visible deeds. A person's actions expose their commitment to Christ. This is illustrated by the analogy of attaching new cloth to old clothing. The old clothing, a visible example of our sinful actions and selfish life, cannot be mended, but must be replaced with the new cloth of righteous living. We must give up our old traditions and attempts to alter Christ's teachings to better fit our earthly concepts and desires. We must accept the new teachings and ordinances of the restored Gospel of Jesus Christ, unaltered by our own beliefs.

As we accept Gospel truths, growing from grace to grace in faith, obedience and light, we prepare ourselves for a glorious resurrection. Eventually, we all will die and put off the old cloth and worn wineskins of our old carnal imperfect fallen bodies of mortality. Like new cloth and new wineskins in the resurrection, our spiritual, perfected, eternal, and glorified bodies will come forth. The saints will walk in new paths where, "they see as they are seen, and know as they are known, having received of his fulness and grace."[675]

Draw Net

This parable of Matthew comes right after the parable of the Pearl of Great Price. This was a very un-Jewish parable and the Jews did not understand it. It was not based on the prophets or the stories of the Pentateuch. In it, the Lord teaches that the Gospel net draws in all types of people, who are symbolized by fish. After the nets are drawn ashore, the catch is separated, and the bad fish are cast away, referring to the end of the world at Christ's Second Coming.

"Again, the kingdom of heaven is like unto a net, that was cast into the sea, and gathered of every kind: Which, when it was full, they drew to shore, and sat down, and gathered the good into vessels, but cast the bad away. So shall it be at the end of the world: the angels shall come forth, and sever the wicked from among the just, And shall cast them into the furnace of fire: there shall be wailing and gnashing of teeth."[676]

We see here that the reach of the missionary work of the Church is like a great net, gathering in all kinds of people. But to be a member of God's church is not enough. Some are fully converted to Jesus Christ, but others are drawn to it for the sociality, or welfare programs, or their faith is in the missionaries who taught them the Gospel. All of these are a way to start, but all must come fully unto Christ to be saved. When the Savior returns, which is at the end of the world, or the destruction of the wicked, all those who are of the world will be burned, and the wicked will be cast into spirit prison. This separates the just from the unjust. The good fish are gathered and the bad cast away. We should prepare now for the day of our resurrection and the Lord's Second Coming, for this life is the day for men to perform their labor of conversion. Those who wait will incur the wrath of a just God and reap a negative harvest based on the law of restoration.

Invitation to the Wedding Banquet

This parable was given sometime after Christ's triumphant return to Jerusalem and prior to His betrayal and crucifixion. It is a condemnation of the Jews at that time and all those who reject God's invitation through Jesus Christ to come and join the messianic banquet.

"The kingdom of heaven is like unto a certain king, which made a marriage for his son, And sent forth his servants to call them that were bidden to the wedding: and they would not come. Again, he sent forth other servants, saying, Tell them which are bidden, Behold, I have prepared my dinner: my oxen and my fatlings are killed, and all things are ready: come unto the marriage. But they made light of it, and went their ways, one to his farm, another to his merchandise: And the remnant took his servants, and entreated them spitefully, and slew them. But when the king heard thereof, he was wroth: and he sent forth his armies, and destroyed those murderers, and burned up their city. Then saith he to his servants, The wedding is ready, but they which were bidden were not worthy. Go ye therefore into the highways, and as many as ye shall find, bid to the marriage. So those servants went out into the highways, and gathered together all as many as they found, both bad and good: and the wedding was furnished with guests. And when the king came in to see the guests, he saw there a man which had not on a wedding garment: And he saith unto him, Friend, how camest thou in hither not having a wedding garment? And he was speechless. Then said the king to the servants, Bind him hand and foot, and take him away, and cast him into outer darkness; there shall be weeping and gnashing of teeth. For many are called, but few are chosen."[677]

This was given during the passion week, when the conflict between Jesus Christ and the Jewish leaders is growing and will culminate in Jesus Christ's crucifixion. Christ is making abundantly clear that the only way to salvation is through Him. The King is our Father in Heaven. The marriage of His Son is between Christ and the House of Israel. The wedding feast represents the Kingdom of God. God's pre-arranged guest list invites Israel to come to the messianic banquet. But Israel rejects Gods invitation twice and slays His servants the prophets, and His Son! As a result of their rejection, Christ foretells the coming destruction of Jerusalem by Titus and the Roman armies that will occur in 70 A.D. He then sends out His servants to other nations who answer God's call and come to His feast. One comes unprepared, not attired in a wedding garment. God has him bound and cast out into outer darkness, for many are called, but few are chosen.

What does this teach us about the resurrection? The tie to the resurrection is what the parable connotes, for the Kingdom of God is tied directly to the resurrection. It is the eternal abode of His children. God invites all to join Him in His kingdom, which comprises many different glories and types of resurrected bodies. They come and fill the banquet hall and partake of His feast of "fat things." Then one comes who is not prepared, and he seeks to enter God's kingdom without the proper wedding attire. This suggests that all the others have conformed with God's requirements for attending the banquet. "For all who will have a blessing at my hands shall abide the law which was appointed for that blessing, and the conditions thereof, as were instituted from before the foundation of the world."[678] The one unprepared has decided to not follow the prerequisite conditions and is speechless when God holds him accountable. The outcome is disastrous for him. God casts him into outer darkness.

In the day of judgment, some will have refused to repent of their sins, and will remain filthy still.[679] They will be cast out into outer darkness to dwell with Satan, and the spirits that followed him eternally.[680] All must repent who wish to inherit a place in God's kingdom. The sooner we do so, the better off we will be, the quicker will be our spiritual progress, and the greater chance we have of obtaining exaltation in the presence of God. The adage, "don't put off to tomorrow the things you can do today," remains sound advice.

Laborers in the Vineyard

This parable is found only in the Gospel of Matthew. Jesus had just commented on the young man who had riches, and when challenged to sell them and give to the poor, the young man had walked away in sorrow. His shocked disciples, having witnessed this, wondered who could then be saved? Peter upon reflection followed up with this question, "Behold, we have forsaken all, and followed thee; what shall we have therefore?"[681] Jesus explains to Peter the truth about the kingdom of heaven. With God, entrance into His kingdom is possible, but without Him, it is not. All who faithfully labor in the service of God will find salvation—that is their reward.

"For the kingdom of heaven is like unto a man that is an householder, which went out early in the morning to hire labourers into his vineyard. And when he had agreed with the labourers for a penny a day, he sent them into his vineyard. And he went out about the third hour, and saw others standing idle in the marketplace, And said unto them; Go ye also into the vineyard, and whatsoever is right I will give you. And they went their way. Again he went out about the sixth and ninth hour, and did likewise. And about the eleventh hour he went out, and found others standing idle, and saith unto them, Why stand ye here all the day idle? They say unto him, Because no man hath hired us. He saith unto them, Go ye also into the vineyard; and whatsoever is right, that shall ye receive. So when even was come, the lord of the vineyard saith unto his steward, Call the labourers, and give them their hire, beginning from the last unto the first. And when they came that were hired about the eleventh hour, they received every man a penny. But when the first came, they supposed that they should have received more; and they likewise received every man a penny. And when they had received it, they murmured against the goodman of the house, Saying, These last have wrought but one hour, and thou hast made them equal unto us, which have borne the burden and heat of the day. But he answered one of them, and said, Friend, I do thee no wrong: didst not thou agree with me for a penny? Take that thine is, and go thy way: I will give unto this last, even as unto thee. Is it not lawful for me to do what I will with mine own? Is thine eye evil, because I am good? So the last shall be first, and the first last: for many be called, but few chosen."[682]

The householder is Christ. He goes out to the market place at 6:00

in the morning to find laborers to work in His vineyard, which represents the world. He is anxious to start work, for there is much to do. The laborers are His servants, the saints. The Jewish workday was from sunrise to sunset. He offers the first workers one denarius, a Roman soldier's pay for a day, and they went to work. As the day progresses, Christ hires more workers, and though He does not mention the pay, He says, "whatsoever is right I will give you." The harvest ends, and the time comes to pay the laborers what was due them. A surprise occurs, for the last are paid first, and the first are paid last. Christ directs His steward to pay the laborers per this unusual order. The last ones hired for working one hour are given one denarius. The first laborers seeing this expect to be paid more, but when their time comes, they receive the pay they contracted for: one denarius. When they receive it, they murmur against the householder for paying the last laborers the same as they the first received. The householder is forced to defend himself, though he had dealt fairly with them according to their agreement. Many are called, but few are chosen.

In the context of the resurrection, the message is that in the kingdom of God, in this case the highest degree of the celestial kingdom, all will receive the same reward. Through the mercy and grace of Jesus Christ, all saints who prove themselves worthy will receive exaltation. Those who are worthy of this will be made equal in all that God has as joint heirs with Christ.[683] "[T]hen shall they be above all, because all things are subject unto them. Then shall they be gods, because they have all power, and the angels are subject unto them...For strait is the gate, and narrow the way that leadeth unto the exaltation and continuation of the lives, and few there be that find it, because ye receive me not in the world neither do ye know me."[684] What greater gift can there be, and is it not worth all our effort to obtain it? While "few there be that find it," it is available for all to obtain.

God will reward all His children according to His mercy and love, not by the standards the world applies, but by the standards of heaven. Whether we accept the Gospel early, or late, in the Lord's eyes isn't the determining factor. It is that we answer His call and labor faithfully in His vineyard. We are not in a race to beat someone else, or to claim a prize only a few can obtain. God's gifts and blessings are available to all and all who are worthy will become joint-heirs with Christ. We should draw comfort from the fact that there is an abundance, not a scarcity. We should find motivation in the truth that God's mercy and love exhibited in Jesus Christ's Atonement extends to all of us. We all can obtain God's greatest blessings if we will answer His call and labor faithfully in His vineyard. "Behold, doth he cry unto any, saying: Depart from me? Behold, I say unto you, Nay; but he saith: Come unto me all ye ends of the earth, buy milk and honey, without money and without price. Behold, hath he commanded any that they should depart out of the synagogues, or out of the houses of worship? Behold, I say unto you, Nay. Hath he commanded any that they should not partake of his salvation? Behold I say unto you, Nay; but he hath given it free for all men; and he hath commanded his people that they should persuade all men to repentance. Behold, hath the Lord commanded any that they should not partake of his goodness? Behold I say unto you, Nay; but all men are privileged the one like unto the other, and none are forbidden."[685] Have we answered His call? Are we laboring in His vineyard with our might?

Lowest Seat at the Feast

This parable recorded in the Gospel of Luke reflects Christ attending a wedding, and His humbling of those who, when invited to dine at the wedding feast, sought the best seats in the chief rooms. Through it, Christ teaches a universal truth: God will humble the proud and exalt the humble.

"And he put forth a parable to those which were bidden, when he marked how they chose out the chief rooms; saying unto them, When thou art bidden of any man to a wedding, sit not down in the highest room; lest a more honourable man than thou be bidden of him; And he that bade thee and him come and say to thee, Give this man place; and thou begin with shame to take the lowest room. But when thou art bidden, go and sit down in the lowest room; that when he that bade thee cometh, he may say unto thee, Friend, go up higher: then shalt thou have worship in the presence of them that sit at meat with thee. For whosoever exalteth himself shall be abased; and he that humbleth himself shall be exalted."[686]

This parable reflects an attribute of humility that those who desire a glorious resurrection must cultivate. In the parable, there were a number of rooms at the wedding just as there are multiple kingdoms. In it, some assumed to occupy the highest room, while seeking the honor and praise of society. In a similar way, some make a show of seeking their salvation while basking in the praise of others. Christ's admonition is that we need to approach our salvation in humility, not with pride. True humility is not being weak, and it isn't thinking less of yourself. It's not being outwardly humble, while concealing pride. True humility is the willingness to accept direction, coupled with an eagerness to act upon it. Humility often leads to the service of others and is manifest in service to a cause greater than our own personal ambitions. "How can ye believe, [when ye] receive honour one of another, and seek not the honour that cometh from God only?"[687]

Falling prey to pride can happen so easily. I recall as a young man receiving my mission call to serve in England. My bishop asked me to speak in Sacrament meeting just prior to my departure. I thought: here is my chance to show what I know. I outlined a talk about the Second Coming of Jesus Christ and proceeded to present my thoughts. A number of members came up afterwards and thanked me for my thoughts and desire to serve. I left that Sunday thinking I had really done well, and I was pleased with my efforts. Sounds a bit prideful, doesn't it?

A number of years later, I stumbled upon the outline of that talk. As I read it, I was embarrassed by a number of my comments, and realized some of the things I said were incorrect. In reflecting, I realized that those members were probably not so much impressed with my speaking abilities and knowledge, but with the fact that I was willing to serve a mission. I thought about how it must be for our loving Father in Heaven to see us stumble around in a spirit of pride and self-importance when we know so little about the eternities and our potential. We must forever be diligent to humble ourselves for, "Pride goeth before destruction, and an haughty spirit before a fall."[688] Exaltation will not come to the prideful heart, but to the humble soul.

Sheep and the Goats

The parable of the sheep and the goats is part of the Olivet Discourse, and it is a parable of the last days. It is only found in the Gospel of Matthew. At the end of the parable, Jesus Christ speaks about the need to perform charitable acts in behalf of humankind, such as feeding the hungry, clothing the naked, visiting the sick and infirmed, and ministering to those in prison. TThese all are things that the saints should be engaged in while loving their fellowman. For the purpose of the resurrection, we will focus on the eschatological portion of the parable.

"When the Son of man shall come in his glory, and all the holy angels with him, then shall he sit upon the throne of his glory: And before him shall be gathered all nations: and he shall separate them one from another, as a shepherd divideth his sheep from the goats: And he shall set the sheep on his right hand, but the goats on the left. Then shall the King say unto them on his right hand, Come, ye blessed of my Father, inherit the kingdom prepared for you from the foundation of the world."[689]

When Jesus Christ comes in His glory with all the holy angels, He will set up His kingdom for His millennial reign. The gathering of the Nations shifts the parable to the judgment day where He separates humankind with the sheep on His right hand and the goats on His left.

In the day of judgment following the resurrection, all who inherit a kingdom of God will be on God's right hand. The right hand is a symbol of salvation, honor, power, and it is where Christ reigns in majesty and glory. Those found there are likened to sheep, symbolic of God's flock who heard the voice of their shepherd, Christ. These inherit salvation in a kingdom of God. Having repented of all their sins, they are the children of our God and of Christ.

Those on the left hand are the goats. These Jesus Christ is ashamed to own before the Father. Unlike the sheep, they are not God's flock. They hearkened not to the good shepherd and have gone their own way. These will not inherit a kingdom of God, but will be cast off to outer darkness, where Satan and his host reign. Of this it is written, "And the righteous shall be gathered on my right hand unto eternal life; and the wicked on my left hand will I be ashamed to own before the Father; Wherefore I will say unto them—Depart from me, ye cursed, into everlasting fire, prepared for the devil and his angels."[690]

From this we can see that there will come a day of reckoning for all nations and people. Regardless of what happens in the world around us, the wicked will not prevail and righteousness will eventually triumph. The wicked have their moment in the sun, but God's glory shines eternally on the righteous. This paradoxical illusion we see around us will one day be overturned. This eventual triumph of good was emphasized by Isaiah. He was quoted by the Savior to the Nephites in the New World. Jesus said, "Ye have said: It is vain to serve God, and what doth it profit that we have kept his ordinances and that we have walked mournfully before the Lord of Hosts? And now we call the proud happy; yea, they that work wickedness are set up; yea, they that tempt God are even delivered. Then they that feared the Lord spake often one to another, and the Lord hearkened and heard; and a book of remembrance was written before him for them that feared the Lord, and that thought upon his name. And they shall be mine, saith the Lord of Hosts, in that day when I make up my jewels; and I will spare them as a man spareth his own son that serveth him. Then shall ye return and discern between the righteous and the wicked, between him that serveth God and him that serveth him not."[691] The wicked have their day in the sun during mortality, but eventually they will be held accountable for their works. God will fulfill all His promises and purposes, resulting in the eternal life and exaltation of faithful humankind. Having accepted Jesus Christ and exercised faith in Him, we must endure to the end with good works and patience. Our faith in Him will not be in vain.

Talents

The parable of the three servants and the talents is found in the Gospel of Matthew. It can be seen as a warning to His followers about how they are to care for His kingdom once He is gone. There is also a message to humankind about their focus, and how they should deal with God's gifts.

"For the kingdom of heaven is as a man travelling into a far country, who called his own servants, and delivered unto them his goods. And unto one he gave five talents, to another two, and to another one; to every man according to his several ability; and straightway took his journey. Then he that had received the five talents went and traded with the same, and made them other five talents. And likewise he that had received two, he also gained other two. But he that had received one went and digged in the earth, and hid his lord's money. After a long time the lord of those servants cometh, and reckoneth with them. And so he that had received five talents came and brought other five talents, saying, Lord, thou deliveredst unto me five talents: behold, I have gained beside them five talents more. His lord said unto him, Well done, thou good and faithful servant: thou hast been faithful over a few things, I will make thee ruler over many things: enter thou into the joy of thy lord. He also that had received two talents came and said, Lord, thou deliveredst unto me two talents: behold, I have gained two other talents beside them. His lord said unto him, Well done, good and faithful servant; thou hast been faithful over a few things, I will make thee ruler over many things: enter thou into the joy of thy lord. Then he which had received the one talent came and said, Lord, I knew thee that thou art an hard man, reaping where thou hast not sown, and gathering where thou hast not strawed: And I was afraid, and went and hid thy talent in the earth: lo, there thou hast that is thine. His lord answered and said unto him, Thou wicked and slothful servant, thou knewest that

I reap where I sowed not, and gather where I have not strawed: Thou oughtest therefore to have put my money to the exchangers, and then at my coming I should have received mine own with usury. Take therefore the talent from him, and give it unto him which hath ten talents. For unto every one that hath shall be given, and he shall have abundance: but from him that hath not shall be taken away even that which he hath. And cast ye the unprofitable servant into outer darkness: there shall be weeping and gnashing of teeth."[692]

In this parable, the servants are not equal. This is true of us. None in reality are equal to one another in mortality. All have different abilities, talents, opportunities, and resources. Each servant receives a certain number of talents. Biblical scholars tell us a talent is equal to about seventy-five pounds of gold or silver and was their highest monetary measure. The Lord assesses them and gives them a stewardship based on their capacity. The first gets five talents and earns five more. The second gets two talents and earns two more. These two received talents according to their capacity and worked according to each of their abilities, despite their differences. They were equal in their labor, devotion, and faithfulness. The last gets one talent, but he hides it rather than putting it out to earn more. The first two servants are praised for their efforts. The Lord makes them rulers over more, and they enter into the joy of their Lord. The last is condemned for not growing the value of his stewardship. His talent is taken away, and it is given to the one who had ten. The last servant is then cast into outer darkness.

In terms of the resurrection, this parable's message shows that God will reward those that serve Him faithfully, regardless of their different abilities. Both of the faithful servants enter into the Lord's joy, or His kingdom, and are rewarded. God is no respecter of persons, but loves to bless those who serve Him, whatever their capacity is.[693] Those who come under condemnation are they who do nothing with what they are given. They love Him not, they serve Him not, they know Him not. The lack of effort reflects an attitude at best of indifference, and at worst of rebellion and indolence. They know what God wants, but determine they will not do it. Instead of serving God on His terms, they become a law unto themselves. These have no place in the kingdom of God. It is not where we serve, or what positions we hold, but how we serve that will determine our standing before God.

The story of two individual's service to God highlights this concept. A sister had several callings extended to her for service in the Church, but declined each with an excuse justifying her rejection. Later she said she would be willing to accept a calling to perform service in the Primary. After a few months, she came and said she could no longer serve because she found it disagreeable to her needs. She felt any service she performed should be more for her benefit than for others.

Contrast that with a calling extended to another older sister who was asked to serve as Young Women's President. She said she thought she was a little old for those energetic young women, but she would be happy to serve. There was a problem with moral issues among some of the young women at that time, and her experience and ability were needed to help set things right. She went and worked hard and had a significant impact on the moral attitude of those young women. She used her talents to bless those around her rather than focusing on what she might gain, or what she could or could not do.

Two laborers, each blessed with different capacities, talents, and abilities. Each with opportunities to serve God, and others. One focused inwardly and did little to bless those around her. The second abundantly blessed those who she was called to serve. We should ask ourselves, which more reflects our attitude and service in God's kingdom here on earth, "For thus saith the Lord—I, the Lord, am merciful and gracious unto those who fear me, and delight to honor those who serve me in righteousness and in truth unto the end. Great shall be their reward and eternal shall be their glory."[694]

Ten Virgins

This parable in Matthew has been both intriguing and somewhat enigmatic to those studying the Bible. Christ is the bridegroom, the marriage is to His church and its people, the virgins are the saints, the oil is spiritual readiness, and the groom's appearance is the Second Coming of Christ. We read:

"Then shall the kingdom of heaven be likened unto ten virgins, which took their lamps, and went forth to meet the bridegroom. And five of them were wise, and five were foolish. They that were foolish took their lamps, and took no oil with them: But the wise took oil in their vessels with their lamps. While the bridegroom tarried, they all slumbered and slept. And at midnight there was a cry made, Behold, the bridegroom cometh; go ye out to meet him. Then all those virgins arose, and trimmed their lamps. And the foolish said unto the wise, Give us of your oil; for our lamps are gone out. But the wise answered, saying, Not so; lest there be not enough for us and you: but go ye rather to them that sell, and buy for yourselves. And while they went to buy, the bridegroom came; and they that were ready went in with him to the marriage: and the door was shut. Afterward came also the other virgins, saying, Lord, Lord, open to us. But he answered and said, Verily I say unto you, I know you not. Watch therefore, for ye know neither the day nor the hour wherein the Son of man cometh."[695]

Normally, as part of Jewish tradition, the bridegroom, with some close friends, left his home to go to the bride's home where various ceremonies were performed. This was followed by a procession after nightfall through the streets to his home. The festivities, which could last several days, would then begin at the groom's house. The lamps themselves were not torches, but a round receptacle for the oil. This was placed in a deep saucer, which was fastened by a pointed end, or handle, to a long wooden pole and was lifted up.

In considering the resurrection, there are some conclusions one can draw from this parable. The first is that the virgins have been selected to prepare for Christ's eventual appearance. Five have readied themselves and filled their receptacles with oil, but five brought no oil, perhaps assuming they could fill their lamps later from some common vessel containing oil. Inherent within this is the number two. The number two is symbolic of a separation, or division. There are two classes, one prepared, and one not. All are wearing the wedding garments, suggesting they are followers of the Lord. They are anticipating a glorious reunion with Christ, and to join Him upon His return. They know the wedding is coming. They have seen the signs that herald it. It is night, and darkness reigns. Those who have been entrusted to carry the light to meet Him upon His coming soon rest due to His delayed return. The one group who was prepared brought their own oil. They were spiritually prepared to endure to the end of the world, which is the destruction of the wicked, or the return of the bridegroom. The second group had not readied themselves. These found their lights gone out, and they were unprepared to meet Him. When Christ returns, the time has passed to obtain oil, suggesting a sudden appearance. The separation happens. One group is admitted into the banquet, or God's presence. The other group is turned away.

Those who were prepared have hearkened to a celestial spirit. They have not faltered or diminished their spiritual light. Being prepared, they endured all things and are admitted to God's banquet. They will be resurrected based on the spirit they have obeyed. Those who are unprepared find their spiritual light diminished and they are shut out of the wedding. Their resurrection is to a lower kingdom of glory. Where God and Christ dwell, they cannot come. This parable has a message similar to the parable of the Sheep and the Goats, but with more detail. The message is that we need to continue to be prepared before, during, and after the Bridegroom comes, and He is coming soon!

In reflecting about spiritual preparation, an experience I had during my missionary service came to mind. At the end of my mission in England, I, along with another Elder who had entered the mission at the same time, had the opportunity to attend the London Temple on our way back to the United States. We attended a session and became aware of a wonderful elderly couple from Johannesburg, South Africa. They had saved their entire lives to be able to attend the temple, take out their endowment, and be married under priesthood authority for eternity. Being at the temple was the highlight of a long life of service to God. The husband was a postal delivery man and lost his job due to taking needed time off for their trip. He had sold his motor bike, which he used for postal deliveries, to help cover their travel costs. But their sacrifices seemed as nothing to them compared to the blessings of the temple. They were staying in housing at the temple and did not have any funds for needed temple clothing which was also being provided. They were happy, humble, and filled with love. Like the five wise virgins, they had filled their lamps with spiritual readiness, had sacrificed all to help prepare themselves to meet the Bridegroom, and were filled with love and gratitude. They had prepared. Have we?

The Sower

The Parable of the Sower is found in all three synoptic Gospels: Matthew, Mark, and Luke. It is sometimes called the Parable of the Soils. When Christ's disciples heard it, they were unsure what it meant. They later asked the Master, and He replied that, "unto you it is given to know the mysteries of the kingdom of God: but to others in parables; that seeing they might not see, and hearing they might not understand."[696]

A crowd had gathered to hear Jesus speak from "every city," providing an abundance of souls for the Savior to cast His net among. Evidently, they did not come to see the Messiah or to hear the word of God, but rather they came to marvel and see this strange thing in the land. And among them were the Pharisees and Sadducees, His chief detractors. Hence, He spoke to them in a parable, "that seeing them might not see, and hearing they might not understand." When they heard this, the Jewish leaders would have understood that He was paraphrasing Isaiah. What he did not say to them, but implied by that, was that they were spiritually unable to receive Him and would not.[697] This enflamed their antagonism. Jesus later goes on to give His disciples the interpretation of the parable because their hearts were open to His teachings.

"A sower went out to sow his seed: and as he sowed, some fell by the way side; and it was trodden down, and the fowls of the air devoured it. And some fell upon a rock; and as soon as it was sprung up, it withered away, because it lacked moisture. And some fell among thorns; and the thorns sprang up with it, and choked it. And other fell on good ground, and sprang up, and bare fruit an hundredfold. And when he had said these things, he cried, He that hath ears to hear, let him hear."[698]

The Lord then follows with an interpretation for His disciples. "The seed is the word of God. Those by the way side are they that hear; then cometh the devil, and taketh away the word out of their hearts, lest they should believe and be saved. They on the rock are they, which, when they hear, receive the word with joy; and these have no root, which for a while believe, and in time of temptation fall away. And that which fell among thorns are they, which, when they have heard, go forth, and are choked with cares and riches and pleasures of this life, and bring no fruit to perfection. But that on the good ground are they, which in an honest and good heart, having heard the word, keep it, and bring forth fruit with patience."[699]

The seed, as mentioned, is the word of God or the Gospel. Then He explains that with some, the devil comes along and takes the word, or Gospel, from them. It has no place in their hearts or lives, an indication that Satan claims them as his, and they become part of his kingdom and inherit outer darkness. They do not believe in Christ, and hence cannot be saved since salvation only comes through Him. These are the Sons of Perdition.

We next see a group whose seeds fall upon the rocks. The soil is deep enough for them to take root, but as the scorching sun of life shines upon them they wither and "fall away" indicating a failure to endure to the end. These can be likened to those who inherit the telestial kingdom of God. They bring forth no fruit but follow their own hearts.

Then the Lord indicates that the next group are those that are overcome by the cares and pleasures of life. The Gospel seed comes into their lives, but as it springs up the weeds of temptation and the world chokes out the truth, leaving them spiritually immature and uncommitted. They "bring no fruit to perfection." It is not enough to just bring forth fruit; the fruit must be brought forth in perfection. The fruit they fail to bring forth is to become spiritually mature, to be sanctified through the Atonement of Jesus Christ, and to inherit celestial glory. They fail to become this perfect fruit. These can be likened to those who will inherit the terrestrial kingdom. They are the good men of the earth, but they are not valiant in their testimony of Christ.

The Lord then describes a fourth group. They are found in the good soil of the Gospel. These which, "In an honest and good heart, having heard the word, keep it, and bring forth fruit with patience." In their diligence and patience, they become spiritually mature, are sanctified, and endure to the end. They bring forth the fruit to perfection that is most desirable. They inherit eternal life with God in the celestial kingdom.

This parable is rich in its allusion to the three degrees of glory and the kingdom of the devil. These are the eventual rewards for humankind following their resurrection and judgment. It shows the importance of the Gospel in each of our lives and the need to fully embrace it. It demonstrates that the process of patiently working out our salvation can result in the fruit of perfection.

Every day, the message of the restored Gospel of Jesus Christ touches someone's life. A number of years ago, a couple I knew became interested in learning more about the Gospel of Jesus Christ. They joyfully listened to the missionaries, and they contemplated being baptized and committing their lives more fully to Jesus Christ. We were thrilled with their progress as we watched the seed of the Gospel spring up and begin to grow. Then we came to the discussion of tithes and offerings. They were troubled that they would be asked to help build the kingdom of God by donating funds to the Church. We talked about where the monies went, why they were needed, and how this would call down the blessings of heaven. They grew distant and became hard to contact. Finally, we met and they said they were unwilling to support their budding faith with a financial commitment. We were saddened, and we thought how they were like the seeds that fell upon the rocks and had withered because they had no root when the first test of their faith came. Where have the seeds of the Gospel fallen in our lives? Have they taken root? What are they bringing forth as a harvest?

Unjust Steward/Manager

The parable of the Unjust Steward (Manager) has been a challenge to understand for many. It is a parable Jesus taught His disciples about a manager who was about to be fired, but who gained favor with his master's debtors by discounting what was owed. To gain insight into what the Lord was trying to teach His disciples, I think it helps to turn to the Amplified version of the Bible.

"Now Jesus was also saying to the disciples, "There was a certain rich man who had a manager [of his estate], and accusations [against this man] were brought to him, that this man was squandering his [master's] possessions. So he called him and said to him, 'What is this I hear about you? Give an accounting of your management [of my affairs], for you can no longer be [my] manager.' The manager [of the estate] said to himself, 'What will I do, since my master is taking the management away from me? I am not strong enough to dig [for a living], and I am ashamed to beg. I know what I will do, so that when I am removed from the management, people [who are my master's debtors] will welcome me into their homes.' So he summoned his master's debtors one by one, and he said to the first, 'How much do you owe my master?' He said, 'A hundred [a]measures of [olive] oil.' And he said to him, 'Take your bill, and sit down quickly and write [b]fifty.' Then he said to another, 'And how much do you owe?' He said, 'A hundred [c]measures of wheat.' He said to him, 'Take your bill, and write eighty.' And his master commended the unjust manager [not for his misdeeds, but] because he had acted shrewdly [by preparing for his future unemployment]; for the sons of this age [the non-believers] are shrewder in relation to their own kind [that is, to the ways of the secular world] than are the sons of light [the believers]. And I tell you [learn from this], make friends for yourselves [for eternity] by means of the wealth of unrighteousness [that is, use material resources as a way to further the work of God], so that when it runs out, they will welcome you into the eternal dwellings. "He who is faithful in a very little thing is also faithful in much; and he who is dishonest in a very little thing is also dishonest in much. Therefore if you have not been faithful in the use of earthly wealth, who will entrust the true riches to you? And if you have not been faithful in the use of that [earthly wealth] which belongs to another [whether God, or man, and of which you are a trustee], who will give you that which is your own? No servant can serve two masters; for either he will hate the one and love the other, or he will stand devotedly by the one and despise the other. You cannot serve both God and mammon [that is, your earthly possessions, or anything else you trust in and rely on instead of God]."[700]

The Lord first places the setting in the world as we know it. A manager is unfaithful in fulfilling his role over his master's estate. Realizing that he is about to be fired, he mourns over his lack of opportunities for future work. He then decides that he can secure help from his master's debtors by discounting what they owe. The Savior then observes that those businessmen of the world are shrewder in their relationships with one another than the saints. He then changes the setting and goes on to say that we need to use our resources to further the kingdom of God, so that when those resources run out, or when life is over, we will be welcome in God's kingdom. If we cannot be faithful over the use of the world's riches, how will God be able to entrust us with the riches of eternity? If we cannot be faithful in the use of others' wealth, who will entrust us with anything of value? We cannot serve both God and the world.

By drawing a parallel with the world around us, the Lord is teaching us what we need to focus on: the kingdom of God. We need to use the resources we obtain in this life, which are in reality not our own, to further the work of salvation. By doing so, one puts themselves in a position to obtain the riches of eternity, or a celestial resurrection. If we cannot be faithful in using the world's wealth for God's work, which in its entirety won't buy a crust of bread in the celestial kingdom, how can we be trusted to share in all that God has, and dwell with Him to enjoy the true riches of eternity? "For how knoweth a man the master whom he has not served, and who is a stranger unto him, and is far from the thoughts and intents of his heart?"[701] The Pharisees' reaction to the Savior's message was to deride and scorn the Lord for His foolishness, for they were covetous.[702]

This parable should inspire us to reflect on our daily walk in life. Where are our priorities, and what are our hearts focused on? How are we using our time, talents, and resources to further the work of salvation? Do we focus mainly on our careers, societies lure of fame, the pleasures of this world, or how to make more money, like the Pharisees who scorned our Lord? Do we have a good balance between God, our family, and work, with a Christ-centered life? If yes, keep it up. If not, what do we need to change?

In considering a Christ-centered life, I thought of a high priest in our ward who had struggled with thyroid cancer for a number of decades. He honorable served in the Navy on a nuclear powered ship. His office was above the reactor as I remember. His wife had divorced him, and he had left the Navy to raise his children as a single father. Now his kids were grown and he was often alone. He had trouble walking even with a cane, and he no longer could drive since his eyesight was now impaired. His cancer medicines had become ineffective in halting the spread of his cancer. Yet he had a gregarious personality and a warm handshake. When you went to pick him up, he would greet you with a big smile and say, "Freddie is ready!" He never complained about his circumstances or his pain. Despite his difficulties, his priority was the Gospel and his service in the Church. He would often make copies of music, Church articles, or talks that he thought would benefit someone. "This one's a goodie," he would say and then give it to them. When asked how he was doing, he often replied, "God has been good to me."

One day, Freddie failed to answer his phone and a friend came to check on him. He was lying on the floor where he had fallen. An ambulance was called, and he was rushed to the hospital where he died of a heart attack. He lived a Christ-centered life despite his difficulties, and left a hole in everyone's heart who knew him. Freddie was indeed ready for the eternities; are we?

Wheat and Weeds

This parable found in the Gospel of Matthew is one of the few where we have a record of Christ's explanation to His disciples. It has similarities to the parable of the Wheat and the Tares, but it seems to have a different focus.

"Another parable put he forth unto them, saying, The kingdom of heaven is likened unto a man which sowed good seed in his field: But while men slept, his enemy came and sowed tares among the wheat, and went his way. But when the blade was sprung up, and brought forth fruit, then appeared the tares also. So the servants of the householder came and said unto him, Sir, didst not thou sow good seed in thy field? from whence then hath it tares? He said unto them, An enemy hath done this. The servants said unto him, Wilt thou then that we go and gather them up? But he said, Nay; lest while ye gather up the tares, ye root up also the wheat with them. Let both grow together until the harvest: and in the time of harvest I will say to the reapers, Gather ye together first the tares, and bind them in bundles to burn them: but gather the wheat into my barn."[703]

He followed this parable with an explanation to his disciples. "Then Jesus sent the multitude away, and went into the house: and his disciples came unto him, saying, Declare unto us the parable of the tares of the field. He answered and said unto them, He that soweth the good seed is the Son of man; The field is the world; the good seed are the children of the kingdom; but the tares are the children of the wicked one; The enemy that sowed them is the devil; the harvest is the end of the world; and the reapers are the angels. As therefore the tares are gathered and burned in the fire; so shall it be in the end of this world. The Son of man shall send forth his angels, and they shall gather out of his kingdom all things that offend, and them which do iniquity; And shall cast them into a furnace of fire: there shall be wailing and gnashing of teeth. Then shall the righteous shine forth as the sun in the kingdom of their Father. Who hath ears to hear, let him hear."[704]

This parable teaches that until the Second Coming of Christ, the wicked will be allowed to grow along with the righteous. They grow right next to them, not across from them or separated from them, but so close that their roots intertwine. This is the condition of our world today: the wicked are seemingly intertwined with the righteous. The parable also teaches us that it will not always be so, for at Christ's Second Coming, the destruction of the wicked, or end of the world, will occur.[705]

As the Lord taught Joseph Smith, "For the hour is nigh and the day soon at hand when the earth is ripe; and all the proud and they that do wickedly shall be as stubble; and I will burn them up, saith the Lord of Hosts, that wickedness shall not be upon the earth."[706] These will be cast into spirit prison to await the second resurrection and the judgment at the end of the world. There among them will be weeping, and wailing, and gnashing of teeth as they reflect on what awaits them. But the righteous will arise, be crowned with glory, and shine forth as the sun in a glorious resurrection.

We may ask, in what way are we intertwined with the wicked? What unrighteous influences do we find in our homes or our lives? How can we remove those influences and keep them from choking and uprooting us? I asked myself this question. Recently, I went to see a PG-13 movie which was well made and impressively directed. It was filled with sci-fi violence, and the plot was woven around a being who had unusual powers—almost godlike. In one scene, after defeating an enemy, they came down from the heavens with light streaming from them. I thought: what am I doing here? I do not subscribe to violence, nor can I fathom believing in an imaginary superhuman and their ability to save us. In a simple way, the roots of the tares were trying to intertwine with my Gospel-based faith of the one divine being to walk this earth, Jesus Christ. The movie scenes robbed me of the peace, joy, and tranquility I valued. Perhaps some would see this as a small thing, but the feelings that were engendered by that movie where not positive, nor did they draw me closer to our Heavenly Father. Out of small things proceeds that which is great, both for good and evil.

Summary

Although the parables couch eternal truths in stories and do not represent the simplicity with which the Savior taught the Gospel in the early days of His ministry, there still are truths to be learned from them in relationship to the resurrection.

From the parable of the Cloth and Wineskin, we learn that we must be careful of the outside doctrines and embrace the Gospel of Jesus Christ in simplicity. We must walk in a newness of life to be worthy of a glorious resurrection. In the Draw Net, we see that the Gospel net pulls in a variety of people. But it is not enough to just become a member. Failure to be truly converted will result in one becoming separated from the righteous and reaping disaster in the resurrection. The Invitation to the Wedding Banquet teaches us that all are invited to the Lord's banquet, but we must fully live the Gospel and repent if we would hope to enter into God's kingdom in the resurrection. The parable of the Laborers shows us that God rewards His children in mercy and love. In the Lord's eyes, whether we accept the Gospel early or late isn't the determining factor, rather it is that we answer His call and labor in His vineyard, which will impact our ability to obtain a glorious resurrection. The Lowest Seat at the Feast demonstrates that in the resurrection, exaltation will not come to the prideful heart, but to the humble soul. We must always watch for the sin of pride in our lives.

In the Sheep and the Goats, we learn there will come a day of reckoning for all nations and peoples at the resurrection. Regardless of what happens in the world around us, the wicked will not prevail and righteousness will triumph. The Parable of the Talents teaches us that in the resurrection, God will reward those who serve Him faithfully, regardless of their different abilities, a concept that should give us all hope. The parable of the Sower is rich in its allusion to the three degrees of glory and the kingdom of the devil, which are the eventual rewards of humankind. It shows the importance of the Gospel in each of our lives, and the need to fully embrace it. We learn that the process of patiently working out our salvation can result in the fruit of perfection in the resurrection. The Parable of the Ten Virgins demonstrates the message that we need to continue to be prepared before, during, and after the bridegroom comes. The oil of spiritual readiness is essential to our salvation. With the Unjust Steward/Manager, the Lord draws a parallel to the world around us in teaching us that we need to focus on the kingdom of God. We need to use the resources we obtain in this life, which are in reality not our own, to further the work of salvation if we would obtain our desires in the resurrection. It should cause us to reflect on our lives and help us find ways to increase our commitment to Christ. The Wheat and the Weeds parable illustrates the reality that until the Second Coming of Christ, the wicked will be allowed to grow alongside the righteous: but at Christ's coming, they will be burned, and in the day of judgment, the wicked will be cast off.

Each of the truths found in these parables can help us in our process of becoming more like our Savior and Redeemer and preparing for Christ's Second Coming. He is coming soon. Preparation proceeds power, the power to come forth in the First Resurrection clothed with glory, immortality, and eternal life.

CHAPTER 15

CONCLUSION

*There is no excellence in all the world which
can be separated from right living.*

~ David Starr Jordan

ALL TRUTH IS not of equal value. The most important knowledge comes from God and leads to our eternal salvation and exaltation. Thus, the search for understanding and insight into the resurrection is of inestimable value. During your search, what type of reader have you been: the sponge, funnel, strainer, or sieve? If the sieve, what precious Gospel flour have you garnered and what will you make of it? Does it give you hope or comfort, or does it provide a catalyst for action by helping you to comprehend your divine potential? God does not want a people who simply know the truth. He wants a people that through living it have become what the truth engenders. In the end, when we all stand at the judgment day, it won't be so much about what we have learned, but what we have become. The more we have become like Christ, the greater the reality is that we will obtain eternal life and exaltation. All have this potential to experience the joy and wonder of eternity in the celestial kingdom of God with their families.

We are all at different points in our efforts to obtain exaltation. Despite our past success or failure in becoming more like Christ, the fact that today finds us on the path headed towards eternal life is the key. If followed, this process of growing line upon line and going from one grace to another, will eventually lead us to realize our divine potential and become joint heirs with Christ. We will adore God and Christ, and be filled with their light, love, and glory eternally. We have the ability and opportunity to accomplish this through the loving grace of our Savior, Jesus Christ. He has already suffered for all the sins of humankind and the debt of justice is paid for all who have faith in Him and repent. Nothing we do will add to, or take away from, that reality. What matters is whether we will take advantage of the opportunity that His Atonement provides.

I recall a family member saying to me that the Gospel was "one hat that fits all" approach to humanity. The reality of the Gospel is that God's expansive "hat" blesses all His children with the desires of their hearts. It has been so from the beginning. We all will ultimately decide our own fates and receive a reward according to our desires. Some will desire more and obtain all that God has for those who love and follow Him. Others will fall short. It is my hope that the truths contained within this book will help all of us understand and gain our eternal exaltation and all that God has in store for those that love and follow Him.

Remember what Jacob taught his brethren: "Therefore, cheer up your hearts, and remember that ye are free to act for yourselves—to choose the way of everlasting death, or the way of eternal life. Wherefore, my beloved brethren, reconcile yourselves to the will of God, and not to the will of the devil and the flesh; and remember, after ye are reconciled unto God, that it is only in and through the grace of God that ye are saved. Wherefore, may God raise you from death by the power of the resurrection, and also from everlasting death by the power of the atonement, that ye may be received into the eternal kingdom of God, that ye may praise him through grace divine."[707] Let us all press forward trusting in Christ, and one day we will rejoice together in the highest degree of the celestial kingdom of God with our Lord and Savior, having obtained the pearl of great price, our exaltation. For we can do all things through Jesus Christ who strengthens us.

About the Author

Steven P. Garrett is a member of the Church of Jesus Christ of Latter-day Saints and has spent many years studying and writing about the resurrection. He makes his home in Washington State with his wife, has four children, enjoys gardening when it is not raining, and painting when it is.

The genesis of this book began with the premature death of his beloved sister and his experiences presiding over more than a dozen funerals. Despite a wealth of information available about the resurrection no one source existed that encapsulated or fully discussed it. This in turn led to his writing THE HOLY RESURRECTION ARISING IN GLORY. More information can be found at his website, theholyresurrectionarisinginglory.com.

Endnotes

The Purpose of this Book

1   The IH Monogram includes the Greek letters iota (I) and eta (H or η), which are the first two letters of the word Jesus in Greek "Ιησους" pronounced (yay–soos) or Yehoshua saves, and was a shorthand for His name.

2   *TPJS*, 296.

3   *TPJS*, 324.

4   D&C 93:33.

Chapter 1

5   Abraham 3:18.

6   D&C 29:27–28.

7   See headings: Eternal Progression and Celestial Offspring.

8   Moses 1:39.

9   D&C 14:7.

10   Matthew 13:45–46.

11   D&C 6:13.

12   1 Thessalonians 5:9.

13   In D&C 76:96–98 it speaks of these three kingdoms as all being kingdoms of glory and part of God's realm.

14   D&C 76:88, 138:57–59.

15   See heading: Celestial Offspring.

16   For example: Romans 1:16; Ephesians 1:13; Philippians 2:12; 1 Thessalonians 5:9; 2 Timothy 2:10; Hebrews 5:9; D&C 6:3, 11:3, 27:18; Mosiah 4:6–7; Alma 26:36; 3 Nephi 18:32; etc.

17   See heading: The Resurrection Help Us Know God.

18   Alma 11:45.

19   Alma 11:43–44; 2 Nephi 9:12.

20   Exodus 23:14–16.

21   1 Corinthians 15:20.

22   2 Nephi 2:8–9.

23   James 1:18.

24   Jacob 4:11.

25   D&C 84:102.

26   See heading: Numbers.

27   Helaman 14:17.

28   Alma 41:3–4.

29   Alma 41:2.

30   D&C 88:22–24.

31   D&C 130:18.

32   2 Nephi 9:13.

33   Alma 41:15.

34   For example: John 14:15, 15:10; 1 John 5:3; 1 Nephi 15:25; Mosiah 2:22; D&C 29:3, 82:7, etc.

35   Matthew 5:48.

36   1 John 1:10.

37   Ephesians 2:8.

38   3 Nephi 12:48.

39   *Liber XXIV Philosophorum*, II.

40   D&C 130:22.

41   Hebrews 12:29; Joseph Smith declared, "God Almighty Himself dwells in eternal fire; flesh and blood cannot go there, for all corruption is devoured by the fire." *TPJS*, 367.

42   D&C 20:17–18.

43   *TPJS*, 345–346.

44   *TPJS*, 347.

45   Psalm 30:5.

46   See heading: The Resurrection and Receiving a Fullness of Joy.

47   Alma 21:9.

48   Mosiah 16:6–7.

49   This is what the righteous anticipated while awaiting Christ's appearance in the Spirit World following His death. See D&C 138:16–17.

50   D&C 29:36–37.

51   2 Nephi 9:8–9.

52   D&C 45:17, 138:50.

53   D&C 93:33–34.

54   Alma 11:37; See also: Ephesians 5:5.

55   This is the fate of the Sons of Perdition who have rejected Christ and His Atonement, although they will briefly return to God for judgement. See D&C 76:41–44.

56   As John the Revelator proclaimed, "And God shall wipe away all tears from their eyes; and there shall be no more death, neither sorrow, nor crying, neither shall there be any more pain: for the former things are passed away." Revelation 21:4.

57   Parley P. Pratt, *Key to the Science of Theology*, 60.

58   D&C 76:8.

59   In part this joy is what the Lamanites experienced, while Nephi and Lehi were in their midst, and they were surrounded by pillars of fire after repenting. The Book of Mormon records, "and they were filled with that joy

which is unspeakable and full of glory." Helaman 5:44.

60   See heading: Numbers.

61   Abraham 3:22–23; Abraham is shown the spirits of humankind before the world was.

62   D&C 131:7-8.

63   Revelation 12:7-9. Abraham describes the effect of rebellion while in our pre-earth life in terms of humankind's estates of existence. See Abraham 3:26–28.

64   Alma 12:24, 34:32.

65   Mosiah 16:10; Alma 5:15.

66   For those born after the Millennium begins, death and the resurrection occur simultaneously. They pass from their second estate without re-entering the spirit world and leaving their bodies in the grave, and they immediately begin their third estate of immortal existence in eternity. See D&C 63:51. Some have suggested that since during the Millennium people are changed in the twinkling of an eye, that death no longer exists. But that is not what the scriptures teach. Also, that view narrowly defines death by our current standards. They cite D&C 101:29, which says, "And there shall be no sorrow because there is no death," but that clearly has to do with pre-mature death as referred to in verse 30 of that section which says, "In that day an infant shall not die until he is old; and his life shall be as the age of a tree." Verse 31 goes on to say that during the Millennium, "when he dies he shall not sleep, that is to say in the earth, but shall be changed in the twinkling of an eye, and shall be caught up, and his rest shall be glorious." In other words, in the Millennium when one dies they will not suffer burial, or the sorrows that accompany death. They will simultaneously die and leave their mortal state by being resurrected. But that change of leaving behind mortality, or dying and being resurrected, happens in a twinkling of an eye.

67   Alma 11:45.

68   Mosiah 16:10.

69   D&C 88:15.

70   D&C 88:16.

71   John 11:41–44.

72   John 4:46–51.

73   1 Kings 17:20–22.

74   3 Nephi 28:36–40.

75   *JST* Genesis 14:32.

76   For example: Hebrews 11:5; Moses 7:21; *JST* Genesis 14:34; 2 Kings 2:11; D&C 7:1–6.

77   *TPJS*, 170–171.

Chapter 2

78   Alma 12:12, 41:4; Mosiah 16:10; Alma 5:15, 40:2, 41:4; 3 Nephi 28:8.

79   1 Corinthians 15:42; 2 Nephi 9:7; Mosiah 16:10; Alma 5:15, 40:2, 41:4.

80   1 Corinthians 15:44; Alma 11:45; D&C 88:27.

81   Mosiah 15:22, 18:9; Revelation 20:5–6.

82   D&C 76:85.

83   Matthew 27:52; Helaman 14:25; D&C 29:26.

84   Alma 13:29; D&C 9:14.

85   Matthew 28:7; 2 Nephi 26:1; D&C 18:12.

86   Philippians 3:21; D&C 138:14.

Chapter 3

87   Alma 38:9.

88   Mosiah 5:7.

89   D&C 93:21.

90   Ether 3:14.

91   John 1:1.

92 Mosiah 18:2.

93 Matthew 28:18.

94 Revelation 1:18.

95 Isaiah 14:16–17.

96 Korihor is an good example of Satan's ultimate lack of support. See Alma 30:58–60.

97 Mosiah 3:17.

98 2 Nephi 9:13.

99 Luke 24:10–11, 38–39; John 20:25.

100 Isaiah 9:2.

101 2 Nephi 2:19; Genesis 3:23–24.

102 2 Nephi 9:6.

103 Helaman 14:16–17.

104 Mormon 9:14.

105 Alma 7:11–13.

106 Helaman 14:18.

107 D&C 19:16–17.

108 D&C 138:59.

109 Helaman 14:18.

110 D&C 88:33 .

111 See heading: Sons of Perdition Resurrection Timing and Nature.

112 John 5:8.

113 John 5:14.

114 John 5:5.

115 Luke 7:12–15.

116 Luke 17:12–14.

117 Matthew 9:20–22.

118 The clearest illustration in the New Testament of how the doctrine of

works and grace are intertwined was given by Jesus Christ during His mortal ministry. In the metaphor of the vine and branches, Christ teaches that He is the vine and that without Him, humankind (the branches), cannot bear fruit or do anything. In nature the branches must abide in the vine otherwise they wither and die. They cannot bring forth fruit without the vine. Similarly, our spiritual nourishment comes through the grace of Christ. Christ's grace provides the means or spiritual strength for us to bring forth fruit. We must abide in Him otherwise we wither and die spiritually. See John 15:1–8.

119   Mark 10:21–22.

120   Mark 10:26–27.

121   Moses 7:59.

122   Mosiah 2:21.

123   James 2:26.

124   Moroni 10:32.

125   D&C 88:34.

126   D&C 93:11–12, 20.

127   Moroni 7:47–48.

128   D&C 20:30–31.

129   Alma 27:28

Chapter 4

130   Alma 12:25.

131   Ezekiel 37:12–13; See also: Job 19:26; Daniel 12:2.

132   2 Nephi 2:8.

133   Mark 12:18.

134   Acts 23:8.

135   See Alfred Edersheim, *The Life and Times of Jesus The Messiah*, 749.

136   See the *Apocrypha* 2 Maccabees 1:24–29, where parts of the eighteen blessings are rehearsed in a prayer offered by Neemias and the priests to God.

137   David Instone-Brewer, "The Eighteen Benedictions and the Minim before 70 CE," *The Journal of Theological Studies* 54, no. 1, 25–44.

138   John 11:25.

139   D&C 138:15–17.

140   Abraham 3:22–23.

141   John 1:3–4.

142   Ether 3:14.

143   2 Timothy 3:16.

144   Ephesians 4:11–12.

145   D&C 84:20. To say it another way, God's power to exalt others is manifest in His ordinances.

146   D&C 88:34; See also: Helaman 3:35 where the Nephites' hearts were sanctified, "because of their yielding their hearts unto God."

147   Moroni 10:5.

148   http://www.theharrispoll.com/in-the-news/harris-polls/Americas-Belief-in-God.html.

149   http://www.religionnewsblog.com/14273/most-Americans-don't-believe-in-the-resurrection.

150   http://www.bbc.com/news/uk-england-39153121.

151   Proverbs 1:7.

152   2 Nephi 2:27.

Chapter 5

153   D&C 76:96–98.

154   D&C 76:16–17.

155   D&C 76:85. See also: D&C 63:17–18.

156   D&C 76:64.

157   D&C 45:54. See also: Mosiah 15:24.

158   D&C 76:71–72.

159 D&C 76:51–53, 69. Also see heading: Celestial Resurrection Timing and Nature.

160 D&C 76:72–75, 79. Also see heading: Terrestrial Resurrection Timing and Nature.

161 See D&C 76:17 for the resurrection of the Just, and John 5:29 for the resurrection of Damnation.

162 D&C 88:102.

163 D&C 76:100–101, 110. See also: Telestial Resurrection Timing and Nature.

164 See heading: Sons of Perdition Resurrection Timing and Nature.

165 Alma 40:11–13.

166 *DS*, vol. 2, 229–230.

167 Alma 11:45.

168 D&C 76:70–71,81.

169 Mormon 9:3–5.

170 See heading: Resurrection a Type of Judgement.

171 Orson Pratt, *The Seer*, 274.

172 D&C 76:112.

173 D&C 88:22.

174 See: Bruce R. McConkie, "The Seven Deadly Heresies," *Classic Speeches*, 175. See also: *The Teachings of Spencer W. Kimball*, 49; Melvin J. Ballard, *The Three Degrees of Glory*, 35–36; George Albert Smith, "Semi-Annual Conference Report" (October 1945), 172.

175 Alma 3:27.

176 D&C 1:36, 43:29, 88:92.

177 Mormon 3:20.

178 D&C 38:5.

179 Revelation 20:11.

180 Revelation 20:12.

181 Revelation 3:5. The scriptures often refer to those who gain exaltation as being written in the book of life. See D&C 132:19; Revelation 21:27.

182 Alma 5:57.

183 See heading: Sons of Perdition Timing and Nature.

184 Revelation 20:14-15. See also: Revelation 13:8 where those who worship the Beast, or the devil, are not written in the book of life.

185 D&C 128:7.

186 D&C 88:2.

187 Alma 11:37; See also: Alma 42:24; Helaman 8:25.

188 Mormon addresses the need to repent to inherit any of God's kingdoms when he speaks of those who repent as being saved, while there will be others who are cast out from God's presence, implying the latter do not repent. The former having done good receive everlasting life and the latter having done evil receiving everlasting damnation. Mormon uses these two situations to signify a separation between those who are part of God's realm and inherit a kingdom of glory versus those who are cast off from God's presence to become part of Satan's realm and inherit everlasting damnation, Helaman 12:23–26. Likewise Nephi speaks of the need for those who belong to the kingdom of the devil to be stirred up to repentance or the devil will grasp them in his everlasting chains. Showing that the unrepentant sinner belongs to Satan's kingdom, 2 Nephi 28:19, 23. Also see heading: Sons of Perdition Resurrection Timing and Nature.

189 Alma 41:11.

190 1 Samuel 16:7.

191 Alma 41:13.

192 Melvin J. Ballard, "*The Three Degrees of Glory,*" 15.

193 2 Nephi 25:23.

194 Joshua 24:15.

195 D&C 138:51.

196 *JD* 15:137.

197 *JD* 15:139.

198 See heading: Terrestrial Resurrection Timing and Nature.

199 See heading: Telestial Resurrection Timing and Nature.

200 Wilford Woodruff, "Obtaining the Spirit of God," *Millennial Star*, vol. 67, no. 39, 612.

201 The Book of Mormon prophets often speak of the fact that we need to repent in this life, or we will reap damnation. They do this emphasizing that when we reach the judgment day, and we have remained in our same wicked state—terrible will be our fate. This stresses the urgency to repent and improve now versus at a later date. They do not address the time between death and the resurrection, and a person's ability to change within that intervening period. For example, we read, "And now, as I said unto you before, as ye have had so many witnesses, therefore, I beseech of you that ye do not procrastinate the day of your repentance until the end; for after this day of life, which is given us to prepare for eternity, behold, if we do not improve our time while in this life, then cometh the night of darkness wherein there can be no labor performed. Ye cannot say, when ye are brought to that awful crisis, that I will repent, that I will return to my God. Nay, ye cannot say this; for that same spirit which doth possess your bodies at the time that ye go out of this life, that same spirit will have power to possess your body in that eternal world," Alma 34:33–34. Here, Amulek infers that our final state will reflect our attitude when we leave this life. He describes the spirit world as a, "night of darkness wherein can no labor be performed."

Certainly, contained in this scripture is the message to repent now, do not delay, or you may find eternal damnation your reward. A fitting warning from a Prophet to all people. Prior to the Savior's mission to the Spirit World, there were two realms in the spirit world with no movement between them: paradise for the righteous, and spirit prison for everyone else who died. Missionary work at that time was not going on in spirit prison, nor a call to repent. It was indeed a night of darkness for the wicked spirits wherein no labor could be performed. Later Alma in speaking of these two realms said, "Now this is the state of the souls of the wicked, yea, in darkness, and a state of awful, fearful looking for the fiery indignation of the wrath of God upon them; thus they remain in this state, as well as the righteous in paradise, until the time of their resurrection," Alma 40:14. Alma and Amulek's statements fit the spirit worlds conditions at that time. Later, after Christ's death, while in the spirit world, He bridged the gap between these two realms as His body lay in a tomb. Missionaries now could visit those in spirit prison and proclaimed the Gospel of repentance to them, D&C 138: 36–37. We know people can repent in the spirit world and are taught that in the scriptures, D&C 138:30–34. Alma and Amulek's words are a clear call to repent now for this is the time to prepare to meet God. It is also a warning that how we feel when we leave this life will be how we feel when entering the spirit world. But it does not mean that how we leave this life seals our eternal fate. An indicator, yes; a certainty, no.

202   See 2 Nephi 26:25–27; D&C 133:67.

203   D&C 138:30–34.

204   2 Nephi 9:13.

205   D&C 130:18.

206   Neal A. Maxwell, "*The Promise of Discipleship*," 100.

207   3 Nephi 18:32.

208   D&C 130:18–19.

209   Joseph F. Smith, *Gospel Doctrine*, 58.

210   Bruce R. McConkie taught the truth that God progresses as His kingdoms increase and His dominions multiply, not in the sense that he learns new truths and laws. He knows all things and has all power," Bruce R. McConkie, "The Seven Deadly Heresies".

211   *TPJS*, 347–348. The covenant God made with Abraham that his seed should continue both in and out of the world, and would be as innumerable as the stars, is a continuation of the works of God, "wherein he glorifieth himself," D&C 132:30–31.

212   We are told that, "The glory of God is intelligence, or, in other words, light and truth," D&C 93:36. The Lord's glory not only comprises intelligence and truth but light itself. Glory is a physical substance that pervades all things and manifests itself in the form of light. We are told that Christ, "ascended up on high, as also he descended below all things, in that he comprehended all things, that he might be in all and through all things, the light of truth; Which truth shineth. This is the light of Christ," D&C 88:6-7. Likewise, as

we increase in intelligence and truth we increase in glory or light for, "That which is of God is light; and he that receiveth light, and continueth in God, receiveth more light; and that light groweth brighter and brighter until the perfect day," D&C 50:24. As we progress in glory or light we become more like our Lord whose glory the sun is written as being typical of, D&C 76:70.

213   Abraham 3:26.

214   D&C 88:60; See also: John 15:8; Moses 1:39.

215   See heading: Celestial Offspring.

216   D&C 19:7, 10–11.

217   D&C 76:44. There was an ancient belief that a worm burrowed into one's tooth and its turning and twisting caused a toothache. When it rested or died, the toothache stopped. A worm that did not die would mean unending anguish. In a similar vein, an unquenched fire would mean unending guilt and sorrow.

218   Abraham 3:26.

219   D&C 58:29.

220   D&C 84:74.

221   D&C 132:6.

222   D&C 132:25.

Chapter 6

223   Mosiah 15:21.

224   See heading: Timing of Humankind's Resurrection.

225   D&C 29:26; Isaiah 26:19.

226   Helaman 14:17.

227   D&C 1:38.

228   D&C 29:24–25.

229   D&C 77:2–3.

230   Joseph Fielding Smith, *Answers to Gospel Questions*, vol. 2, 51.

231   Moses 7:48.

232   D&C 29:9–11. In Isaiah 24:21-22 we read that at the Lord's Second Coming He will punish, "the host of the high ones that are on high, and the kings of the earth upon the earth…and [they] shall be shut up in the prison." Indicating that at the Second Coming the proud and lifted up, along with the wicked, will be cleansed from the earth and put into the spirit prison.

233   Revelation 21:1.

234   D&C 88:17–18, 20.

235   The earth, at one point in its existence, was in the presence of God. In Abraham 5:13, we read that time for Adam in the Garden of Eden was after the Lord's time, for he had not appointed unto Adam a different measurement or reckoning of time. Following the fall of Adam, the earth fell from the presence of God and humankind's measurement of time became 1,000 years for a day in the Lord's time. See Facsimile 2 Fig. 1 in conjunction with Abraham 3:9.

236   D&C 88:19.

237   John A. Widtsoe, ed., *Discourses of Brigham Young*, 101.

238   D&C 11:28.

239   D&C 76:43.

240   N. B. Lundwall, *The Vision Eternity Sketched In A Vision From God*, 158.

241   Alma 26:16.

242   *TPJS*, 199.

243   *DS*, vol. 2, 292.

244   Alma 40:23.

245   Luke 24:39.

246   The Savior's scars were tokens of His divine mission and are shown at various times as a witness to those He appears to. Joseph Fielding Smith said, "It can hardly be accepted as a fact that these wounds have remained in his hands, side, and feet all through the centuries from the time of his crucifixion and will remain until his Second Coming. But they will appear to the Jews

as a witness against their fathers and their stubbornness in following the teachings of their fathers." See *DS*, vol. 2, 292. They are not an indication of scars, or wounds being present with humankind in the resurrection.

247   D&C 77:2.

248   Genesis 49:29.

249   Genesis 49:31.

250   Judges 2:8–10.

251   *TPJS*, 295.

252   Joseph Fielding Smith, *Answers to Gospel Questions*, vol. 2, 100.

253   D&C 137:10.

254   Moroni 8:12.

255   Joseph F. Smith, *Gospel Doctrine*, 455–456.

256   D&C 29:49–50.

257   Moroni 8:22.

258   See 1 Corinthians 15:50.

259   *TPJS*, 367.

260   *DBY*, 372; See also: Orson Pratt, *The Seer*, 274; Heber C Kimball, *JD* 3:107-108.

261   Moses 1:27.

262   Enoch is another example where in vision his intellect was expanded, and he beheld all the inhabitants of the earth, Moses 7:21–24. Also, where the prophet Abinadi tells us that following His Atonement Jesus Christ saw all His seed, or all those who have accepted Him and His Gospel, again demonstrating the expansion of one's comprehension following the resurrection. Mosiah 15:10–11.

263   *JD* 16:363.

264   Moses 7:31.

265   Moses 7:41.

266   *JD* 1:293.

267 D&C 76:94.
268 3 Nephi 17:3–4.
269 *JD* 21:263.
270 Acts 1:9.
271 3 Nephi 11:8.
272 John 20:19.
273 *JS-History* 1:30.
274 *JS-History* 1:32.
275 *JS-History* 1:17.
276 D&C 50:24.
277 D&C 78:19.
278 Luke 24:15–16.
279 D&C 110:3.
280 Genesis 18:2–10.
281 Exodus 24:9–11.
282 Luke 24:41–43.
283 D&C 27:5–14.
284 Moses 4:25.
285 Revelation 7:16–17.
286 John 2:7–10.
287 Matthew 14:19–21.
288 Revelation 21:3–5.
289 Alma 24:14.
290 Moroni 7:30.
291 For example: D&C 128:20; Alma 30:53; Moses 1:12–14.
292 D&C 129:1–9.
293 For example: Genesis 16:7–11; Luke 1:28–38; 1 Nephi 12.

294 Moroni 7:31.

295 See D&C 133:17; Mosiah 3:2–22.

296 D&C 13:1, 128:21.

297 For example: Exodus 33:2–10; D&C 88:105–114, 103:18–20.

298 For example: Abraham 3:20; Acts 5:19; Luke 22:43.

299 D&C 128:20.

Chapter 7

300 1 Corinthians 13:12.

301 1 Corinthians 15:22–23.

302 Matthew 27:52–53.

303 *TPJS*, 188.

304 3 Nephi 23:7–10.

305 Mosiah 15:21–22.

306 D&C 133:54–55.

307 See 3 Nephi 28:40, where it indicates that the three translated Nephites are to be resurrected at Christ's Second Coming when He judges the world. John the Beloved was also to tarry until the Lord would come in His glory, D&C 7:3. This would indicate that others who were translated since Christ's coming in the flesh will also experience the resurrection at this time.

308 D&C 45:44–45; See also: 1 Thessalonians 4:16.

309 D&C 43:18; See also: D&C 88:98.

310 Orson Pratt, *The Seer*, 2 vols., 280.

311 D&C 133:46–49.

312 D&C 29:11; Article of Faith 1:10. During the millennium Christ and the resurrected saints will probably not dwell here on the earth, but with those who have previously been resurrected, and will visit the earth from time to time. Joseph Smith commented, "While in conversation at Judge Adams' during the evening, I said, Christ and the resurrected Saints will reign over the earth during the thousand years. They will not probably dwell upon the earth, but will visit it when they please, or when it is necessary to govern it." *TPJS*,

268.

313   D&C 63:50.

314   D&C 88:96.

315   See D&C 63:20–21; Articles of Faith 1:10; 2 Peter 3:10–13. This change is not the same as what will occur at the end of the earth when it will be celestialized.

316   D&C 101:31.

317   Alma 40:25.

318   D&C 88:28–29.

319   See D&C 59:2, 78:15; Moses 7:56. It is also called a "Crown on Righteousness," 2 Timothy 4:8; D&C 25:15, 29:13, or a "Crown of Glory," D&C 104:7; 1 Peter 5:4.

320   D&C 76:51–52.

321   Ibid.

322   D&C 76:87.

323   D&C 29:27.

324   D&C 88:20, 63:20.

325   D&C 131:1.

326   D&C 76:55, 58–60. See also: D&C 76:92 that states the vision of the celestial kingdom was where God the Father reigns upon His throne, which excels in all things, which is in the highest degree of the celestial kingdom.

327   D&C 131:2–4; Likewise, the inhabitants of the terrestrial and telestial Kingdom are limited in their progression.

328   D&C 76:56–57; Elder B. H. Roberts, in speaking of the Gospel, said, "If it teaches that in the great future men will become kings and priest unto God, it teaches also that women will become queens and priestesses. If it teaches that a woman is dependent upon an eternal union with man in order to attain to a fullness of exaltation and glory in heaven, it teaches, no less emphatically that man is equally dependent upon woman for a fullness of glory and exaltation. To one accepting "Mormon" theology, the sexes are

not made to walk separately and alone, either in time, or in eternity, but hand in hand." See B. H. Roberts, "The Church of Jesus Christ of Latter-day Saints at the Parliament of Religions, Part 5, Woman's Place in Mormonism," *Improvement Era* 2 (October 1899), 900.

329 D&C 76:58.

330 Romans 8:16–17; D&C 76:59.

331 D&C 132:20.

332 D&C 130:10–11.

333 D&C 130:9.

334 D&C 88:27–28.

335 See heading: The Resurrection and Receiving a Fullness of Joy.

336 D&C 76:67.

337 Moses 7:19.

338 D&C 78:20–22.

339 D&C 93:21.

340 D&C 76:53.

341 D&C 88:2.

342 The temple ordinances were revealed following the receipt of Doctrine & Covenants Section 76, and therefore are not included in it. This does not nullify the requirement to receive them.

343 *TPJS*, 331.

344 *TPJS*, 309.

345 *DS*, vol. 2, 190.

346 D&C 137:10.

347 2 Nephi 25:23.

348 In addition, Jacob and Isaac have entered into their exaltation and sit upon thrones, D&C 132:37.

349 D&C 132:29.

350 D&C 137:2.

351   D&C 132:19.

352   Claire Middlemiss, *Cherished Experiences From The Writings Of President David O. Mckay*, 59–60.

353   D&C 132:16–17.

354   D&C 136:37.

355   D&C 46:8–9.

356   D&C 132:7–8.

357   D&C 132:15–16.

358   D&C 132:15–18.

359   *TPJS*, 300–301.

360   D&C 50:5. See also: Benson, Ezra Taft, "To the Single Adult Sisters of the Church," *Ensign* (November 1988).

361   D&C 132:14.

362   D&C 76:5–6.

363   D&C 132:24.

364   D&C 130:21.

365   D&C 131:2–4.

366   D&C 132:19.

367   D&C 132:30; The Abrahamic Covenant was where God covenanted with Abraham that he would receive lands of inheritance, have a numerous posterity in and out of the world, which would be greater than the sands of the sea, have the Gospel and priesthood, and bless the nations of the earth. See Genesis 12:1–3, 17:5–6; Abraham 2:9–11, 3:14.

368   Parley P. Pratt, *Autobiography of Parley P. Pratt*, 329–330.

369   Melvin J. Ballard, *The Three Degrees of Glory*, 11–12.

370   See heading: Celestial Offspring.

371   Orson Hyde drew an interesting diagram showing the patriarchal order in the kingdom of God.

In the accompanying editorial, Elder Hyde said, "The above diagram shows the order and unity of the kingdom of God. The eternal Father sits at the head, crowned King of kings and Lord of lords. Wherever the other lines meet, there sits a king and a priest unto God, bearing rule, authority, and dominion under the Father. He is one with the Father, because his kingdom is joined to his Father's and becomes part of it." Orson Hyde, "A Diagram of the Kingdom of God," *Millennial Star* 9 (15 January 1847), 23.

372   *TPJS*, 330.

373   D&C 124:25–31.

374   *DBY*, 399.

375   *JD* 15:139.

376   This welding link in the dispensation of the fullness of times encompasses the whole and complete union of all keys, powers, and ordinances of all dispensations D&C 128:18.

377   D&C 128:15.

378   D&C 76:81, 86–87.

379   Bryant S. Hinckley, *Sermons and Missionary Services of Melvin Joseph Ballard*, 257.

380   Moses 7:39.

381   Ibid.

382   During His mortal ministry Jesus Christ spoke of the fact that no one had gone up to heaven–yet, but that the Son of Man had come down from heaven. See: John 3:13.

383   John 20:17.

384   Moses 7:56–57.

385   It appears the resurrection of both celestial and terrestrial spirits occurred after the time Christ arose. Who then continued the great missionary work among the vast numbers of telestial spirits that remained in the world of spirits? Parley P. Pratt gave us insight into this in the *Key to the Science of Theology*, when he wrote concerning resurrected beings, "Angels are ministers both to men upon the earth and to the world of spirits. They pass from one world to another with more ease and in less time than we pass from one city to another." Perhaps the resurrected angels of God played a role among the disembodied spirits in prison preaching the Gospel of Jesus Christ in conjunction with the spirits of the righteous who died shortly after Christ's resurrection. See Parley P. Pratt, *Key to the Science of Theology*, 106.

386   D&C 88:99.

387   Zechariah 14:17-19.

388   D&C 45:54.

389   D&C 88:30.

390   D&C 76:78.

391   D&C 76:77.

392   See heading: All Who Inherit God's Kingdoms Must Repent.

393   D&C 76:74.

394   D&C 76:75.

395   D&C 76:79.

396   D&C 76:86.

397   Matthew records that at the time of Christ's Second Coming it is the "Unjust" who will be destroyed and ushered into the spirit world, Matthew 13:49–50.

398   2 Peter 2:9.

399   D&C 76:110.

400   D&C 76:85.

401 D&C 88:100–101.

402 D&C 76:106.

403 D&C 76:98.

404 D&C 76:109.

405 D&C 76:86.

406 D&C 76:110.

407 D&C 29:27.

408 See heading: All Who Inherit God's Kingdoms Must Repent.

409 D&C 88:31.

410 D&C 76:82–84.

411 D&C 76:99–100.

412 D&C 76:103.

413 Wilford Woodruff, "Obtaining the Spirit of God," *Millennial Star*, vol. 67, no. 39, 612.

414 The Little Season, or Little Period, begins following the Millennium. During it, humankind will once again deny God, D&C 29:22. Hence, telestial beings will once again be on the earth. The length of time the Little Period covers is unknown. At this time Satan gathers his armies from the spirit world and on the earth for the final time to battle Michael and his armies. At the end of it, Satan and his followers will be defeated and cast into their own place, D&C 88:111–114; Revelation 20:7–10.

415 Mormon 9:2.

416 D&C 88:102.

417 Mosiah 5:10.

418 D&C 19:5.

419 D&C 29:44–45; Mosiah 16:1-2, 5.

420 D&C 88:35.

421 D&C 38:6.

422 Alma 40:13; D&C 29:28.

423   D&C 76:36.

424   D&C 133:71–73.

425   D&C 76:37.

426   D&C 43:33.

427   3 Nephi 28:34–35.

428   D&C 76:31–32.

429   Matthew 12:31.

430   D&C 132:27.

431   D&C 42:18.

432   Alma 30:60.

433   D&C 19:2–3.

434   Matthew 6:21.

Chapter 8

435   Elder James A. Talmage felt it was April 6th, B.C. 1, J. Reuben Clark Jr. thought it was December of B.C. 5 or early B.C. 4, and Bruce R. McConkie favored an earlier 5 B.C. date. Other non-LDS scholars have picked varying dates.

436   See Matthew 2:1-20 showing Herod was alive when Jesus Christ was born.

437   See Jeffrey R. Chadwick, "Dating the Birth of Christ," *BYU Studies Quarterly*, vol. 49, no. (2010).

438   3 Nephi 8:5–23.

439   3 Nephi 8:2, 5.

440   The death of Jesus Christ is recorded in the four Gospels as having occurred at the start of the Passover festival. See Matthew 26–27; Mark 14–15; Luke 22–23; John 13–19.

441   Interestingly, if Jesus Christ died on April 6th, then the date of the Restoration of the Church of Jesus Christ of Latter-day Saints, like the mythical phoenix, symbolically becomes a new creature born out of the ashes

of His death.

442   See Jeffery R. Chadwick, "Dating the Death of Jesus Christ," *BYU Studies Quarterly*, vol. 54 no. 4 (2015).

443   It is important to remember that between 1BC and 1AD there is only one year, not two.

444   Matthew 12:38–40.

445   *DS*, vol. 1, 128.

446   Deuteronomy 17:6.

447   Matthew 18:16. See Ether 5:4, where three witnesses will establish the truth of the Book of Mormon.

448   Luke 1:39–44.

449   Luke 2:6–7.

450   Matthew 27:56.

451   Mark 16:1–6.

452   Matthew 28:8–9.

453   Mark 16:9.

454   John 10:18.

455   Matthew 27:50–51.

456   3 Nephi 8:6–7.

457   3 Nephi 8:17.

458   1 Nephi 19:12.

459   Matthew 27:57–60.

460   Matthew 27:65–66.

461   See Daniel 6:17 for an example of this practice.

462   In the Gospel of Peter, an apocryphal work, it says the tomb was marked by seven wax seals. Brown, Raymond., Trans., "Gospel of Peter," 33. The cork shaped rock could be rolled on wooden poles.

463   A Roman watch normally consisted of two to four soldiers who stood guard for a six–hour shift. See Amplified Version Acts 12:4; Scripture

quotations taken from The Amplified Bible, Copyright © 1954, 1958, 1962, 1964, 1965, 1987 by Lockman Foundation. All rights reserved. Used by permission (www.lockman.org).

464   Matthew 28:4.

465   Matthew 28:11–15. The fact that some guards presented themselves to the chief priest suggests the number of soldiers that guarded the tomb were more than two. Interestingly the Gospel of Peter indicates the tomb was guarded by two by two guards on every shift. Brown, Raymond., Trans., "Gospel of Peter," 35.

466   The actual punishment administered was determined by a soldier's superior officer and could depend on their past service, circumstances, and whether it occurred in a time of peace or war, etc.

467   Mark 16:2–4.

468   Matthew 28:5–8.

469   John 20:2.

470   John 20:8.

471   John 20:10.

472   John 20:11–16.

473   Mark 16:9.

474   Amplified Version John 20:17; Ibid, 178.

475   John 20:17.

476   Matthew 28:9–10.

477   Matthew 28:16–18.

478   Deuteronomy 16:3.

479   Isaiah 53:4–5.

480   Some Hebrew scholars differ as to the meaning and validity of the Afikoman tradition at the time of Jesus Christ. A good overview is Paul Sumner's article, "He Who Is Coming The Hidden Afikoman," http://www.hebrew-streams.org/works/judaism/afikoman.html.

481   1 Corinthians 11:24.

482   John 6:48.

483   See Chart of Jesus Christ's Time in the Tomb.

484   See Katzir, Reshit., "The Wave Sheet Offering."

485   Ezekiel 37:5.

Chapter 9

486   Matthew 28:13.

487   John 20:13

488   Matthew 28:13

489   Edwards, William D., et all. "On the Physical Death of Jesus Christ." *Journal of the American Medical Association* (March 21, 1986), 1455–63.

490   Luke 24:11.

491   Luke 24:36–43.

492   See heading: Two Angels at the Tomb.

493   In Matthew Mary Magdalene and the other Mary are present. In Mark the two Mary's and Salome are present. In Luke Mary Magdalene, Mary the mother of James, Joanna, and other women are present at the tomb.

494   Chester Beatty Library. http://www.csntm.org/About/RecentProjects/Chester-Beatty-Library. Written in Greek, it is from a codex (sewn and folded book) rather than a scroll.

495   Rylands Library. http://textus-receptus.com/wiki/Rylands_Library_Papyrus_P52. Written in Greek, it is probably from a codex (sewn and folded book) rather than a scroll.

496   This is the earliest record of the ancient Church's creed, which many believe was written in about 33–35 A.D., proclaiming Christ's atonement, death, and resurrection. Paul probably obtained it when he visited Jerusalem and spoke with the Apostles following his conversion, Acts 9:26–28.

497   Mark is believed to have been written first by about 60 A.D. Luke no later than 62 A.D. Matthew is thought to have been written in the 60s. John is also believed by some to have been written in the late 60s but most scholars place it later. For a discussion of this see: Blomberg, Craig L. *The Historical*

Reliability of the Gospels. Second Edition, Downers Creek, Illinois: Intervarsity Press, 2007, P 25–26.

498   Flavius Josephus, *Jewish Antiquities*, 18.3.3 §63. Note: Some believe that the statement about Jesus Christ did not totally originate with Josephus, but that a simpler statement concerning Christ did, which was modified later. For another Roman historian's description of events surrounding early Christians and Christ see: Complete Works of Tacitus. Tacitus. Alfred John Church. Annals. 15:44.

499   Pliny, Letters. Trans. William Melmoth, rev. W.M.L. Hutchinson, vol. 2, X:96.

500   John 21:25.

501   Luke 1:1.

502   There were many things written about Christ that have not survived the passage of time. For example, according to Irenaeus, Papias was "a hearer of John and a companion of Polycarp." He lived in the 1st century A.D. and wrote a five-book treatise on the sayings of Jesus Christ. See Eusebius, *The Ecclesiastical History*, 3.39.1.

503   3 Nephi 11:14–15.

504   D&C 76:22–24.

Chapter 10

505   Matthew 28:2–5.

506   John 20:12.

507   *JST* Matthew 28:1–3.

508   Luke 24:4–6.

509   Mark 16:9–11.

510   Matthew 28:9–10.

511   Luke 24:9–11.

512   Luke 24:34.

513   Luke 24:18; 1 Corinthians 15:5.

514	Luke 24:15–21.
515	Luke 24:25–26.
516	Luke 24:31–32.
517	Luke 24:36–43.
518	Luke 24:48.
519	John 20:24–29.
520	John 21:2–3.
521	John 21:5–7.
522	Luke 5:4–11.
523	Luke 22:34.
524	John 21:15–17.
525	Matthew 28:16–20.
526	1 Corinthians 15:6.
527	1 Corinthians 15:7.
528	Luke 24:50–52.
529	Acts 1:6–12.
530	Acts 7:55–56.
531	Acts 1:3.
532	Acts 22:5–10; See also: Acts 9:3–6.
533	1 Corinthians 15:8.
534	Revelation 1:14–18.
535	3 Nephi 11:8–10.
536	3 Nephi 11:13–15.
537	3 Nephi 26:13.
538	3 Nephi 27:1–2.
539	3 Nephi 27:7–8.
540	3 Nephi 16:3; See also: 3 Nephi 17:4.

541   Mormon 1:15.

542   Ether 12:39.

Chapter 11

543   D&C 20:12.

544   See, "The Living Christ: The Testimony of the Apostles," The Church of Jesus Christ of Latter-day Saints (https://www.lds.org/ensign/2000/04/the-living-christ-the-testimony-of-the-Apostles-the-church-of-jesus-christ-of-latter-day-saints?lang=eng).

545   A powerful testimony of Jesus Christ was given by Elder Bruce R. McConkie, see: Bruce R. McConkie, "The Purifying Power of Gethsemane," *Ensign* (May 1985). Elder David B. Haight related a dream he had of a panoramic view of the Saviors life, sacrifice, and atonement, see: David B. Haight, "The Sacrament—and the Sacrifice," *Ensign* (November 1989). Elder Spencer W. Kimball related a dream of George F. Richards' of the Council of the Twelve that he had of the Savior, see: Spencer W. Kimball, "The Cause Is Just and Worthy," *Ensign* (May 1974). See also: Gordon B. Hinckley, "Special Witnesses for Christ," *Ensign* (May 1984) and Thomas S. Monson, "I Know That My Redeemer Lives," *Ensign* (May 2007), 25.

546   *The Utah Genealogical and Historical Magazine*, 5:62. https://archive.org/stream/utahgenealogical1914gene#page/62/mode/2up/search/neibaur.

547   Alfred Douglas Young, *Autobiographical Journal*, 1808–1842, 4–5.

548   *JD* 11:10.

549   *JS-History* 1:16–17.

550   D&C 110:1–4.

551   D&C 76:21–24.

552   N. B. Lundwall, *The Vision Eternity Sketched In A Vision From God*, 11.

553   Leroi C. Snow, "An Experience of My Father's," *Improvement Era*, 677, 679; punctuation and capitalization modernized.

554   Mark F. McKiernan and Roger D. Launius, eds., *An Early Latter Day*

Saint History The Book of John Whitmer Kept by Commandment, 66–67.

555   *HC*, vol. 1, 335.

556   As cited in Bryant S. Hinckley, *The Faith of Our Pioneer Fathers*, 226–227.

557   Orson F. Whitney, "The Divinity of Jesus Christ," *Improvement Era* (January 1926), 224–225.; See also: *Ensign* (December 2003) punctuation, capitalization, and spelling standardized.

558   Bean, Rebecca Rosetta Peterson, recorded talk at Salt Lake City fireside fall 1964. Women's Manuscript Collections, MSS SC 2273, 12–13.

559   *JH* (October 10, 1883).

Chapter 12

560   D&C 93:13.

561   Benjamin Franklin, *The Autobiography of Benjamin Franklin*, vol. IX.

562   Psalm 139:10.

563   Proverbs 15:3.

564   3 Nephi 27:26.

565   Matthew 6:6.

566   Revelation 3:15–16.

567   1 Samuel 13:14.

568   A jot and tittle refer to the smallest marks of the Hebrew written language. It denotes something small and insignificant.

569   Matthew 6:1.

570   Matthew 6:4.

571   Matthew 5:27–28.

572   Matthew 5:38–39.

573   3 Nephi 11:29–30.

574   Moroni 7:45–47.

575   Hosea 10:12.

576	Romans 8:5–6.
577	D&C 93:30.
578	D&C 88:74.
579	Bruce R. McConkie, *Mormon Doctrine*, 539.
580	Galatians 5:22–23.
581	Alma 5:11–13.
582	Joseph F. Smith, *Gospel Doctrine*, 65.
583	Ezekiel 11:19–20.
584	D&C 64:34.
585	Mosiah 4:6–7.
586	See 3 Nephi 11:11, 17:2; John 5:19–20, 30, 14:10.
587	Ether 12:27.
588	D&C 93:20.
589	D&C 59:21.
590	D&C 58:43.
591	D&C 82:7.
592	2 Nephi 4:31.
593	D&C 63:15.
594	D&C 19:16.
595	Ephesians 4:32.
596	D&C 64:9–10.
597	D&C 58:42.
598	Matthew 22:37–40.
599	Moroni 7:46.
600	Moroni 7:47–48.
601	Amplified Version 1 Timothy 1:5; Ibid, 178.
602	Matthew 16:25–26.

603   James 1:27.

604   3 Nephi 9:19.

605   D&C 59:8.

606   Matthew 23:11.

607   D&C 18:11.

608   N.B. Lundwall, ed., *A Compilation Containing the Lectures on Faith*, 58.

609   Matthew 5:16.

610   See 2 Corinthians 9:6–7; Moroni 7:6–11.

Chapter 13

611   For a more in-depth study of symbols, see Alonzo L. Gaskill, *The Lost Language of Symbolism: An Essential Guide For Recognizing And Interpreting Symbols Of The Gospel*.

612   Revelation 13:8.

613   Moses 5:5–7.

614   John 10:14, 27.

615   See Matthew 15:24; Luke 15:4.

616   John 21:15–17.

617   Matthew 25:33.

618   Matthew 4:19, 13:47.

619   Romans 6:4.

620   D&C 128:12.

621   D&C 45:47, 56:1.

622   See 1 Nephi 22:11; D&C 136:22.

623   See 3 Nephi 27:19; Revelation 7:14.

624   For example: Matthew 6:22; 3 Nephi 13:22–23; D&C 88:67.

625   See 2 Nephi 9:44; Psalm 33:18.

626   For example: Revelation 14:14; D&C 76:108.

627   D&C 88:107; Moses 7:56.

628   Matthew 5:8.

629   Matthew 6:21, 12:35.

630   See Romans 14:11; Philippians 2:10–11; D&C 88:104.

631   D&C 95:6.

632   D&C 50:23.

633   Romans 13:12; Ephesians 5:11.

634   Alma 40:13.

635   D&C 82:5; Moses 7:26.

636   3 Nephi 8:19.

637   Revelation 4:2–3.

638   Genesis 9:13–15.

639   Revelation 4:4.

640   Alma 13:11.

641   Revelation 6:4.

642   Revelation 3:5; See also: Alma 5:21.

643   Revelation 19:8.

644   Examples are: 1 Nephi 8:5; Matthew 28:3; *JS-History* 1:31.

645   Revelation 7:14-15.

646   D&C 6:3.

647   D&C 88:45.

648   Psalms 19:1.

649   1 Corinthians 8:6.

650   3 Nephi 12:48.

651   Matthew 25:32–33. Another example is there are only two churches, 1Nephi 14:10.

652   Matthew 12:40.

653   Revelation 11:8–11.

654   See Matthew 24:31; Revelation 7:1; 2 Nephi 21:12.

655   3 Nephi 16:5.

656   Revelation 13:18.

657   Moses 3:2.

658   Matthew 18:22.

659   See Chart of Resurrection Timing.

660   Examples of eight being a new beginning are: Genesis 21:4; 1 Peter 3:20; John 20:26; D&C 68:27; 1 Nephi 17:4; Ether 3:1.

661   1 Nephi 17:4.

662   D&C 68:25–27.

663   Matthew 28:1–6.

664   Matthew 10:1–5.

665   Revelation 14:3; See in conjunction with D&C 77:11.

666   3 Nephi 18:7.

667   1 Corinthians 15:29.

668   D&C 128:13.

669   Alma 30:44.

670   Daniel 12:2–3.

Chapter 14

671   Matthew 12:24.

672   Matthew 13:10–15.

673   Mark 2:21–22.

674   The Greek can be translated as bottle, or wineskin. Other translations use wineskin, which seems more appropriate.

675   D&C 76:94.

676   Matthew 13:47–50.

677   Matthew 22:2–14.
678   D&C 132:5.
679   D&C 88:35.
680   D&C 133:70–73.
681   Matthew 19:27.
682   Matthew 20:1–16.
683   Romans 8:16–17.
684   D&C 132:20, 22.
685   2 Nephi 26:25–28.
686   Luke 14:7–11.
687   John 5:44.
688   Proverbs 16:18.
689   Matthew 25:31–34.
690   D&C 29:27–28.
691   3 Nephi 24:14–18.
692   Matthew 25:14–30.
693   Acts 10:34.
694   D&C 76:5–6.
695   Matthew 25:1–13.
696   Luke 8:10.
697   Isaiah 6:8–12.
698   Luke 8:5–8.
699   Luke 8:11–15.
700   Amplified Version Luke 16:1–13; Ibid, 178.
701   Mosiah 5:13.
702   Luke 16:14.
703   Matthew 13:24–30.

704   Matthew 13:36–43.

705   *JSM* 1:4.

706   D&C 29:9.

Chapter 15

707   2 Nephi 10:23–25.

BIBLIOGRAPHY

Bibliography- Articles and Magazines

Bean, Rebecca Rosetta Peterson, recorded talk at Salt Lake City fireside fall 1964. Women's Manuscript Collections, MSS SC 2273. L. Tom Perry Special Collections, Harold B. Lee Library, Brigham Young University, Provo, Utah.

Benson, Ezra Taft. "To the Single Adult Sisters of the Church." *Ensign*, November 1988.

Chadwick, Jeffrey R. "Dating the Birth of Christ," *BYU Studies Quarterly* 49, no. 4, 2010.

———. "Dating the Death of Jesus Christ," *BYU Studies Quarterly* 54, no. 4, 2015.

Edwards, William D., et all. "On the Physical Death of Jesus Christ." *Journal of the American Medical Association* (March 21, 1986), 1455–63.

Haight, David B. "The Sacrament—and the Sacrifice." *Ensign*, November 1989.

Hinckley, Gordon B. "Special Witnesses for Christ." *Ensign*, May 1984.

Instone-Brewer, David. "The Eighteen Benedictions and the Minim before 70 CE." *The Journal of Theological Studies* 54, no. 1 (April 2003): 25–44.

Kimball, Spencer W. "The Cause Is Just and Worthy." *Ensign*, May 1974.

McConkie, Bruce R. "The Purifying Power of Gethsemane." *Ensign*, May 1985.

———. "The Three Pillars of Eternity." Devotional address given at Brigham Young University, 17 February 1981.

Monson, Thomas S. "I Know That My Redeemer Lives." *Ensign*, May 2007.

Neibaur, Alexander. *The Utah Genealogical and Historical Magazine*, April 1914.

Roberts, B. H. "The Church of Jesus Christ of Latter-day Saints at the Parliament of Religions, "Part 5, Woman's Place in Mormonism, *Improvement Era*, October 1899.

Semi-Annual Conference Report, Salt Lake City: Deseret Book Co., October 1945.

Snow, Leroi C. "An Experience of My Father's." *Improvement Era*, September 1933, 677.

Whitney, Orson F. "The Divinity of Jesus Christ." *Improvement Era*, January 1926.

Bibliography - Books

Amplified Version of the Bible. Grand Rapids: The Zondervan Corporation, 1995.

Ballard, Melvin J. *The Three Degrees of Glory*. Ogden Tabernacle, 1922.

Blomberg, Craig L. *The Historical Reliability of the Gospels*. Second Edition. Downers Creek, Illinois: Intervarsity Press, 2007.

Edersheim, Alfred. *The Life and Times of Jesus The Messiah*. Peabody: Hendrickson Publishers Marketing, LL, 2014.

Eusebius. *The Ecclesiastical History. Dcocumenta Catholica Omnia*, http://www.documentacatholicaomnia.eu/03d/0265-0339,_Eusebius_Caesariensis,_Church_History,_EN.pdf.

Franklin, Benjamin. *The Autobiography of Benjamin Franklin*. Public Domain Books, Kindle Edition.

Journal History of The Church of Jesus Christ of Latter-day Saints. Salt Lake City: Historical Department Archives, The Church of Jesus Christ of Latter-day Saints.

Journal of Discourses. Liverpool: R. James, 26 Volumes.

Gaskill, Alonzo L. *The Lost Language of Symbolism: An Essential Guide For Recognizing And Interpreting Symbols Of The Gospel*. Salt Lake City: Deseret Book Co., 2003.

Hinckley, Bryant S. *The Faith of Our Pioneer Fathers*. Salt Lake City: Deseret Book Co., 1956.

Hinckley, Bryant S. *Sermons and Missionary Services of Melvin Joseph Ballard*. Salt Lake City: Deseret Book Co., 1949.

Josephus, Flavius. *Antiquities of the Jews*. Translated by William Whiston. Edinburgh: William P. Nimmo.

Lundwall, N.B., ed. *A Compilation Containing the Lectures on Faith*. Self-Published. Salt Lake City.

———. *The Vision Eternity Sketched In A Vision From God*. Salt Lake City: Bookcraft Publishing Co.

Maxwell, Neal A. *The Promise of Discipleship*. Salt Lake City: Deseret Book Co., 2001.

McConkie, Bruce R. *Mormon Doctrine*. Salt Lake City: Bookcraft, 1958.

———. "The Seven Deadly Heresies." *Classic Speeches*, Provo,

Brigham Young University Press, 1994.

McKiernan, Mark F. and Roger D. Launius. *An Early Latter-Day Saint History: The Book of John Whitmer Kept by Commandment*. Independence: Herald Publishing House: Independence, 1980.

Middlemiss, Claire. *Cherished Experiences from The Writings Of President David O. Mckay*. Salt Lake City: Deseret Book Co., 1976.

Millennial Star. Liverpool: Church of Jesus Christ of Latter-day Saints, 1840–1970.

Pliny, Letters. Trans. William Melmoth, rev. W.M.L. Hutchinson, 2 vols. Cambridge: Harvard University Press, 1935.

Parley P. Pratt, *Autobiography of Parley P. Pratt*, Parley P. Pratt Jr., ed. Chicago: Law, King & Law, 1888.

———. *Key to the Science of Theology*. Salt Lake City: Deseret News Printers and Publishers., 1915.

Pratt, Orson. *The Seer*. 2 vols. S. W. Richards, 1853.

Smith, Joseph F. *Gospel Doctrine*. Salt Lake City: Deseret Book Co., 1959.

Smith, Joseph Fielding. *Answers to Gospel Questions*. 3 vols. Salt Lake City: Deseret Book Co., 1979.

———. *Doctrines of Salvation*. Edited by Bruce R. McConkie. Salt Lake City: Bookcraft Publishing Co., 1955.

Smith, Joseph Fielding, ed. *Teachings of the Prophet Joseph Smith*. Salt Lake City: Deseret Book Co., 1972.

The History of The Church of Jesus Christ of Latter-day Saints. 7 vols. Salt Lake City: Deseret Book Co.,1974.

Witdsoe, John A, ed. *Discourses of Brigham Young* Salt Lake City: Deseret Book Co., 1954.

Young, Alfred Douglas. *Autobiographical Journal 1808–1842*. Copied by Brigham Young University, 1958.

Bibliography - Websites

Brown, Raymond, trans. "Gospel of Peter." http://www.earlychristianwritings.com/text/gospelpeter-brown.html.

Chester Beatty Library. http://www.csntm.org/About/RecentProjects/Chester-Beatty-Library.

Katzir, Reshit. "The Wave Sheet Offering." http://www.hebrew4christians.com/Holidays/Spring_Holidays/First_Fruits/first_fruits.html.

"Most Americans don't believe in the resurrection." Religion News Blog. http://www.religionnewsblog.com/14273/most-Americans-don't-believe-in-the-resurrection.

"Resurrection did not happen, says quarter of Christians." BBC News. http://www.bbc.com/news/uk-england-39153121.

Rylands Library. http://textus-receptus.com/wiki/Rylands_Library_Papyrus_P52

Sumner, Paul., "He Who Is Coming The Hidden Afikoman." http://www.hebrew-streams.org/works/judaism/afikoman.html.

Complete Works of Tacitus. Tacitus. Alfred John Church. William Jackson Brodribb. Sara Bryant. edited for Perseus. New York. Random House, Inc. Random House, Inc. reprinted 1942. Annals. 15:4. http://www.perseus.tufts.edu/hopper/text?doc=Perseus%3Atext%3A1999.02.0078%3Abook%3D15%3Achapter%3D44.

The Book Of The Twenty-Four Philosophers. http://themathesontrust.org/papers/metaphysics/XXIV-A4.pdf.

"The Living Christ: The Testimony of the Apostles, The Church of Jesus Christ of Latter-day Saints." https://www.lds.org/ensign/2000/04/the-living-christ-the-testimony-of-the-Apostles-the-church-of-jesus-christ-of-latter-day-saints?lang=eng.

"U.S. Belief in God down, belief in theory of evolution up." UPI Home/Health News. https://www.upi.com/US-belief-in-God-down-belief-in-theory-of-evolution-up/24081387762886/.

INDEX

A

Abraham
    abrahamic covenant, 103
    buried with his ancestors, 72
    exalted, 97–98
    footnote, 211, 367
    hosted three holy men, 81
Adam
    expulsed from garden, 26
amidah, 35
anecdotes
    a man's conversion, 59
    broken bones, 78
    Bob a celestial personality, 99
    chinese brochure, 38–39
    Dan faithful in adversity, 11–12
    effects of gravity, 117
    employee non–repayment loan, 184
    forgotten suit coat, 10–11
    Fred a navy officer, 229–230
    investigators and tithes and offerings, 226–227
    lights went out, 40
    london temple, 223–224
    mission illustration boards, 36
    mission talk, 216–217
    mobster son of perdition personality, 119
    neptune society, 73
    one hat fits all, 235

PG-13 movie, 231–232
shacho, 174–175
skeptical family member, 105–106
suffering purifies, 71
telestial personality, 115–116
terrestrial personality, 112
the garden, 179–180
two individuals respond to callings, 221
youth postponing repentance, 54
animals
in various kingdoms, 67–68

B

Ballard, Melvin J.
communication between kingdoms, 107
dream, 164
eternal increase, 103
repentance, 55
bible
early papyri, 138
when written, footnote 497
book of life, 52–53
book of sanctified, 53
books, other, 52–53

C

chaata'ah
adultery, 176
call to live a higher law, 177
giving alms, 176
missing the mark, 175-176
revenge, 176–177
Christ, Jesus
author of salvation, 24–25
divine prototype, 23
firstfruit, 5, 130, 133
foreordained, 24
increases in glory, 62
law of witnesses, 123
left God's presence, 109

message about perfection, 9
　　restoration vrs resurrection, 17
　　returns to God's presence, 109
　　reverses entropy, 69
　　rich young man, 29
　　right hand have eternal life, 2
　　sign of Jonas, 125
　　witnesses of key events, 123–133
Christ, Jesus atonement
　　all power, 24
　　keys of death and hell, 24
　　overcomes death, 25–26
　　overcomes fall of Adam, 26
　　overcomes first spiritual death, 26
　　overcomes second spiritual death, 26–27
　　receives keys of resurrection, 24,125
　　saves perfectly, 24
　　saving grace, 28–31
Christ, Jesus birth
　　born december 5 B.C., 123–124
　　D&C 20 1 A.D. confusion, 123
　　different dates of birth, 123
Christ, Jesus death
　　april 6th 30 A.D., 125
　　burial, 127, 129, 132, 136
　　cataclysms, 127
　　control over, 133
　　disciples doubt, 139, 143
　　historical and medical evidence, 136–137
　　Mary visits tomb, 126, 129, 130
　　number in roman watch, footnote 463
　　sealing of sepulchre, 127 128
　　Simon Peter and John visit tomb, 129
　　tomb marked by seven seals, footnote 462
　　touch me not, 130
　　women come to anoint, 128–129
Christ, Jesus resurrection
　　april 9th 30 A.D, 125
　　day of death and resurrection, 125
　　jewish belief spirit hovers 3 days, 124
　　jewish day ends at sunset, 124

communication
    between kingdoms, 106–107

D

damnation
    eternal, 62–63, footnote 188, 201
    not justified by Christ, 45
    resurrection of, 113, 116
death
    first overcome for all humankind, 26
    second overcome by atonement and repentance, 26–27
    type of judgement, 47

E

earth
    earth return to God's presence, 69
    existed near God, footnote 235
    resurrected, 68
    ultimately die, 68
    Elements, not all resurrected, 75
Elijah
    arose at Christ's resurrection, 91
    raised widow's son, 17
    returns at second coming, 91
    translated, 18
    temple work fulfills mission, 104
eternal damnation, 62
eternal life
    definition, 2–3
    God's greatest gift, 2
    is to inherit God's life, 2
    occupy kingdom of God, 2
    right hand of Christ, 2, 21, 52
    synonymous with salvation, 3
eternal progression, 60–62
exaltation
    limitless pie, 62
    many opportunities extended, 57
    requires grace, 29
existence

states of, 15–16
    first estate, 16
    second estate, 16
    second estate not limited to mortality, 56–57
    third estate, 16, 61

F

feast of firstfruits
    barley offering, 4, 132–133
    high priest reads from Ezekiel, 132
    pentecost, 132
feast of unleavened bread, 131
firstfruit
    defining, 4–6
    Jesus Christ, 5, 131–133
    jewish festival, 4
Franklin, Benjamin, thirteen traits, 170

G

gateways, three transitional, 16–18, 126, 197, 202
grace
    definition, 28–30
    footnote 118
    must conform lives, 30
    not making up the difference, 29
    works cannot save, 30

H

hasidut, 177–178
Herod, death 4 B.C., 123
Hyde, Orson, patriarchal order, footnote 371

I

illustrations
    celestial resurrection timing, 190
    Christ's post mortal appearances, 142
    first resurrection, 43
    God's realm and Satan's realm, 87
    humankind's resurrection timing, 89

Jesus Christ time in tomb, 125
Moses 7 resurrection teachings, 108
schedule of juxtapositions, 21
second or last resurrection, 45
sons of perdition resurrection timing, 116
telestial resurrection timing, 113
terrestrial resurrection timing, 107
world religions, 40

J

joy,
    absence of bodies bondage, 13–14
    resurrection and fullness, 14–15
judgement
    all thing written, 173
    at death, 47–48
    book of life, 52
    final, 51–53
    resurrection a partial, 49–50
    types records in, 52
justification, 30
juxtapositions
    examples, 20–22
    pairs, 22
    synonyms and verbs, 22

K

keys
    difference between spirits, 85
    three grand, 84–85
    righteous spirits sent on missions, 85
kingdom, celestial
    bodies quickened celestial glory, 94
    children saved in, 74
    communicates with terrestrial, 119
    mentally challenged saved, 74
    qualities, 94
    receive a crown, 94
    three degrees within, 95–98
kingdom, celestial highest degree

Abraham obtained exaltation, 97
book of sanctified, 96
church of Enoch and Firstborn, 95
circling rings of fire, 98
D&C 76 and highest degree, 95
earth residence, 98
eternal posterity, 2, 62, 64, 102–104
general assembly, 95
highest degree, 95–100
marriage, 100–102
new and everlasting covenant of marriage, 101
spirit children, 103
spiritual body, natural body, 95
vision of holy city, 98
welding link, 104–106
kingdom, celestial other degrees
    not much known, 99–100
    remain single, 99
kingdom, Satan's
    blaspheme against Holy Ghost, 118
    live on planet of no light, 117
    pre-meditated murderer, 118
    sons of perdition do not repent, 117
    sons of perdition, 116–119
    those who commit unpardonable sin, 118
    works destroyed at end of earth, 119
kingdom, telestial
    arise after the just rise, 113
    cannot dwell with God, 114
    don't accept gospel, 113
    Holy Ghost administers, 114
    live on another world, 114
    last resurrection, 113
    must repent, 114
    no testimony of Christ, 113
    qualities and traits, 114–115
    receive salvation, 3
    Wilford Woodruff sees vision of, 115
kingdom, terrestrial
    arise at Christ's first coming, 109
    cannot enter God's presence, 111

communicates with telestial, 112
nature and traits, 111–112
inherit another world, 111
Jesus Christ ministers to, 111
knew no law, 44
must repent, 111
quickened by terrestrial glory, 111
resurrected by divine decree, 56
right hand of Christ, 111

kingdoms, no movement between, 50–51

M

mankind, eternal beings, 2
marriage
    celestial, 100–102
    new and everlasting covenant, 100
    abrahamic covenant, 103
    welding link, 104–106
Maxwell, Neal A., spirit world part of second estate, 59
McConkie, Bruce R., obedience, 51, 181, foonote 210
McKay, David O., vision of holy city, 98
millennium
    burial cease but not death, 94, footnote 66
    changed in a twinkling of an eye, 89, 110–111, 120
monogram, IH, footnote 1

P

Papais, footnote 502
parables
    pearl of great price, 2–3
    prolonged Jesus ministry, 207
    uses of, 207–208
parables, cloth and wineskins
    cannot mix old and new, 208
    focus is our thoughts and motivation, 209
    give up old traditions, 209
    review of, 208–209
    should be bottle versus wineskin, 208–209
    warning about pharisees and sadducees, 208
parables, draw net

refers to second coming, 204
  review, 210
  separates just from unjust, 204
parables, laborers in vineyard
  abundance versus scarcity, 215
  all receive same reward, 214
  review, 212–215
  value of denarius, 214
parables, lowest seat
  approach salvation in humility, 216
  mission talk, 216–217
  review, 215–217
parables, sheep and goats
  judgment day separates, 217
  left hand goats, 217
  review, 217–219
  right hand sheep, 217
parables, talents
  God rewards all equally, 220
  review, 219–221
  two individuals respond to callings, 221
parables, ten virgins
  division between wicked and righteous, 48
  lamps round receptacle on pole, 222
  London temple, 223–224
  review, 221–224
  two classes, 223
parables, the sower
  investigators tithes and offerings, 226–227
  seed is the word, 225
  review, 224–227
  three kingdoms, 225–226
parables, unjust servant, focus kingdom of God, 295
parables, unjust steward
  business men shrewd, 228
  Fred a navy officer, 229–230
  review, 227–230
  use resources for kingdom, 229
parables, wedding feast
  condemnation of Israel, 210–211

    given during passion week, 211
    must conform to God's laws, 212
    review, 210–212
    wicked cast out, 212
parables, wheat and tares, 20
parables, wheat and weeds
    PG-13 movie, 231–232
    review, 230–232
    wicked grow beside righteous, 231
paradise, little children enter, 48
passover
    afikomen, 132
    met in upper room to observe, 131
    Christ symbolically purging disciples, 132
    leaven symbol of decay, 131
perfection
    after resurrection, 9
    defining, 8–10
    not obtainable in mortality, 8–9
pharisees
    believed in resurrection, 156
    dead roll in cavities, 34
    receive the sign of Jonas, 125
    rejected Christ's message, 229
    stirred up Jews, 152
plan of happiness, 18
poems
    flowers, 201
    footprints in the sand, 31
    He is risen, 122
    I walked a mile with pleasure, 83
    the seed shop, 204
    the vision, 69
    there is not death, there are no dead, 171–172
Pratt, Orson
    affections increased, 77
    classes of bodies in resurrection, 50
    graves opened at second coming, 92
    locomotion increased, 103
    vision enlarged, 60
Pratt, Parley P.

angels minister to spirits, footnote 385
eternal man, 15
eternal posterity, 103

R

repentance
    all must repent, 53–55
    mortality best time, 55
restoration, law of
    applies to animals, 68
    characteristics when die restored to us, 54
    defining, 6–8
    earthly experiences remain, 7
    premortal experiences restored, 7
    restores characteristics and knowledge, 7
    restores physical bodies, 7
    restores to God's presence, 6
    wicked restored based on evil works, 27
resurrection
    absence frustrates God's plan, 13
    absence means death permanent, 13
    actions affect, 50
    animals in, 66–68
    children in, 74
    definition, 4
    earth, 68
    eternal importance, 13–14
    everything that has a spirit resurrected, 67
    extent of, 65–70
    first resurrection defining features, 44
    four beasts, 67
    fulness of joy after, 13, 14–15
    God resurrected exalted man, 4, 10–11
    helps know God, 10–12
    immutable event, 66
    juxtapositions for, 20–22
    laws one obey affects, 50
    likeness of baptism, 205–206
    morning of first, 46–47
    need to reach potential before, 51

    no resurrection no atonement, 14
    only once, 49
    pre-earth life knowledge returned at, 58
    priesthood ordinance, 55–56
    receive desires of heart in, 51
    role in salvation, 12–13
    saints arise at time of Christ, 109
    second estate ends at, 59
    state of conscience affects, 49–50
    table fellowship in, 80–82
    three grand keys, 84–85
    timing of humankinds, 88–90
    taught in all ages, 33–36
    type of judgement, 49–51
    versus restoration to life, 17
    versus translation, 17–18
    world's failure to recognize, 39–41
resurrection, bodies in
    appear as in mortality, 71
    arise from the grave, 70–72
    arise where buried, 72–73
    classes of bodies in resurrection, 50
    different types of bodies, 49–50
    impossible to destroy body, 73
    nature of bodies important, 49
    need physical bodies, 13
    no deformity in, 70
    not all elements resurrected, 75
    Savior's scars tokens, footnote 246
    without physical bodies become like Satan, 13
resurrection, capabilities
    ability to eat, 80–82
    hunger and thirst no more, 82
    imbued with glory, 79–80
    increased capabilities, 75–77
    no pain or suffering, 83–83
    pass through physical objects, 78–79
    power over gravity, 78
    power to show or hide glory, 80
resurrection, celestial
    arise again at second coming, 89, 91–92

    Bob a celestial personality, 99
    discussion of, 90–95
    saints arose at time of Christ, 91
    timing, 90
    translated arose at time of Christ, 91
    translated arise again at second coming, 92
resurrection, first
    inherit celestial and terrestrial kingdom, 44
    nature of, 43–44
    resurrection of the just, 44
    title, 46
resurrection, preparation
    chaata'ah or missing the mark, 175–177
    consecration, 191–193
    five P's, 173–175
    forgiveness, 186–187
    hesidut or loving kindness, 177–178
    keeping the commandments, 183–185
    law of proliferation, 179–181
    law of the harvest, 178–179
    loving all, 187–189
    obedience, 181–183
    repentance, 185–186
    sacrifice, 190–191
    service, 189–190
    shekhinah, 172–173
resurrection, second
    also called last resurrection, 44, 45–46, 113
    arise by divine decree, 56
    inherit telestial or Satan's kingdom, 45
    telestial on God's right hand, 45, 120
    timing of, 113
    vision of, 56, 115
resurrection, sons of perdition
    discussion of, 116–119
    mobster son of perdition personality, 119
    not saved through atonement of Christ, 117
    on God's left hand, 46, 117
    only ones second death applies, 118
    part of Satan's kingdom, 117
    part of second resurrection, 45–46, 113

timing of, 116
resurrection, taught, 33–36
resurrection, telestial
    damnation or unjust, 113
    discussion of, 113–116
    on God's right hand, 45, 120
    part of second resurrection, 45–46, 113
    telestial personality, 115–116
    Timing, 113, 120
resurrection, terrestrial
    at Christ's first coming, 109–110
    discussion of, 107–112
    terrestrial personality, 112
    timing, 107, 110–111
resurrection, theories denying
    bible is fabricated, 139–140
    discrepancies lin bible accounts, 137–138
    disciples stole Him away, 134–135
    others stole Him away, 135
    tomb not empty, 135–136
    unconscious when removed from cross, 136–137
    Vision hypothesis, 137
righteous, living transformed at second coming, 93

S

sadducees
    did not believe resurrection, 34 , 156
    receive sign of Jonas, 125
    stirring up people against Christ, 152
salvation
    definition, 3–4
    God's efforts to bring, 36–39
    greatest of God's gifts, 3
    resurrections role in, 12–13
    saves no one in sin, 53
    salvation, God's efforts
    cleanse and sanctifies, 38
    created earth, 37
    gift of Holy Ghost, 38
    provided Jesus Christ, 37

provided pre-earth life, 36–37
provides ordinances, 38
provides scriptures and prophets, 37–38
sanctification, 29, 30
Satan
    appears in opposition to God's work, 84
    does not possess intelligence, 61
    gathers armies for final battle, footnote 414
    has kingdom of no glory, 43, 45, 116
    he and followers cast out of heaven, 35
    inherits endless punishment, 62
    lost all through disobedience, 183
    masquerades as prince, 24–25
    number 666 perfect representation of, 202
    no power over translated beings, 17
    plants tares, 21
    three grand keys to expose, 84–85
    unrepentant inherit his kingdom, 45
second coming
    bring previously resurrected at, 91
    eath cleansed, 68
    graves opened, 92
    judgment day of Christ, 52, 92
    living transformed, 93
    righteous caught up, 92
    saints who have died resurrected, 91–92
    translated beings resurrected, 92
shekhinah, 172–173
Smith, Joseph
    arise from grave as laid down, 70
    baptism likeness of resurrection, 196
    baptismal font similitude of grave, 205
    book, and book of life, 53
    cannot be saved without all ordinances, 96
    children raised in the resurrection, 74
    Christ visit earth in millennium, footnote 312
    desire to die among saints, 72–73
    God created mankind, 10
    God dwells in eternal fire, footnote 41
    God dwelt on a earth, 10
    Jesus does what saw Father do, 61

    learn how to be Gods, 10
    many bodies of the saints arose, 90
    no immaterial matter, 15
    receive keys of resurrection, 56
    resurrection consoling, 11
    sacrifice of all required, 192
    study the resurrection, XIV
    temple work for dead, 104
    translated being's habitation, 18
    translated beings, 18
    vision in grove, 159–160
    vision with Oliver Cowdery, 160
    vision with Sidney Rigdon, 160–161
Smith, Joseph F.
    children raised in resurrection, 74
    proper application of knowledge, 61
    sacrifice of all required, 192
    temple work for dead, 104
Smith, Joseph Fielding
    baptized, after death go to paradise, 48–49
    Christ's wounds after resurrection, footnote 246
    impossible to destroy body, 73
    Christ received keys of resurrection, 125
    no deformity in resurrection, 70
    not all receive temple work, 97
    resurrection and creatures, 68
    righteous, not wicked go to paradise, 48
sons of perdition
    mobster son of perdition personality, 119
    not saved, 69
    not written in book of life, 52
    parable of sower includes, 225
    resurrected after little period, 89, 116
    traits and attributes, 117–119
spirit prison
    can accept the gospel while in, 58
    includes terrestrial spirits, 108
    outer darkness can mean spirit prison, 48
    remain in until repent, 108–109
    discussed, 48
    wicked who die in millennium enter, 113–114

symbols
    baptism, 196–197
    birth and death, 197–198
    definition, 195
    heavenly orbs, 200
    nature, 200
    sacrament, 204–205
    seasons, 203–204
    vicarious work, 205–206
symbols, animals, 195–196
symbols, body parts, 198
symbols, color, 198–200
symbols, numbers
    eight, 90, 181, 203
    four, 43, 90, 202
    one, 203
    seven, 38, 90, 202
    six, 202
    three, 15, 19, 118, 202
    three and one/half, 202
    twelve, 203
    two, 20, 43, 201, 222–223, footnote 248

T

tamin, 9
teleios, 9
Trajan, 139
translation, 23–24

U

unrepentant, 40, 117, footnote 188

W

witnesses, ancient
    Cleopas and another, 145–146
    eleven apostles and disciples jerusalem, 147–148
    eleven apostles galilee, 149–150
    eleven apostles mount of olives, 151
    five hundred, 150

James, 150–151
John on patmos, 153
Mary Magdalene, 143–144
Mary, Joanna, Salome, and other, 144
Paul on road to damascus, 152–153
seven apostles sea of tiberius, 148–149
Simon Peter, 145
Stephen's stoning, 152
ten apostles and disciples, 146–147
two angels at tomb, 142–143
witnesses, ancient other
book of mormon prophets, 155
lost ten tribes, 155
nephite twelve, 154–155
temple, 153–154
witnesses, law of, 126
witnesses, modern day
Alexander Neibaur, 157–158
Alfred Douglas, 158–159
Frederick G. Williams, 159
Joseph Smith and Oliver Cowdery, 160
Joseph Smith and Sidney Rigdon, 160–161
Joseph Smith grove, 159–160
Lorenzo Snow, 161–162
Lyman Wight, 162–163
meeting high priests, 163–164
Melvin J. Ballard, 164
Orson F. Whitney, 164–165
other, footnote 544
Rebecca Bean, 165–167
school of prophets, 167–168
Woodruff, Wilford, 56, 115

Y

Young, Brigham
ancestors revealed by revelation, 105
earth return to God's presence, 69
elements brought together in resurrection, 75
keys of the resurrection, 55–56
need for temples, 104–105

www.ingramcontent.com/pod-product-compliance
Lightning Source LLC
Chambersburg PA
CBHW021355290426
44108CB00010B/246